W9-ASH-110

PN   Noble, Peter.
1995.9   The Negro in films.
.N4
N6
1969

89021766

WITHDRAWN

THE DAVID GLENN HUNT
MEMORIAL LIBRARY
Galveston College
Galveston, Texas

DAVID GLENN HUNT
MEMORIAL LIBRARY
GALVESTON COLLEGE

The Negro in Films

THE
NEGRO IN FILMS

by

PETER NOBLE

KENNIKAT PRESS
PORT WASHINGTON, N. Y. 11050

DAVID GLENN HUNT
MEMORIAL LIBRARY
GALVESTON COLLEGE

TITLE PAGE

Clinton Rosemond in *They Won't Forget*, directed for Warners by Mervyn Le Roy (1937).

THE NEGRO IN FILMS

First published 1948
Reissued 1969 by Kennikat Press

Library of Congress Catalog Card No: 76-79306
SBN 8046-0525-4
Manufactured in the United States of America

CONTENTS

CONTENTS—*continued*

ACKNOWLEDGMENTS

For help and advice in collecting some of the material and illustrations the author wishes to express his gratitude to the following :—

The United States Office of War Information, Washington.
The Motion Picture Academy of Arts and Sciences, Los Angeles.
Iris Barry, The Film Library, Museum of Modern Art, New York.
Leon Hardwick, of the International Film and Radio Guild, Los Angeles.
Walter White, of the National Association for the Advancement of Coloured Peoples, U.S.A.
Ernest Lindgren and Norah Traylen, of the National Film Library, British Film Institute, London.
Dr. Lawrence Reddick, Curator of the Schomberg Collection, New York Public Library.
Dave and Jack Goldberg, Negro Marches On Inc. Hollywood.

And also to :—

Carl Van Vechten, Margaret Marshall, Bill Batchelor, Clarence Muse, Jack Griggs, Andrew Neatrour, Norah Mumford, Louis Golding, Mervyn McPherson, Ernest Player, David Jones, Monja Danischewski, Katherine Dunham, Alan Tucker, Marjorie Booth, Dr. Alain Locke, Gayne Dexter, Thorold Dickinson, Roger Manvell, Selby Howe, Lena Horne, Stella Wilkes; and to Mary Stone and Oswald Frederick for help in compiling the Index.

LIST OF ILLUSTRATIONS

5

CHAPTER ONE

INTRODUCTION

" The influence of the screen for good or evil cannot be overestimated. As a propaganda medium it is the most powerful of agents. Napoleon said he feared one newspaper more than a thousand bayonets. What would he have said had he lived in the age of the cinema ? "
WILLIAM PERLMAN, in " *The Movies On Trial* " (Macmillan 1936)

" The treatment of the Negro by the movie is inaccurate and unfair. Directly and indirectly it establishes associations and drives deeper into the public mind the stereotype conception of the Negro. By building up this unfavourable conception, the movies operate to thwart the advancement of the Negro, to humiliate him, to weaken his drive for equality and to spread indifference, contempt and hatred for him and his cause. This great agency for the communication of ideas and information, therefore, functions as a powerful instrument for maintaining the racial subordination of the Negro people."
DR. LAWRENCE REDDICK *in* " *The Journal of Negro Education,*"
Summer Number, 1944.

" When will Hollywood producers have the moral courage to give a true-to-life version of Negro characters when they are intimately associated with white characters ? "
" *New York Age,*" *February, 1945.*

How has the Negro been portrayed on the screen ? And to what extent has this depiction contributed towards the continued existence of a colour bar in the United States of America (and to a far less extent in Europe) ? The treatment of the Negro in Hollywood films, paralleling as it does his treatment in American life, has long been noted for its injustice. For, like much American fiction, the film tends to interpret the Negro, his mind, his outlook, his way of life, in a way which is calculated to justify his exploiters. When slavery was abolished and after the black man began to use his vote, go to school, and work in field and factory, the myth of Negro inferiority and, later, of his innate brutality was created, for his exploiters feared him. To an extent they still do. The bulk of Hollywood's output in the past thirty years has in consequence pointed out, in varying degrees of subtlety, those racial characteristics which supposedly indicate Negro inferiority and refer continually to his historic position of abject subservience to the white man. From " The Birth Of A Nation " to " Gone With The Wind " it has been the same sorry tale of discrimination.

Cinema audiences regard the coloured man as a clown, a buffoon, an idiot and a superstitious fool ; and their feeling of contempt for him is a result of the manner in which he is invariably portrayed on the screen. The ordinary filmgoer has his whole outlook formulated by the film ; politically, socially, intellectually he forms his opinions unconsciously through direct and indirect film propaganda. And in this instance the screen, an extremely powerful instrument for moulding opinion, has continually utilised its power to nurture among audiences this feeling of contempt, good-natured or otherwise, for those who happen to possess skins of a different shade. In forcing coloured actors and actresses to depict ignorant servants, lazy janitors, superstitious toilet-attendants, nit-wit maids, valets, shoe-shine boys, faithful retainers, tramps and no-accounts, and Uncle Tom rôles of every description, the film producers are merely carrying out a policy which seems to them to be a natural one—the debasement of the Negro, in the public mind, to that of an inferior. None of these film-characters is allowed to demonstrate a lively intelligence ; all are merely cinematic puppets, empty-headed, grinning dolts with conversation consisting of those so-called " quaint " inanities with which all filmgoers are by now familiar.

Robert Stebbins aptly pointed out the following in *New Theatre*, July, 1935 : " The Negro's activity in the Hollywood film is confined to fleeting shadows of him as a lazy servant (' Judge Priest '), a boot-black, a newsboy, a stableboy (' Broadway Bill,' ' Reckless,' ' Princess O'Hara '), or a coachman who has been made to look ridiculous (' Mississippi '). He is also a repulsive, mis-shapen zombie in ' The Lost World,' a voodoo-maddened villain bent on exterminating the white race in ' Black Moon,' or at best a benighted prisoner intoning the ubiquitous spiritual in the death house while the hero is being prepared for his walk along the ' last mile ' (' The Last Mile,' ' The Criminal Code,' ' If I Had A Million ')".

Margaret Farrand Thorp, in her book *America at the Movies* (Faber, 1946), is a little more charitable to Hollywood.

She observes : " The producer is ready to protect the Negro and avoid stirring race hatreds by keeping off the modern screen such villainous Negroes as appeared in Griffith's ' The Birth Of A Nation,' but the best he thinks he can do beyond that is to make the Negro so amusing and agreeable that an audience is always pleased at the appearance of a black face. A Negro may also appear in a position where he excites no laughter, but sympathy. The Negro janitor suspected of the murder in ' They Won't Forget ' is the best example of this class. He is probably the most realistic Negro, thanks to the script, but also to remarkably fine acting, that the screen has seen. The all-Negro ' The Green Pastures,' for all its originality and, at some points, elevation, permitted, however, a certain feeling of superiority on the part of the audience."

The cinema is fifty years old, and has completed half a century of mass entertainment of a kind approached previously by no other form of art. And although it is, perhaps, stressing a somewhat tiresome truism to repeat here that the film is the most considerable influence for instilling ideas into its vast audiences, it would be well to draw attention at the very beginning of this book to what motion picture pioneer Thomas Edison once truthfully said : " Whoever controls the film industry controls the most powerful medium of influence over the public." And, as Donald Slesinger put it more recently in his chapter " The Film and Public Opinion " in *Print, Radio and Film in a Democracy*, edited by Douglas Waples : " We must confess that we are only at a beginning of an understanding of the educational and propaganda possibilities of the film. We know something about producers, little about exhibitors, less about the audience. We know that a lot of administrative and economic problems must be solved before the film achieves its maximum usefulness. We don't know what the ' symbol ' is in a motion picture ; or, if the symbol is composed of light waves, whether a sound or slogan will be needed to produce action. We know, or think we know, that a film is addressed by a few to many, and that as ' many ' increases we are reduced to entertainment, as the lowest common denominator. But we don't know how much education or propaganda an entertainment film can carry. We know little, but we are working. Government and industry, alone and together, are experimenting. Researchers are studying. When the data are in, we are certain that the film will turn out to be, potentially, the most powerful medium of communication."

The film· has since the very commencement of its meteoric rise to world popularity unconsciously propagated certain ideas, and consciously and carefully propagated others. Among the latter is the idea that Negroes, specifically the coloured peoples of America, and generally the rest of the world, are in every way inferior to white people, specifically the citizens of the United States of America. The cinema is, of course, not alone in disseminating this form of bias ; the Press, the radio, and to an extent the drama have each over a long period made their dubious contributions to racial intolerance. But since the motion picture commands such an immense world-wide audience and with the years appears to increase formidably in influence and power, an examination of at least one of its more sinister aspects of influence would seem to be long overdue.

Admittedly, Hollywood's attitude to the question of the Negro minority in the United States has been for many years something of a reflection of the attitude of average America. However, it may be logically contended that if film producers had, from the very first, endeavoured to portray the screen Negro in a less unsympathetic light, or had tried in any way to ease racial tension, it would have constituted an invaluable help towards the betterment of relations between the American man-in-the-street and his erstwhile slave. Hollywood would probably retort that its films are not designed as " propaganda," but in the following pages it is proposed to indicate, with appropriate evidence, that the opposite is precisely the case. Film propaganda has, in fact, wrought great dis-service to the Negro cause, and the manner in which coloured actors are shown on the screen has affected to a truly remarkable extent the reaction of audiences all over the world to coloured people in their own country and elsewhere. (It is, indeed, a fact that numbers of English families during the war expressed amazement, on meeting Negro soldiers of the U.S. Army stationed in this country, that they were ordinary and likeable human beings and not the illiterate, ignorant, sub-human creatures depicted for so many years in American films !) Apparently Hollywood, however, does not even *recognise* the existence of a race problem. An indication of this is given by the Production Code of Ethics of the motion picture industry, set up by the former Hays Office and containing the only stated rules and guide for Hollywood film-making, which mentions the word " race " only once, and this in the section forbidding the depiction in films of " miscegenation " (sex relationship between the white and black races).

The problem of the Negro is really the problem of the whites ; (did not that eminent Jewish author, Louis Golding, write somewhere about " the Gentile problem " ?). It is white people everywhere who have the power to change attitudes ; it is they who could bring a new spirit of tolerance to the American scene. That they are not aided to do so by the newspapers, the cinema, the radio—and some United States laws—has been made clear from contemporary history. But if the powerful Hollywood machine for moulding mass opinion had originally been turned full blast against all forms of racial intolerance, anti-Negroism, and other less prominent facets of Fascism, then who knows to what degree this might have affected the attitude of filmgoers everywhere ?

The Negro is not the sub-human dolt that Hollywood would have us believe he is. Here are a few facts. The 1940 Bureau of Census Statistics shows that there were in the U.S.A. at that time three thousand five hundred and twenty-four physicians and surgeons ; two thousand three hundred and thirty-nine college presidents and professors ; one thousand and fifty-two lawyers and judges ; one hundred and thirty-two thousand one hundred and ten craftsmen and foremen in industries ; and six thousand eight hundred and one trained nurses. This is surely an indication that the coloured American is an ordinary human being ? But not according to Hollywood, as we shall see.

In his valuable pamphlet *Educational Programme for the Improvement of Race Relations in Motion Pictures, Radio, the Press and Libraries* (which will often be referred to in this book), Dr. Lawrence D. Reddick, Curator of the Schomberg Collection at the New York Public Library, gives a list of what he describes as the principal stereotypes of the Negro in the American mind. They are as follows :—

1. The savage African.
2. The happy slave.
3. The devoted servant.
4. The corrupt politician.

11

5. The irresponsible citizen.
6. The petty thief.
7. The social delinquent.
8. The vicious criminal.
9. The sexual superman.
10. The superior athlete.
11. The unhappy non-white.
12. The natural-born cook.
13. The natural-born musician.
14. The perfect entertainer.
15. The superstitious churchgoer.
16. The chicken and water-melon eater.
17. The razor and knife " toter."
18. The uninhibited expressionist.
19. The mental inferior.

As Dr. Reddick points out, these stereotypes supplement each other though they are sometimes mutually contradictory.

The purpose of the following pages is to follow up Dr. Reddick's assertions, to examine in some detail the way in which the Negro has been depicted in certain films, from the early 1900's up to the period of the Second World War, and particularly to point out to what extent Hollywood's attitude to Negro film characters has improved latterly. It is not too late for film producers to atone for their many years of injustice to the coloured peoples of the world, and it is hoped that in some small measure this book will help to clear away the clouds of misunderstanding and race prejudice which still exist today.

CHAPTER TWO

THE NEGRO ON THE STAGE

" The old portrayals of the Negro's way of life have had their day as fantastic caricatures. With few exceptions, plays about Negroes have been two grades above the Minstrel stage—the cork is missing but the spirit is there. This has created an apathy on the part of the Negro, who is averse to patronising the theatre which reveals him as a happy-go-lucky race in rompers. We of the American Negro Theatre are trying to present a true conception of our lives and to emulate, if we can, the integrity and dignity of artists who have reached out for us : Paul Robeson, Marian Anderson, Richard Wright, Dorothy Maynor, Canada Lee, Langston Hughes and others."

ABRAM HILL, *director of the American Negro Theatre, 1946.*

" Perhaps the greatest victory for the Negro, in terms of establishing his equality with the white man inside the theatre itself, was Paul Robeson's becoming the first Negro Othello in Broadway history—and achieving a triumph in the role."

" *Negro Digest*," *June, 1945.*

The Negro entered the entertainment world in the same manner in which he entered the social life of the United States of America—through the back door. During the slavery days he was not allowed to work in the theatre proper, except as a servant to an actor or as a worker behind the scenes. Later on his only connection with entertainment came through minstrel shows. It was through his contact with these amateur concerts and afterwards with the vaudeville theatre that the coloured performer began to make himself recognised in the early years of the nineteenth century. And after the Civil War, when thousands of freed slaves found their way to the Northern cities, there followed an influx of coloured talent into musical shows staged in New York, Chicago, Philadelphia and elsewhere. From this it was but another step to the twentieth century, and so into motion pictures, although Negro actors did not really begin to come into their own until the invention of the talking film. The coloured actor's progress on the American stage will be traced briefly, since it provides the background to his subsequent entry into films. [Recommended for a detailed study of the subject is the book, "The Negro In The American Theatre," by Edith J. R. Isaacs (Theatre Arts, New York, 1947)].

In the first hundred years of slavery the South had witnessed scores of minstrel shows, performed in the evenings by Negro workers on the plantations. Participants in these spontaneous concerts began to be known as " nigger minstrels." (The word " nigger " has since tended to become a derogatory term for a Negro and its use today is still considered an insult.) In the professional theatre there were as yet no coloured performers, although various so-called " nigger minstrel shows " were put on in the vaudeville theatres of big cities, in which these minstrels were actually white men in black-face. Black-face acts became extremely popular, in fact, but Negroes themselves could not get on the stage. The Negro necessity for self-expression, however, found certain outlets, and in the early nineteenth century some all-coloured amateur plantation companies began to tour from one plantation to another in the South in a semi-professional capacity. And as early as 1820 a group of amateur Negro actors in New York, known as the African Company, performed to mixed audiences such plays as " Othello," " Richard III " and " Macbeth " in a disused warehouse, a few blocks away from the famous African Free School, founded some thirty years previously. Best-known member of the African Company was James Hewlett, whose Richard the Third was reputed to be outstanding at that time.

The most famous of the early Negro actors was Ira Aldridge, a flamboyant, talented and altogether fascinating personality. Born in New York in 1807, Aldridge toured in Europe continuously from 1825 until his death in 1867, and played Othello with Edmund Kean in London, later touring with him in England and on the Continent for many years. Aldridge plays no specific rôle in the founding of the American Negro Theatre, but his career is interesting in that it demonstrates how a strong-minded, self-educated Negro was able, even in those days, to force his way on to the legitimate stage (though, it may be noted, *not* in the United States). But, in any case, Aldridge was an isolated example, and Negro actors in America and elsewhere did not become generally accepted in the theatre until fifty years after his death.

There seems to be very little on record to indicate that the Negro entertainer made much progress on the American stage from the time of the Reconstruction until we reach the era which has become generally known as the period in which jazz was born, i.e., from about 1890 onwards, but it is certain that great strides were made from the beginning of the present century, when Negroes began to enter both the legitimate and vaudeville theatre in ever-increasing numbers. The period—known as " the jazz era "—of Bob Cole and Bert Williams, J. Rosamund Johnson and George Walker, W. C. Handy—often referred to as " The Father of the Blues "—and others of the early pioneers, gradually gave way to the even more exciting post-war period of the Lafayette Theatre and the beginnings of Negro legitimate drama in New York and elsewhere.

Previously the Negro had proved himself adept in musical shows, being known particularly as comedian, musician, dancer and general figure of fun ; and as such he had his place in this period of American theatrical history. Vaudeville shows and touring musicals composed entirely of coloured performers were, indeed, immense successes in some of the big cities as well as " on the road." This activity was duplicated in the New York and London theatres of the period, for it is well-known that the stage in these cities at that time was largely devoted to the lighter forms of amusement : musical comedy, farces, mostly unsophisticated and often inane entertainment. The black-face tradition was carried on by such stage stars as Al Jolson and Eddie Cantor in literally dozens of shows.

With the coming of the First World War, however, a number of differences in the theatre on both sides of the Atlantic became noticeable, differences which found reflection also in the stirrings of racial consciousness among Negro writers, artists and actors. During the war Lester Walton, a dramatic critic and playwright, leased the New York Lafayette Theatre, where for the next few years various Negro producing concerns played in all types of stage entertainment, from song and dance to grand opera, from comedy to thriller, and with occasional repertory seasons of the great classical plays. The Lafayette Theatre in Harlem will always have a revered place in Negro theatrical history, and most of the honoured names of the modern Negro theatre have played there at various times in the past thirty years. (As I write, in front of me on the wall of my studio is a beautifully-designed theatre poster announcing that the Negro Federal Theatre is presenting its production of Bernard Shaw's " Androcles And The Lion " at the Lafayette Theatre—this is dated 1936—and many similar and original productions have been seen at this historic theatre.)

In 1917 " Three Plays For A Negro Theatre " by Ridgley Torrence, opened in New York, the first Negro plays to be presented outside Harlem. This programme is generally regarded as the pioneer production, although Eugene O'Neill's original drama " The Emperor Jones," which burst upon a startled New York in 1920, was, perhaps, the first modern play to draw widespread attention to Negro potentialities in the field of the legitimate theatre. Charles Gilpin, who had previously played leading rôles at the Lafayette Theatre, varying his stage work with jobs as a lift-man owing to the lack of opportunities for Negro actors at that time, made a great success with his powerful performance in the title rôle of O'Neill's sombre play. This was O'Neill's first great triumph, and no less of a triumph for Gilpin, who now ranks with Richard B. Harrison, Rex Ingram and Paul Robeson in the list of the greatest coloured actors.

Gilpin received high praise from the critics. Indeed, he was the talk of New York for his work in the O'Neill play, and of this period in Broadway theatrical history James Mason, the English actor, writing in the *Daily Mail*, September 14th, 1946, recalled an interesting story concerning Gilpin and John Barrymore. He wrote as follows : " Charles Gilpin, the coloured actor, gave a performance in ' The Emperor Jones ' which was the theatrical sensation of the day. Critics ran out of superlatives and the acting profession felt that the occasion demanded of them some gesture of admiration. A meeting was convened for the purpose of deciding what form this should take. Neither gold watch, it was thought, nor illuminated testimonial would express their feelings adequately.

" Then somebody suggested holding a dinner in Gilpin's honour. This did not go down very well, but among the few who voted in favour was John Barrymore. Was he then not affected by the question of colour, they asked him ? ' Why no,' said Barrymore, ' I have seen the performance three times and the experience has rendered me colour blind ! '

" He was then asked to suggest a formula which would relieve less broad-minded dinner guests of all possible embarrassment.

" ' That's easy,' said Barrymore, ' why don't we all black up ? ' "

Events moved on, but Negro progress in the theatre was slow. In 1930 Elmer Anderson Carter, the editor of *Opportunity*, wrote : " For fifty years the stage has adhered to the Uncle Tom tradition. When the Negro was dramatised, invariably he was a simple old retainer of the Uncle Tom type, with white woolly hair and a quavering voice, extolling the virtues of Missus and Massa ; or he was an ignorant, improvident scamp of the Topsy *genre*, although this was sometimes varied by the use of a black villain in order to provide a suitable object for the exaltation of Nordic supremacy. Even these characterisations were seldom, if ever, interpreted by actual Negroes. White men in black-face, after the fashion of the once-popular minstrel, were selected to depict Negroes. And as a rule they were just about as accurate in their portrayal as they were real in the racial delineation. The use of Negro themes interpreted by actual Negroes is comparatively new to the American stage ; it followed in the wake of the remarkable performance of Charles Gilpin in 'The Emperor Jones.' That Negro themes are capable of successful and stirring dramatic treatment, and that Negro casts can intelligently and sometimes brilliantly interpret these themes can now be attested by the success of such plays as Du Bose Heyward's ' Porgy.' And the number of plays such as ' Black Boy ' and ' Goin' Home,' dealing with various phases of Negro life produced in New York recently indicates the increasing popularity of the Negro actor."

Soon the theatrical spotlight shone on another, and better-known, facet of Negro interpretation, this time the revue. In such productions as " Shuffle Along," and " Dixie To Broadway," delightful Florence Mills, lovable *gamine*, soon came to mean to Negroes everywhere all that was most vivacious and colourful in the Negro race. This brilliant girl also appeared in the wildly successful New York revue " Blackbirds," but unfortunately, she died young, mourned by everyone on the American stage. Florence Mills was, indeed, a severe loss to the Negro theatre. Perhaps no coloured artist (with the possible exception of Robeson) has been so universally beloved.

Conditions improved. Negroes found a ready place for their particular talent in Broadway musicals, and became an accepted part of the American theatrical scene. The Lafayette Company, headed by Clarence Muse, and the Ethiopian Art Players, founded in Chicago, achieved some measure of prominence in their promising attempts to stage dramas of Negro life as well as classics of modern plays, but it was Eugene O'Neill who once more turned attention to the serious endeavour of the Negro theatre. His play " All God's Chillun Got Wings " again featured a coloured man as the central character, and dealt movingly with the problem of inter-racial marriage. The production had great historical significance; a young man who previously had been known only as a great singer of spirituals made his first acting success in this rôle. He was Paul Robeson, whose performance in this play was the first step in a long and glorious career, a career which has led to international fame. Later at the Provincetown Playhouse, known in theatre history as the small experimental stage which first drew attention to the works of O'Neill, one of America's most significant dramatists, was staged a play by another white playwright who seems always to have been in the vanguard of the handful of dramatists who have written worth-while drama for the Negro theatre. His name was Paul Green, the play was " In Abraham's Bosom," which later won the Pulitzer Prize. Featured in the cast were such well-known Negro actors of that time as Frank Wilson, Rose McClendon and Jules Bledsoe (later to become known as the creator of the famous rôle of Joe in Edna Ferber's " Show Boat.") And there were others. A classic of its kind, " Porgy," a play by Du Bose and Dorothy Heyward, was produced by the Theatre Guild in 1928 and ran successfully; it has also been revived in New York and London since that time. Again, one saw that Frank Wilson and Rose McClendon were prominent in a talented cast, while among the new names could be noted Leigh Whipper, later to become a successful Hollywood actor.

During the 1930's a wave of new plays about coloured people swept through the United States. Some, like " Savage Rhythm " and " Never No More," were not markedly successful, but others such as Hall Johnson's " Run Little Chillun," with Fredi Washington and Edna Thomas, were important enough in theme and production to bear revival today. Frank Wilson and Ernest Whitman appeared in an interesting play, " Bloodstream," in 1932. Of their work the critic of *The Stage* wrote : " Both these actors gave performances which rank among the outstanding portrayals of the season. The Negro is frequently an impressive actor because of his racial gifts of voice and vivid dramatisation." (Whitman later made a great success in Hollywood and has appeared in a number of outstanding parts, while Wilson has remained on the New York stage until the present time.) Such plays as John Wexley's " Marching Song," and his sensational " They Shall Not Die," based on the trial of the Scottsboro' Boys (for an alleged rape of white women, which it was proven they did not commit) ; " Stevedore " by Paul Peters and George

Sklar ; Paul Green's memorable chain-gang play " Hymn To The Rising Sun " ; " Mulatto " and " Don't You Wanna Be Free," both by Langston Hughes, all these and others brought to the theatre scene some indication of the deep resentment against injustice and discrimination felt strongly by Negroes themselves as well as white intellectuals and sympathisers with the Negro struggle. A number of political playwrights made their contributions to Left-Wing drama with plays on Negro themes, though none of these caused much of a stir in the American theatre, and often were of only ephemeral interest.

Nevertheless, the Left-Wing theatre played an important part in the development of the Negro on the American stage. As playwright George Sklar remarked in *New Theatre* : " Here for the first time the Negro has been truthfully and realistically portrayed ; here for the first time have we faced his essential problems and struggles. From its very inception the working class theatre has made the Negro issue a paramount one. Such plays as ' Scottsboro, Scottsboro,' ' Newsboy,' ' Black Is Only A Colour,' ' Mass Pressure ' and ' Eviction ' have in their countless performances brought home the truth of the life struggle of the thirteen million Negroes in America. And in the professional theatre it remained for a revolutionary playwright, John Wexley, to write a play like ' They Shall Not Die,' and for a revolutionary theatre, the Theatre Union, to produce a play like ' Stevedore.' "

Mention should, of course, be made of the famous " The Green Pastures," the play by Marc Connelly adapted from Roark Bradford's folk stories of Southern Negroes. Sterling Brown considers that this play is one of the greatest contributions to the Negro-American theatre. It was described as " an attempt to present certain aspects of a living religion in the terms of its believers," and most critics have seen in " The Green Pastures " a statement in simple terms of the relationship of any ordinary person and his God. A biblical story presented on the stage in an original manner, it was an outstanding success which ran for several seasons, (and was later made into a moving film.) Richard B. Harrison played De Lawd. He had previously been known as one of the outstanding coloured players on the American stage, but, like Charles Gilpin, had found some difficulty in continuing a profession in which parts for Negroes were few and far between. His favourite rôle was Shylock in " The Merchant Of Venice," and he had also been a considerable Othello ; " The Green Pastures " brought

19

him to Broadway, and served to introduce him to thousands of playgoers. His success was immediate, and in any group of outstanding Negro actors of the past thirty years Harrison's name must always be included. Others whose acting in Connelly's play was highly praised by the critics were Daniel Haynes, Wesley Hill, Jesse Shipp and Homer Tutt. "The Green Pastures," like "The Emperor Jones," "All God's Chillun Got Wings," "Stevedore," "Native Son," "Anna Lucasta" and "Deep Are The Roots," is a play which marks an important phase in the development of the Negro on the American stage. Each of these has brought the coloured actor nearer to his goal—equality in the theatre.

The Federal Theatre

In February, 1934, Harry Hopkins of the United States Government telephoned Hallie Flanagan, professor of drama at Vassar College, and said : " We've got a lot of actors on our hands. Suppose you come into New York and talk it over." That was the beginning of the famous Federal Theatre, which operated from 1935 until 1939, and which formed one of the most glorious periods in the history of the American stage. With the setting up of the Works Progress Administration in 1935, there came a new approach to the problem of unemployment on the stage, and the United States Government became the biggest play-producing organisation in the U.S.A. The government deplored the fact that there were almost thirty thousand unemployed actors in the U.S.A. ; and their aim was to provide work for these and also to provide entertainment for the many communities which had been denied a glimpse of the living theatre for many years. Hallie Flanagan took over the job of organising the whole Federal Theatre Project, the full and fascinating story of which is told in her book *Arena* (Duell, Sloan and Pearce, New York, 1940).

The Federal Theatre was responsible for discovering many new playwrights, actors and producers, and it also played a considerable part in founding an American Negro Theatre. As Hallie Flanagan states : " It was a period of beginnings, not only of government procedure as related to theatre operation, but of lines of theatre activity never before attempted in this country, or, so far as I know, in any country : the Negro Theatre ; the Bureau of Research and Publication ; the *Federal Theatre*

Magazine ; and the *Living Newspaper*, all of which activities, while stemming from New York, were nation-wide."

The Negro Theatre, under the auspices of the Federal Theatre Project, had units in New York, Chicago, Seattle, Philadelphia, Los Angeles, Boston, San Francisco, and a number of other big cities. Each unit functioned with amazing success. For example, by 1939, a survey of Negro employment in the Chicago Federal Theatre showed that nearly nine hundred Negro actors were employed, seventy-five plays had been produced, and over a hundred different productions of these plays had been given for runs of varying lengths ! Edna Thomas, Harry Edwards, Carleton Moss, Gus Smith and Rose McClendon formed the first committee of Negro theatre workers, under whose guidance the theatre was to flower ; every effort was made by this group to discover and develop Negro actors and playwrights. The productions were directed by Negroes (Frank Wilson and Rose McClendon) and also by whites (John Houseman, Elmer Rice and Orson Welles) as well as by other prominent theatre people in New York and elsewhere.

Houseman and Welles, for instance, produced a version of " Macbeth " in 1935, the first production of the Negro Theatre, which was an instantaneous success, playing for a long period in Harlem and afterwards going on a lengthy tour. After this promising beginning came many more highly interesting and successful productions. One such was " Turpentine," a play exposing the tyranny and injustice of a Southern labour camp system, and of which the *Amsterdam News* wrote : " The downtown public will not be interested in this play because here the Negro is not ' exotic.' Plain working people and their problems are movingly dramatised." Afterwards the critics were lavish in their praise of such productions as " Battle Hymn," " Horse Play " (a Negro children's play), " Heaven Bound," " Haiti," " Walk Together Chillun," " Black Empire," and other new plays by Negro dramatists. The Negro Theatre had arrived with a bang. After a hundred years the coloured actor was at last receiving recognition along with Negro playwrights and producers.

Not only in New York, but in the Southern States various Negro groups sprang up, and notwithstanding the opposition of sections of the Southern Press, they (along with other Federal Theatre shows) drew great audiences in the agricultural districts where

contact with the living theatre had, up to that time, been practically nil.

In Chicago the most original and interesting Negro productions
included such varied theatre-fare as Theodore Ward's brilliant
play " Big White Fog," a swing version of Gilbert and Sullivan's
" The Mikado " and a clever satire " Little Black Sambo."
Things did not always go smoothly, however, and the Federal
Theatre encountered a good deal of opposition to its productions
of the children's play " Little Black Sambo," and also of Ian
Keith's revival, " The Copperhead." Leading the opposition was
the *Chicago American*, which urged in an editorial that readers
should go and see for themselves what they described as " deplorably
dangerous and disrupting plays." But later on the *Chicago Herald
Examiner* was to extend a welcome to the Negro Theatre when
it wrote of the production of " Big White Fog " : " It is a sheer
joy to watch these Federal Theatre Negro players in action.
Their voices are as sweet as honey. They are as much at ease
on the stage as in their own homes." As Hallie Flanagan pointed
out in her book : " ' Big White Fog ' was important because it
was a fine play dealing with an important problem, written by
a Negro playwright." Indeed, it is true to say that Ward's play
was the first real success of a Negro writer in the American theatre.
Up to that time it had been left to white playwrights like Eugene
O'Neill and Paul Green to air racial problems on the stage, but
Theodore Ward was one of the Negro pioneers, closely followed by
Langston Hughes, Conrad Seiler, Richard Wright and others.

By 1938 a Negro production had become the hit of the season
in Chicago. This was " The Swing Mikado," which ran until
the middle of 1939 and caused such a sensation that a Broadway
manager put on his own version of the show, calling his production
" The Hot Mikado." As *Variety* noted : " This is the first time
that a managerial attraction has actually competed with the
Federal Theatre Project." Events moved on, and by 1939 the
Negro Theatre had settled down to a period of solid work, its
most successful units being in Chicago and New York. At the
Lafayette Theatre was staged Conrad Seiler's " Sweet Land,"
which traced the story of the Negro race in the United States,
and also Eugene O'Neill's " Long Voyage Home " and " In The
Zone," Paul Green's " Hymn To The Rising Sun," Frank Wilson's
" Brother Mose " and many others by both white and black

playwrights. And the Negro Theatre was not only active in Harlem. " Stevedore " by Paul Peters and George Sklar was staged in Seattle, Harold Courlander's " Swamp Mud " in Birmingham, Hall Johnson's famous " Run Lil' Chillun " in Los Angeles, John Charles Brownell's " Brain Sweat " in Cleveland, Frederick Schlick's highly original drama " Bloodstream " in Boston, Hughes Allison's " The Trial Of Dr. Beck " in New Jersey, Burton Jones's " Natural Man," in Philadelphia, and so on. Many of these productions interchanged, while others went on extensive tours in rural areas.

But all this encouraging activity was sabotaged when in June, 1939, the Federal Theatre Project came to the end of its short, but eventful career. It was, indeed, a great blow to everyone concerned ; the F.T.P. had been the means of bringing the theatre to the American people, it had put the stage back on its feet, created great new audiences, been responsible for many repercussions which were to lead to worthwhile developments in the next few years of the American Theatre. Hallie Flanagan has said : " The Project was responsible for creating the modern Negro Theatre, since it encouraged Negro playwrights, producers and actors as no other venture had done," and it is certainly true that no other theatre organisation has meant so much to coloured artists. Until 1935 Negro theatres had experienced an intermittent existence. Money was scarce, and coloured actors often had to work in other jobs while waiting for work. The Federal Theatre, however, brought money, opportunity, State assistance, adequate time for rehearsals, enthusiasm, brilliant people, in fact everything a Negro theatre needed to progress and flower. When this beloved Theatre was finally closed, it left behind a great tradition and many memories of fine and exciting productions. The progress of Negro artists on the modern American stage, culminating in Robeson's magnificent " Othello " and the successful " Strange Fruit," "Native Son," "Anna Lucasta," "Deep Are The Roots " and others, is a direct result of the inspired ground-work of Hallie Flanagan and her historic organisation.

As long ago as 1935 playwright George Sklar wrote : " The American theatre has never really given up its minstrel show conception of the Negro. The fiction of that conception has continued from the first ' burnt-cork ' performer down to Amos and Andy today. It was the fiction which played up the mythical idiosyncrasies of colour and made those idiosyncrasies a butt for the white man's laughter. It was the fiction of Sambo, the lazy good-for-nothing, crap-shooting, razor-toting, ghost-ridden, sex-hopped Negro. And although the long tradition of the white actor in black-face was finally broken and the Negro himself allowed to appear on the stage, that fiction still prevails. Cork or no cork, it was still the white man's fabrication of the Negro. And it still persists when you see an Ethel Waters on the stage, a Buck and Bubbles in vaudeville, a Cab Calloway in a night club, or a Stepin Fetchit in the movies. These performers have, consciously or unconsciously, allowed themselves to fall in with that fiction and to be utilised in this way because the commercial theatre allows for no other conception. And even in the legitimate theatre, when the Negro is treated more seriously, the same thing holds true ; in such plays as ' Porgy,' ' Harlem,' ' Singin' The Blues,' and ' Run Lil' Chillun ' we have virtually the same conception of the Negro." The Federal Theatre, in its five years of glorious life, helped to break the stereotype referred to by Sklar, and on the American stage in the past ten years the situation for Negro actors has shown a marked improvement.

The Modern Period

Since 1939 a number of all-Negro productions have been staged in New York, and many coloured actors have become famous on Broadway in such shows as " Cabin In The Sky," " Mamba's Daughters," " Native Son," " Carmen Jones " and others. However, the tendency has been towards the presentation of all-Negro productions rather than plays with mixed casts ; only very rarely has it been the case that a Negro actor has successfully appeared in a good part in a play alongside white actors (the most recent example of this being " Deep Are The Roots," in which Gordon Heath, a brilliant young actor, was outstanding as the Negro soldier, playing the rôle successfully in New York and London.) Rather has it been that all-Negro plays like " Green Pastures " and " Porgy " have been the means of drawing attention to the Negro as actor, not purely on his merits as an *actor*, but rather on his personality as a *performer*.

Some all-Negro plays, produced in New York, have, nevertheless, created minor theatrical sensations, especially in recent years. For example, in 1944 a play was produced in the basement of the Harlem Public Library ; called " Anna Lucasta," it has enjoyed a long run at the Broadway theatre to which it was transferred, and has also been seen in Chicago and other American cities. Written by Robert Yordan, and acknowledged as the most successful Negro " hit " in theatrical history, it has already broken the record of Marc Connelly's " Green Pastures " (which reached six hundred and forty performances on Broadway). Hollywood has made some offers, and it is likely that a film of the play, starring its acting " discovery " Hilda Simms, may soon be made. It is a production of the American Negro Theatre, a co-operative venture consisting of actors most of whom have to earn their living outside the theatre and play only at nights. " Anna Lucasta," however, has put the American Negro Theatre on its feet. In fact, some critics consider that a new era in Broadway history was instituted when the play was produced. As Louis Kronenberger stated in the journal *P.M.* : " For the first time Negro actors and actresses are playing rôles that do not have a racial label. Here is a play not about Negroes, but about *people.*" " Anna Lucasta " is a forceful, down-to-earth comedy-drama of American life that could be lived by both white and coloured people. The play contains no self-conscious racial distortions, and the first-rate production points the versatile talents of the hard-working people behind the American Negro Theatre. It was founded a few years ago by actor Frederick O'Neal and director-playwright Abram Hill, who has since written two plays, " Striver's Row " and " Walk Hard." Recent productions of the Negro Theatre include Theodore Browne's " Natural Man " and " Starlight " by Curtis Cooksey, but ' Anna Lucasta." is its biggest success so far.

" Anna Lucasta " takes its place among the high peaks of Negro progress in the theatre which range from Gilpin's " The Emperor Jones " and Robeson's " All God's Chillun Got Wings " to the more recent " Native Son " and " Big White Fog," Robeson's Othello, Canada Lee's Caliban, James Gow and Arnaud d'Usseau's courageous play "Deep Are The Roots," and the operettas " Porgy and Bess" and "Carmen Jones." For the first time since the Lafayette Stock Company's seasons of a dozen years ago, a thriving Negro theatre takes its place on Broadway. As Claire Leonard remarked in *Theatre Arts*, July, 1944 : " The American Negro Theatre seeks to discover ' something ' inherent in the Negro's native qualities that can be expressed through the theatre. They do not know what it is nor how it will reveal itself. When they recognise it, they will explore and build on and around it. Now they can acknowledge only two native accents : rhythm and naturalness."

The significance of Robert Yordan's play was stressed by a writer in the magazine Ebony, December 1945, who noted : "The triumph of ' Anna Lucasta ' on the Great White Way has, I hope, shattered completely whatever few colour bars remained on Broadway. Negro actors demonstrated that they could do as well if not better than whites in a play written about whites. Coloured stage stars have, at last, cast off all hi-de-ho minstrel stampeding of the ' Shuffle Along ' and ' Blackbirds ' variety to reach full maturity in the theatre. ' Anna Lucasta ' has proved that the colour line is now finished before the footlights. One Chicago critic, Robert J. Casey, noted : ' Perhaps the solution of Chicago's theatre problem is to turn the whole thing over to the Negroes. They seem to know what to do with it ! ' "

The writer is a trifle optimistic, but goes on : " In spite of all their successes, however, coloured stars will face two major problems : how to get their wage level up to that of white actors and how to defeat Hollywood's unwritten rule against decent rôles for Negroes. In the past few years ranking Broadway producers have cleaned up more than two million dollars on low-paid Negro casts, and the talented troupe of ' Anna Lucasta ' gets—to quote Walter Winchell—' the lowest wages on Broadway.' With the play a certainty to be made into a film before long, speculation has been high on whether the movie will be made with a Negro or white cast. Producer John Wildberg has been insisting on the original coloured cast, but to date Hollywood moguls have turned thumbs down. A Hollywood attorney representing Philip Yordan and an interested film company says Southerners would object, *and would not sit through a film showing Negroes in anything but overalls* (Author's italics).

" At bottom the controversy comes back to the key question : Will Hollywood allow Negroes to play everyday, ordinary, human Americans ? The answer has been, and is still, ' No.' Nothing from the cinema capital has given any hope of any change. Whether ' Anna Lucasta ' can overthrow Dixie domination overnight is doubtful, but the ambitious young actors in the cast cannot help dreaming that they will."

From this all-too-brief survey, therefore, it may be seen that although the Negro has made great strides in the theatre in the past fifty years, and although few will deny that his progress has been quite formidable when one remembers that Negroes were rarely seen on the stage at all at the beginning of the present century, the coloured stage artist still tends to be treated in the nature of a performer rather than an actor. When people go to see an all-coloured production they have a tendency to regard it as a piece of " entertainment," as something to be *watched* rather than *felt*. Thus it is submitted that Jim Crow—the expression meaning the practice of social and political segregation of Negroes—unfortunately still exists in the American theatre, though to a far greater degree in the Hollywood film, as we shall note later.

[*Footnote to Chapter One :* " The musical play ' Annie Get Your Gun ' was banned in Louisiana, Alabama, Georgia, Tennessee and other Southern States on the grounds that it ' presents social equality in action,' showing Negroes as being on an equality with whites, and allowing Negro and white dancers to dance together."
News-Chronicle, October 1st, 1947.

CHAPTER THREE

THE NEGRO IN SILENT FILMS

" Before the United States entered the 1914-18 war, Negroes and characters of foreign nationalities appeared in films in a rather unfavourable light. Of all, the Negro was treated most harshly."
LEWIS JACOBS *in* " *The Rise of the American Film.*"
(Harcourt, Brace, 1940)

The Early Period : 1902-1915

The first appearance of Negroes in films occurred in an early production made by trick film pioneer George Méliès in 1902. The film was called " Off To Bloomingdale Asylum," and I quote its description from the Méliès Catalogue : " An omnibus drawn by an extraordinary mechanical horse is drawn by four Negroes. The horse kicks and upsets the

27

Negroes, who falling are changed into white clowns. They begin slapping each other's faces and by blows become black again. Kicking each other, they become white once more. Suddenly they are all merged into one gigantic Negro. When he refuses to pay his car fare the conductor sets fire to the omnibus, and the Negro bursts into a thousand pieces."

It is likely that the Negroes in this early French fantasia were played by white actors. Certainly, with one or two exceptions, in American films in which Negroes appeared until the period following the First World War the black characters were invariably played by whites. In the American film a prejudice against foreigners of all kinds, and especially black men, made its appearance from an early date ; the plot of " The Masher," made in 1907, provides an example of the kind of slapstick movie made at that time which featured Negroes in a derogatory and sometimes insulting manner. The film shows a lady-killer who is unsuccessful in his wooing with everyone with whom he tries to flirt. Finally he becomes successful with a lady wearing a veil, who quickly responds to his flirtation. However, when he makes further advances and lifts her veil, he discovers to his consternation that the lady of his choice is coloured. This is, of course, unthinkable and completely horrifying ! So embarrassed and shocked is the lady-killer that he runs away as fast as his legs can carry him. Other similar films of this period included " The Wooing And Wedding Of A Coon," described by the producers as " a genuine Ethiopian comedy," which unashamedly poked fun and derision at a coloured couple ; and " Fights Of A Nation,' in which a Mexican was caricatured as a treacherous " greaser," a Jew as a briber, a Spaniard as a foppish lover, an Irishman as a quarrelsome beer-drinker, and a Negro inevitably as a cake-walker, buck dancer and razor thrower.

The " Rastus " films were a widely shown series of short comedies, bearing such titles as " Rastus In Zululand " and " How Rastus Got His Turkey," in which the central character was portrayed as a coloured buffoon possessing only the minutest intelligence. These films, and another slapstick series of the same type featuring a similar black clown called " Sambo," enjoyed great popularity in the period before the war. At this time all films in which coloured characters appeared could be divided into two categories : those like the " Rastus " and " Sambo " series which poked fun at the black man, and those which, treating him in the conventional Uncle Tom manner, portrayed him as the devoted slave who " knows his place." Between 1910 and 1914 a number of films were made on the latter theme. An example was "The Octoroon," which dealt with the tragedy of white people with a few drops of Negro blood in their veins, while such productions as " In Slavery Days " and " The Debt " were concerned with the halcyon days of the glorious Old South, in which happy, laughing slaves and genial, tolerant Southern colonels figured largely. In all the films made during this period dealing with octoroons and mulattos the apparent shame and degradation of being even in the smallest degree non-white was exploited to the full, with the obvious implication that there was something practically sub-human in being black. Indeed, in several productions the lesson seemed to be that for the unfortunate mulatto only suicide provided a logical escape from a world in which to be partially coloured was considered an even worse disgrace than to be a full-blooded Negro.

In the early days of films, Sigmund Lubin in Philadelphia produced a number of all-Negro comedies, including the " Sambo" series. One called " Coon Town Suffragettes " concerned itself with ill-natured jibes at some Southern " Mammys," a group of coloured washerwomen who set about organising a militant Negro suffragette movement to keep their no-good husbands out of saloons. " For Massa's Sake," in true Uncle Tom tradition, told the story of a devoted slave who was so fond of his master that he tried to get himself sold in order to pay his beloved white boss's gambling debts. (Needless to say, all the Lubin films and the other films quoted above were great box office successes in the South.)

An interesting early example of the type of comedy featuring Negro characters was " The Dark Romance Of A Tobacco Can," which told the story of a young man about to lose a fortune unless he can immediately produce a wife. He hastily proposes, by letter, to a girl whose name he finds in a can of tobacco, later discovering to his intense discomfiture that she is a coloured girl. Naturally he beats a hasty retreat. And there were others, more ambitious in theme and treatment. " The Debt," made in 1912, was a melodramatic story of a young man who has a child by his white wife and also one by his octoroon mistress. The children grow up, meet and fall in love, only to find out melodramatically on the eve of their marriage that they are brother and sister. The story ends in tragedy. " In Slavery Days," directed by Otis Turner in 1913, shows an octoroon, substituted during childhood for the daughter of the house, who grows up into a half-caste monster and later sells the white girl into slavery. The latter is saved from the slave dealers by her lover and the wicked octoroon is foiled. It is interesting to note that included in the cast of this picture were Robert Z. Leonard, now a well-known Hollywood director, and Margarita Fischer who afterwards became famous as a black-face comedienne and later played coloured rôles in two film versions of " Uncle Tom's Cabin."

" The Judge's Story," produced in 1911, was somewhat different from the usual run of films on Negro themes, and was probably the first movie to give a measure of sympathy to a coloured screen character. It was concerned with a young Negro worker saved from jail by the impassioned plea of a white judge to the jury. The judge had once been rendered a great service by the boy's mother, and in this way he repaid his debt of gratitude, with the result that the coloured youth went free. Obviously the implication was favourable to the white character, but the boy was also depicted in a fairer manner than was usual at that time. In an early Charles Ray film, " The Coward," a coloured minister was portrayed as a sympathetic character ; but this was the exception rather than the rule.

In its issue dated February, 1927, *Picturegoer* stated : " In the early days of comedy-making, they always made one all-black one to every dozen or so others. There was one famous one with blacked-up white players such as Ruth Roland and Marshall Neilan in the cast, while Hughie Mack and Kate Price appeared in several others." It is also probably well-known that Louise Fazenda, for example, commenced her screen career by playing Negro maids and cooks. Later she appeared without her black make-up, and afterwards successfully continued to do so ; other black-face actors, such as Walter Long and Ruth Roland, followed suit. Harold Lloyd acted in a number of early two-reel comedies with a Negro boy known as " Sunshine Sammy," who played Lloyd's amiable stooge. However, he grew up so rapidly that the series was discontinued and Lloyd continued alone, later becoming a popular comedy star. In 1914 an historic attempt was made to star a Negro in a film, the famous stage actor and singer, Bert Williams—with disastrous results. His first picture, " Darktown Jubilee," was badly received by white audiences and even resulted in a race riot in Brooklyn, while in most districts it suffered a severe boycott. Williams, an extremely talented actor, was, therefore, forced to discontinue what might have been a most promising film career.

Uncle Tom's Cabin

As early as 1909, a film had been made of Harriet Beecher Stowe's famous novel *Uncle Tom's Cabin*, directed by Edwin S. Porter, of " The Great Train Robbery " fame, with, of course, a white actor playing the part of Uncle Tom. Originally a stern and sincere indictment of slavery, the novel was altered so much in its filmic transcription that the original theme became confused. The resultant movie was a sentimental tale, mostly concerned with the faithful, dog-like devotion of Uncle Tom for Little Eva, the daughter of his white master. And as this film, which was the first full-length production to exploit the theme of Negro subservience, dealt with the slave in " his proper place," it had a wide success. Five years later another producer made a film version of Miss Stowe's novel, this time with a well-known Negro actor, Sam Lucas, in the title rôle. It was directed by William Daly with a cast including Marie Eline, Irving Cummings (now directing in Hollywood) and a number of Negro stage players in the smaller rôles. Thus, for the first time, a film about Negroes actually used coloured actors, and thenceforth with notable exceptions like " The Birth Of A Nation " and " One Exciting Night " the practice of using burnt-corked whites to play Negro rôles gradually fell into disuse.

The popularity of its theme was such that in 1918 " Uncle Tom's Cabin " was again re-made, this time directed by Searle Dawley and with white actress Marguerite Clark playing both the part of the coloured girl Topsy and the white child Little Eva. It was generally successful, as was yet another version, directed by Harry Pollard for Universal in 1927, and which featured the Negro actor James B. Lowe as Uncle Tom with blacked-up white players as Topsy, Liza, her husband and baby. Margarita Fischer played Liza, and Virginia Grey (now a well-known leading lady in Hollywood) was Little Eva. This, the most recent production, was long delayed due to differences between the director and the Negro actor who had been the first choice for the rôle of Uncle Tom. Charles Gilpin, the talented coloured actor, who had, as we have noted, made a great success on the stage when he created the part of Emperor Jones, was originally engaged to play the leading Negro part in a new version of the well-known story. Gilpin, an intelligent, proud and sensitive person, had many heated discussions with director Pollard on the manner in which the novel should be filmed and the beloved Negro character portrayed. Finally, as a protest, Gilpin left the cast and returned to New York, where it is said he went back to his old job as lift-man rather than play a well-paid screen rôle, the treatment of which, in his opinion, helped to malign his people. One can only applaud the integrity of Gilpin, and perhaps hope that his action will be emulated in future by other Negro stars when they are offered parts capable of causing harm and distress to their race.

It is, perhaps, somewhat surprising that dramatisations and film versions of " Uncle Tom's Cabin " have provoked much criticism from Negroes themselves, since the book, when published, had a great deal to do with the changing of public opinion on the question of slavery, and has long been considered as an anti-slavery novel, in fact the first of the great abolitionist works. However, in the past hundred years or so the struggle for Negro liberation has arisen to a much more intense level. The Uncle Tom who possessed the qualities of brotherly love and humility was, in his time, an argument against slavery, but Negroes have in recent years discovered militancy, and the meek Beecher Stowe character now offends the sensibilities of most coloured thinkers, writers and workers. In the eyes of most Negroes, Uncle Tom has long been a figure of contempt, and his name associated with a kind of submissive, servile, passive Negro, the " good nigger " who would not fight against oppression. The coloured American has changed. He does not want kindness and sympathy so much as he passionately desires justice and fair play, which is why the term " Uncle Tom " has in a hundred years come to mean all that is considered most contemptible in Negro mentality.

Actually the treatment of Uncle Tom in the finished Universal film, with James B. Lowe substituting for Charles Gilpin, seemed to be more sympathetic and progressive, so it would appear that

Gilpin's protests had had some effect. As Edith Isaacs remarks, in *Theatre Arts*, August, 1942 : " Uncle Tom in this 1927 version seems to wear his ball and chain with a difference." In all, there were some half a dozen different films made from Miss Beecher Stowe's historic novel, and even as I write there is some controversy going on in Hollywood concerning the proposed production of yet another version, which is being strongly resisted by Negro opinion.

The Birth Of A Nation

> " The North London Film Society opens its new season in October, when 'The Birth Of A Nation,' a classic of the silent days, will be screened. The film will be shown unabridged and will include the scenes which were once banned because they were alleged to be anti-Negro, and which caused riots in America."
> " *North London Observer," September 27, 1946.*

If " Uncle Tom's Cabin " was the first full-length picture to give prominence to Negro subservience, the first important full-length film to devote much of its content to Negro villainy was the famous " The Birth Of A Nation." It is not my intention here to analyse D. W. Griffith's monumental achievement in terms of its admittedly considerable artistic merit, but to concentrate solely upon one aspect—its extraordinarily vicious anti-Negro bias. Director Griffith was himself a Southerner, steeped in an atmosphere of racial intolerance, and brought up with the conventional Southern States attitude to the coloured man. In the majestic sweep of Thomas Dixon's strongly partisan novel *The Clansman* he probably saw perfect material for a large-scale epic. The resultant production was technically and artistically far ahead of any other movie of that period, for it must be acknowledged that Griffith was a cinematic genius and certainly the pioneer in employing a number of vital techniques in film-making which are in general use in the studios today. Nevertheless, however great the workmanship, however inspired the direction and however remarkable the acting and production of " The Birth Of A Nation," the fact remains that for sheer bias and distortion this film heads the considerable list of American motion pictures which have consciously maligned the Negro race.

Perhaps it would be as well to deal in some detail here with this truly historic film. Its great theme covered the eventful period of the American Civil War, tracing the histories of two families, one from the North and another from the Southern town of Piedmont. We are shown the palatial homestead of the Southern family, the Camerons, with the usual pretty picture of the indulgent master and the devoted slaves. The Stonemans, the family from the Northern State, and the Camerons are good friends, and, indeed, Ben Cameron falls in love with Elsie Stoneman and their marriage seems imminent. Then comes the Civil War, and the film traces their necessarily ill-fated love-story, for Southerner Cameron becomes a colonel in the Confederate Army, while Elsie is the daughter of a leading Northern politician, whose main political platform is the abolition of slavery. The bitterness of the Civil War drives the young lovers apart, and with the Confederate Army facing defeat, their love seems destined to be destroyed. Later, Cameron, the " Little Colonel," is wounded and captured in battle by Stoneman's son, and is in danger of being shot as a traitor ; but is eventually released through the intervention of Elsie, who still loves him, and his mother, both of whom plead with Lincoln on his behalf. There are many stirring scenes of the final months of the Civil War, but at last we see the final peace settlement, with the fanatical Northerners demanding harsh terms and carrying their victory into even harsher realisation.

Follows the Reconstruction Period, with Stoneman arriving in Piedmont with Elsie, and taking up his abode next door to the Camerons, who now regard him with distaste. The Northern politician has been appointed adviser to Silas Lynch, the Lieutenant Governor of the district, and quickly he proceeds to bring his ideas of " revenge on the South and complete emancipation for all Negroes " into full play. (Incidentally, " Stoneman " is said to be based upon an actual political figure of the period, Thaddeus Stevens, who also figured more recently in William Dieterle's film " The Man On America's Conscience," released in the United States under the title of " Tennessee Johnson." Griffith portrayed this character with very little attention to the true facts, and Dieterle was also attacked by the Negro Press for his unfair conception of the well-known abolitionist.)

The sympathy of the entire film is with the South, though this is not unnatural since Griffith was born in Kentucky ; but his understandable partisanship provides no real excuse for the deliberate distortion and, indeed, his almost malevolent disregard of the real historical facts. His treatment of Stoneman, the progressive, liberal-minded abolitionist, is symptomatic of his narrow and prejudiced outlook. The Yankee politician is depicted by Griffith as a villainous careerist, egotistically insincere, whose avowed plans for the betterment of Negro life and conditions are shown to be fired only by personal ambitions and a deep hatred of the South. With the " renegade " Negro leader, Silas Lynch, he is seen plotting to enforce a " black stranglehold " (Griffith's own description) on the defeated Southern States. The mulatto, Lynch, is also shown as a character of the utmost villainy. His lust extends not only to power, it seems, but also to Elsie, and in the final reel of the film the inevitable rape attempt occurs, following the politician's refusal to allow the mulatto to marry his daughter. (This latter incident provided yet another subtle dig at the " Northern liberal," who, while fighting for Negro emancipation and considering that blacks were the social equal of whites, still refused to allow his daughter to marry a man with Negro blood in his veins.) The pathological obsession of some Americans with the Negro rape of white women is remarkable, and seems to have occurred with astonishing frequency in American literature of the past hundred years. Griffith's " The Birth Of A Nation " marked its first appearance on the screen.

His treatment of mulattos, those " unfortunates " who possess both white and Negro blood, is interesting in its vehemence. Not only does he depict Silas Lynch in the most unfavourable light, but he also introduces another half-caste, Stoneman's servant and mistress, who is revealed as a scheming, envious, entirely unpleasant creature, yearning for the time when she can treat whites not as equals but as *inferiors*. Hatred and malevolence are constantly reflected in her dark, evil face when she meets white politicians in Stoneman's house, and in one astonishing scene, she literally writhes with hate, spitting fury and vowing vengeance on Stoneman's guests and friends for continuing to treat her as a servant rather than as the politician's " unofficial " wife. And there is much more in the same vein. Mulattos receive from Griffith even worse treatment, it would appear, than full-blooded Negroes.

To continue with the plot of " The Birth Of A Nation," Lynch and the politician eject all the white Southerners from positions of power and prominence, and substitute ignorant, ill-educated Negro types. From the programme notes given out at the first performance of the film comes Griffith's description of the following scenes : " The rule of the carpet-baggers begins. The Union League, so-called, wins the ensuing State election. Silas Lynch, the mulatto, is chosen Lieutenant Governor, and a legislature with carpet-bag and Negro members in overwhelming majority loots the State. Lawlessness runs riot. Whites are elbowed off the streets, over-awed at the polls, and often despoiled of their possessions."

And the above is an accurate picture of events in the actual film. We see swaggering black toughs elbowing white women off the pavements and indulging in similar brutalities to all the white citizens. The new *regime* of " Northern progressiveness " brings, according to Griffith, an even worse tyranny than existed previously when the white landowners were in power. There follows much talk of a " Black Empire " and of Negro plans for the complete suppression of the South, and such is Griffith's directorial power that we find ourselves believing him when he draws the situation in the final reel as being fraught with hideous disaster for the formerly well-to-do, and equally well-meaning, whites in the defeated South. They are, it seems, threatened by the plundering, raping and looting of their sub-human ex-slaves. But help is at hand. A new and heroic band of Southerners springs up, led by ex-colonel Ben Cameron, an organisation of ex-Servicemen, a group which will put to rights all the injustices of the Northern rule. This new army of courageous and chivalrous heroes will bring justice (and with it the terror of the hangman's rope) to every Negro in the South. And the name of the organisation ? None other than that dreaded and terrifying body, the now notorious Ku Klux Klan !

By night they ride in their white hoods, lynching, murdering, whipping and threatening. By sheer force, intimidation, tyranny and terrorism the black citizens of the Old South are driven from office, even from the polls, afraid to use their hard-won votes, afraid to take further advantage of their new-found privileges. Since, however, the Negroes have been depicted throughout the film's length in the worst possible light, the inevitable con-clusion reached by cinemagoers is that their persecution by the Ku Klux Klan is only part of their just deserts. Indeed, audiences running into millions must have left the cinema with this conclusion.

" The Birth Of A Nation " showed starkly that the question of historic accuracy did not trouble Griffith overmuch. There was no attempt at truth, and certainly not justice, as may be seen in the following instances. Time and again we are shown the " good niggers," the trusted and faithful Negro slaves who still cling devotedly to the Camerons through times of war and defeat, and hate the free North, preferring slavery in the South. No doubt at that period in the history of the U.S.A. these types of black retainers did in fact exist, but it was inevitable that Griffith concentrated all his patronising sympathy upon these Uncle Tom characters while showing all other black men as vicious rebels and killers. Gus, for example, a " renegade " Negro, formerly employed as a servant in the Camerons' household, is seen at the end of the war as a swaggering soldier in the coloured militia occupying the town of Piedmont. Inevitably he is a hard-swearing, hard-drinking, glowering and lustful scoundrel, and just as inevitably he tries to rape the white heroine Flora Cameron, eventually driving her to suicide in a brutal attempted-rape scene. (Gus was played by a white actor, Walter Long, noted for his tough and villainous appearance, made even more hideous, incidentally, by the liberal application on his features of what appeared to be black boot polish. Other white actors played leading coloured characters, for apparently Griffith would not employ Negro actors to play parts of any significance, even though they be villains.)

Another scene shows the newly formed Negro Parliament in session. Here " the new tyrants of the South " hold sway. They concern themselves with passing measures preventing white citizens from holding any important offices, lounging back in their chairs with their bare feet up on their desks, a bottle of whisky in one hand and a leg of chicken in the other. These " politicians " are not interested in affairs of State ; they desire only revenge on their former white masters and content themselves with planning retaliation, the while intimidating white girls in the gallery with nods, winks and lewd suggestions. This is how Griffith handles the first historic attempts by the former slaves to govern themselves in that tragic post-war period. His monstrous caricatures of coloured politicians, officials, army officers, soldiers and servants in " The Birth Of A Nation " rival anything seen on the screen since that time.

The final reel of this monumental film sees the Ku Klux Klan riding into town and sweeping the blacks out of Piedmont, scattering the frightened Negroes in a magnificently directed crowd scene. The black bullies are tamed by the hooded heroes ! In one sequence a group of coloured soldiers are besieging a hut where the proud and heroic Cameron family have fled and are fighting for their lives. As the murdering blacks, with bulging eyes and frothing mouths, are breaking down the door for the final kill, the white-hooded Ku Klux Klan sweep over the hill to a burst of Wagnerian music and in an exciting and impressive sequence save the white family from the Negro terror. Such a distortion has, indeed, to be seen to be believed ; many younger filmgoers who have been told about " the great film, ' The Birth Of A Nation ' " are by no means aware of its almost unbelievable viciousness. And, although it must be admitted that Griffith's epic has an honoured place in film history and may still be regarded technically as a landmark in film production, it deserves scant recognition nowadays from more enlightened cinema audiences. Even regarded as a period piece, it is still capable of causing harm.

As historian Lewis Jacobs says of " The Birth Of A Nation," in his book *The Rise of the American Film* : " The film was a passionate and persuasive avowal of the inferiority of the Negro. In viewpoint it was, surely, narrow and prejudiced. Griffith's Southern upbringing made him completely sympathetic towards author Thomas Dixon's exaggerated ideas and the fire of his convictions gave the film a rude strength. At one point in the picture a title bluntly editorialised that the South must be made ' safe ' for the whites. The entire portrayal of the reconstruction days showed the Negro, when freed from his white domination, as an ignorant, lustful villain. Negro Congressmen were pictured drinking heavily, coarsely reclining in Congress with bare feet upon their desks, lustfully ogling the white women in the balcony. Gus, the Negro servant, is depicted as a renegade when he joins the emancipated Negroes. His advances on Flora, the ' Little Colonel's ' sister, and Silas Lynch's proposal to the politician Stoneman's daughter, are overdrawn to make the Negro appear obnoxious and audacious. The Negro servants who remain with the Camerons, the dignified Southern family, on the other hand, are treated with patronising regard for their faithfulness, and the necessity of the separation of Negro from white, with the white as the ruler, is passionately maintained throughout the film. The social implications of this celebrated picture aroused a storm of protest in the North."

Griffith had the impudence to insert an epilogue to the film, reading—" The establishment of the South in its rightful place is the birth of a new nation. . . . The new nation, the real United States, as the years glided by, turned away for ever from the blood lust of war and anticipated with hope the world millennium in which the brotherhood of love should bind all the nations." And after this production, which was an incitement to racial intolerance (and worse), Griffith went on to make the famous " Intolerance," which condemned the very things most apparent in his previous film. Perhaps he was never fully aware of his own shortcomings ?

At any rate a storm of indignation arose after the first showing of " The Birth Of A Nation," a storm which continued through the war years and well into the 1920's. It is said that later on Griffith relented somewhat concerning the cruelty of his portrayal of the Negro in this historic film ; and in 1918, in his " Greatest Thing In Life," he inserted a sequence in which a dying Negro soldier cried for his mother and a white comrade kissed him as he died. This shamelessly sentimental scene was, as Richard Watts, Jr., remarked, in *New Theatre*, November, 1936, " a pretty shoddy and futile effort to make up for what he had done in his film of Dixon's novel *The Clansman*."

In New York, " The Birth Of A Nation " was banned for a time, and it was also refused a licence for exhibition in Connecticut, Illinois, Kansas, Massachusetts, Minnesota, New Jersey, Wisconsin, Ohio and many other states. Such prominent people as Oswald Garrison Villard, Jane Addams and Charles Eliot, President of Harvard, spoke bitterly and often against the showing of the film. Rabbi Stephen Wise declared that it was " an intolerable insult to the Negro people." The Liberal magazine *The Nation* described the film as " improper, immoral and injurious, a deliberate attempt to humiliate ten million American citizens and to portray them as nothing but beasts." Historians were quick to point out the many inaccuracies in the film, and generally the effect upon intelligent people was one of antagonism and indignation. Griffith was shocked by this opposition and rose to the defence of his film with a pamphlet entitled *The Rise and Fall of Free Speech in America*, which included quotations from those magazines and newspapers which had endorsed the film, but which did not attempt to answer the accusations of race prejudice. He was greatly incensed by the attack on his beloved film and for many years referred to the public protest as deliberately unfair. But the movie deserves all the protests made against it, then and now.

As Dr. Lawrence Reddick points out in *The Journal of Negro Education*, Summer, 1944 : " The film's justification of the Ku Klux Klan was at least one factor which enabled the Klan to enter upon its period of greatest expansion, reaching a total membership of five million." A contemporary American film critic, Richard Watts, Jr., states in *New Theatre* : " As a completely partisan account of a particularly ugly chapter in American history, ' The Birth Of A Nation ' still possesses a certain stunning power. But its cruel unfairness to the Negro is an inescapable blot upon it." And the English film critic Oswell Blakeston declares, in *Close Up*, August, 1929 : " As a spectacle Griffith's production was awe-inspiring and stupendous, but as a picture of Negro life it was not only false, but it has done the Negro irreparable harm. And no wonder, since it was taken from a puerile novel, *The Clansman*, a book written to arouse racial hate by appealing to the basest passions of the semi-literate." Many leading critics on both sides of the Atlantic agreed with the above statement.

Prominent in the movement against the showing of the film was the National Association for the Advancement of Coloured Peoples, which did a great deal of valuable work in this direction, canalising the protests of Negroes and enlightened white organisations and individuals everywhere. As late as 1931 the film was banned in Philadelphia after the Mayor had declared it " prejudicial to peace between the black and white races." Nevertheless, in spite of all the public action taken against the film, " The Birth Of A Nation " was an enormous financial success, establishing D. W. Griffith as the greatest film director of his time and exerting a considerable influence upon the millions of people who saw it. It is to be regretted that a film which still occupies something of a place of honour in the list of memorable achievements of the cinema could bear such responsibility for a great and incalculable harm. Thirty

**HAZEL SCOTT and LENA HORNE
in *By Hook Or By Crook***

years ago it constituted an incitement to race riot, and seeing it today still tends to leave a nasty taste in one's mouth.

Incidentally, this controversial picture was revived in New York in 1942, despite the protests of Negroes everywhere, but eventually due to the opposition of the Negro Press, the picture was withdrawn after a run of a few days. Afterwards Lowell Mellett, Chief of the Bureau of Motion Pictures of the Office of War Information, assured the Press that his office would seek to prevent future exhibition of Griffith's film ; and since that time it has been shown only by film societies in the U.S.A. and Britain.

The Post-War Period

Hollywood movies began to come into their own after the First World War, and Negro actors were used much more often, though invariably in the rôles of servants, bell-boys, tramps and inferiors of every description. In 1922, D. W. Griffith made " One Exciting Night," perhaps the first, certainly the most striking, example of the use of the Negro as the contemptible comic relief. This comedy is a noteworthy instance of how a director steeped in anti-Negro prejudice can influence his audience. The Negro character in " One Exciting Night " (played, incidentally, by a white man in black-face since the director would still not use a Negro actor) commenced the long line of those well-known screen puppets, the cowardly black men whose hair turns white or stands on end when they meet danger in any form. We know them well by now ; they are afraid of the dark, of thunderstorms, of firearms, of animals, of police, and so on. Griffith was the pioneer in portraying the coloured man as a figure of contempt, and for his treatment of the Negro character in " One Exciting Night " he must be accorded the dubious honour of having commenced the long, long trail of celluloid depicting the Negro as a frightened, shivering wretch, lily-livered, weak-kneed, stupid and almost bestial. In " The Birth Of A Nation " he portrayed the coloured man with hatred, and seven years later, in " One Exciting Night," with contempt. Griffith had, indeed, made some " progress."

Above : CALEB PETERSON, REX INGRAM, LENA HORNE, DOOLEY WILSON and LEON HARDWICK. Below : FRANK SINATRA and The Charioteers.

As Lionel Collier remarked nearly twenty years afterwards, in " *Picturegoer and Film*

Weekly," October 5th, 1940 : " When, years ago, D. W. Griffith made ' One Exciting Night,' he started a cycle of films which has never ceased. The ingredients are familiar : one haunted house, one scared Negro, one hero partially frightened, one heroine, one villain, and so on. . . ."

I shall not deal too fully here with the spate of jungle pictures and films about " darkest Africa " which appeared in the 1920's. Each of these movies used large numbers of Negroes to form the living background to the acting of the white stars, and each one without exception portrayed the black man as a savage, a cannibal or a head-hunter. These types of films had a certain significance in the fact that they helped to spread the general belief that all black men were brutes whose rightful home was the jungle and certainly not in " civilised " America, where they could count themselves lucky even to be tolerated by the whites. (But it must also be admitted that many coloured actors like Rex Ingram and Noble Johnson made their initial appearances on the screen in such jungle films as " West Of Zanzibar," " Black Journey," " Diamond Handcuffs " and " Samba," thereby obtaining their first experience of the film medium, and sometimes going on to play larger, more important and—though rarely—more sympathetic rôles in further movies.)

It was in the silent film days that Hal Roach's famous series of " Our Gang " comedies first appeared. In these a coloured child was always featured as part of the gang, and " Farina," as he was called, became a popular and much-loved screen character in the United States and over here. It has been stated by other writers that " Farina," and later on, " Stymie," were treated generally as the butt of the gang's humour and that the " Our Gang " series takes its place in the story of screen prejudice. For example, that well-known film critic, the late Harry Allan Potamkin, asserted : " The treatment of Farina is typical of the theatrical acceptation of the Negro as clown, clodhopper or scarecrow, an acceptation which is also social. No objections have been raised by the solid South to Farina's mistreatment by the white children (to me a constantly offensive falsehood and unpardonable treachery of the director)."

To some extent Potamkin's remarks were justified, but it is only fair to add that in the opinion of many other critics a great deal of good has been done by these comedies, which incidentally, still continue to be produced today and remain as popular with both coloured and white audiences as they were twenty years ago. Firstly, and I consider this significant, the black child is part of a gang, one member of an otherwise white social group. He is treated, in most essentials, on equal terms with the other children, for they, like all small children, are young enough not to possess the prejudices of their parents. The coloured and white children play together, have many adventures together, share their successes and bear their misfortunes equally, and this, I submit, is most commendable. Broadly speaking, the coloured child functions usually in these short comedies on an equal plane with the other children and there can be no doubt that these otherwise innocuous Hal Roach comedies have played their part—although an admittedly minor part—in helping towards an understanding of the Negro and his family. Richard Wright, in his autobiography *Black Boy*, tells us that coloured children were never allowed to play near white children, and certainly never *with* them. And this, no doubt, is true in most Southern communities, where segregation is ruthlessly observed from childhood. Therefore, for a large number of popular Hollywood films with a very wide appeal to indicate dozens of times, in a series lasting over a number of years, that there is no serious objection to white and coloured children playing together, seems to me to be a significant point, perhaps overlooked by those writers and critics who claim that the " Our Gang " films feature in the pattern of cinematic discrimination.

Dr. Lawrence Reddick lends some support to this contention when he says : " Comparatively speaking, the record of the ' Our Gang ' series for fair play was well above the average. Some of the films may be classified as pro-Negro in that the humour and pathos which come to children were presented without any apparent angling. The children were not separated. They played together, easily and naturally, though in some of the films there was a tendency to place the Negro child in a somewhat more ridiculous or subservient position. The Negro child actors, with one exception, were brilliant and winsome. Even now film fans speak with enthusiasm of ' Sunshine Sammy,' ' Farina ' and ' Stymie.' ' Buckwheat ' did not come off so well nor was he (or she) so well cast. Occasionally, Negro movie fans would protest about a line here or a situation there, but on the whole

' Our Gang ' maintained itself as one of Hollywood's few contributions to better Negro-white relations."

An indication of how during the 1920's certain of the more popular screen magazines viewed the presence of the Negro in films can be gauged from this extract from an article titled " Black Laughter," which appeared in *Picturegoer*, of February, 1927 : " There is something irresistibly contagious about the wide grin of the darkie. Perhaps it is the flash of white teeth against their ebony background that makes it so effective and evokes an immediate answering guffaw. Perhaps it is merely tradition, associated with the many nigger minstrels of one's youth, but black faces and comedy usually go together on the screen. When the darkie is frightened he is apt to roll his eyes and shake like a jelly, and the effect is nearly as funny as when he is pleased. And the best (*sic*) part of D. W. Griffith's ' One Exciting Night ' was the darkie, in this case not a darkie at all, but an exceedingly well-known ' black-face comedian.' The Negro is so much a part of the daily life of America that he is seen in at least fifty per cent. of their films in his natural capacity of lift-man, railway guard, porter, boot-black, etc., and nigger ' mammys ' also abound, and even faithful darkie butlers. Negro humour has its own particular flavour ; it sometimes appears in sub-titles, but it does not appeal to everybody when written as much as it does when acted. The American Negro's fondness for watermelon has been well-exploited too, along with most of his other foibles. No film of the Old South is complete without its coloured members of the cast. Sometimes they are not comedy creations, however. In ' The Birth Of A Nation,' the Negro appears in a very sinister guise, and there have been many instances of huge, terrifying black men appearing in sea stories. Very few screen orgies are seen in which Negroes are not well to the fore."

The above is almost irresistible in its naïveté. But there were other more responsible critics, such as Robert Herring, who wrote at that time in *Close Up* : " There ought to be serious Negro films since there are Negro novels and plays and poems. There ought to be because the Negro is marvellously photogenic and the cinema is equally an affair of blacks and whites. There ought to be because here is a race which has, in a short time, expressed itself vitally in literature and the consideration of that literature shows that the qualities which make it so vital are exactly those which films demand."

From " The Birth Of A Nation " to " The Jazz Singer " there were dozens of films produced in which coloured actors were seen, and some thirty or so productions with Negro *themes*, none, however, with any particular significance. Possible exceptions included such movies as " Free and Equal," a direct appeal to intolerance, which attempted to capitalise on the eternal theme of Negro inferiority ; and an adaptation of Edward Sheldon's play " The Nigger," starring William Farnum. The latter film was a puerile attempt to foster even more racial hatred than already existed in American social life. " Broken Chains " followed in the traditions of " The Birth Of A Nation " and showed the Negro as a murderous and scoundrelly agitator. And there were others ; but, generally speaking, Negroes appeared in films of the 1920's either as servants or savages. Only very occasionally did a director or a screenwriter take it into his head to produce work in which a Negro featured as a real character (and even when this happened he was always shown in an unfavourable light, pictured inevitably with one of two alternatives : hatred or contempt).

Among Negro writers and intellectuals themselves opinions differed as to their progress in the cinema. Geraldyn Dismond wrote in *Close Up*, August, 1929 : " The Negro actor and the part he has played in the development of the American movie is one of the most interesting phases of one of America's greatest industries. Because no true picture of American life can be drawn without the Negro, his advent into the movie was inevitable ; but also because of the prejudices which have hampered and retarded him since his coming to America, his debut was delayed. The Negro entered the movies through a back door labelled ' Servants' Entrance.' However, beggars cannot be choosers, and it is to his credit that he accepted the parts assigned to him, made good and opened the door for bigger things."

But Elmer Anderson Carter was not reassured, and replied as follows, in his magazine *Opportunity* : " Traditional racial attitudes in America have proven a tremendous obstacle in the way of those whose creative instincts lead them to see the beauty and pathos in Negro life. Motion picture producers will hesitate long before they attempt anything in the nature of a new evaluation of the Negro. America is conservative to the point of reaction

47

about ideas—especially ideas on the so-called race problem.
Therefore, it is probable that the screen will follow in the paths
of least resistance, for on that path the box office lies." His
prophecies were to be realised for a good many years to come.
In Hollywood, however, things were to move fast, for a great turning
point in the progress of the film as an art form had come with the
discovery of talking pictures, bringing with it an awareness of the
part the coloured actor could play in the development of sound
on the screen.

CHAPTER FOUR

THE COMING OF THE SOUND FILM

" Our idea of the Negro is about as Negroid as Al Jolson,
and no more."

KENNETH MACPHERSON, *Editor, " Close Up," August, 1929.*

" Hollywood can only visualise the plantation type of Negro—
the Negro of ' Poor Old Joe ' and ' Swanee Ribber.' It is absurd
to use that type to express the modern Negro as it would be to
express modern England in the terms of an Elizabethan ballad."

PAUL ROBESON in *" Film Weekly,"* September 1st, 1933.

On August 6th, 1926, at the Warner Theatre in New York,
a new era was born—the sound film was pioneered
by the Warner Brothers. Since 1900 many inventors,
including Thomas Edison and Lee De Forest, had been experimenting with recorded sound, and as early as 1923 Phonofilms,
the first sound-on-film system, invented by De Forest, had been
introduced into cinemas as a novelty interlude. But in 1926,
the Warners' programme of seven short vocal and musical subjects
and their feature " Don Juan," with John Barrymore, demonstrated
that a miracle had arrived—music and song could be heard on
the screen. Immediately Warner Brothers' Vitaphone productions
was established, and the Broadway singing star Al Jolson was
signed to appear in their first feature film using the new system.
This was " The Jazz Singer " in which Jolson's songs were to
be recorded, though no attempt was to be made yet to record
actual dialogue.

When this film was shown in 1927 it made history, for as Jolson crossed the screen to sing his song the microphone picked up an *ad lib* line, " Say Ma, listen to this," and the packed first night audience roared their approval. Talking films had come to stay. In " The Jazz Singer," and later on " The Singing Fool," Al Jolson, famous on the stage for many years for his black-face singing and Negro impersonations, sang such songs as " Mammy " with his face smeared in the traditional burnt cork. The Negro had arrived in talking pictures—as a black-face comedian ! This may be considered ironically significant since the Negro actor's film career for a number of years followed in the same tradition : white men in black-face, or coloured men in inane black masks—on the screen it amounted to the same thing.

During the early 1930's all-coloured stage productions such as " Blackbirds " and " Porgy," produced in New York and elsewhere, had spot-lighted the Negro's capabilities as a song and dance performer.   Hollywood, which had enthusiastically entered the era of the talking film and was recklessly signing up all available musical comedy talent, was quick to realise the commercial potentialities of Negro entertainers, with a consequence that in many early " all talking, all singing, all dancing epics," numbers of Negro singers, dancers and jazz musicians imported from the New York stage and night clubs were featured prominently. Such names as Stepin Fetchit, Hazel Jones, " Snowball," and later Ethel Waters, Nina Mae McKinney and " Sleep' n' Eat " came to the fore, bringing with them a recurrence of the popular myth that the American Negro was a happy, laughing, dancing imbecile, with permanently rolling eyes and widespread, empty grin.   In films too numerous to mention actors like Fetchit demeaned themselves, bringing Negro dignity to its lowest common denominator.   " Stepin Fetchit has dawdled and shuffled through identical performances in a number of Hollywood films as if he were bent on demonstrating the descent of the Negro from a lower order of the animal kingdom."   So wrote film critic Robert Stebbins in *New Theatre* in 1935.   It is recorded that this actor made (and subsequently lost) a great fortune playing stupid " darkies " and, not unnaturally, other Negro actors followed suit.   Even today, it is saddening to note, there still exist those coloured players who gag and grimace their way across the screen in Stepin Fetchit tradition.

Hearts In Dixie

By 1929 no film had succeeded in giving any real indication of the Negro's immense acting ability. The first of Hollywood's all-coloured films, " Hearts In Dixie," directed by Paul Sloane for Fox, promised much, but we were given no new slant on Negro life and thought, just the same old hackneyed routine. The story was so slight as to be almost non-existent, but apparently we were to be compensated for this by a succession of endless musical numbers, spirituals, prayer meetings, cotton-picking and the like. The film could have been a turning-point for coloured players, and was produced with a great blare of publicity. It was eagerly awaited by Negroes everywhere, but unfortunately did not succeed in living up to its promise. Nevertheless it takes its place in this brief history, since it was the pioneer all-Negro film made in Hollywood. And, in *Opportunity*, April, 1929, film critic Robert Benchley gave it as his opinion that this film demonstrated that " in the Negro the sound picture had found its ideal protagonist." Was he right ?

Once again we had the Southern plantation in " dear old Dixie," a place obviously beloved more by Hollywood than by Negroes themselves. Again we were introduced to the faithful black plantation workers, toiling hard in the cotton fields all day, and relaxing at night by singing, dancing and generally making merry under the benevolent eye of the white master, always held in such affection by his black servants. Stepin Fetchit typifies the lazy, good-for-nothing but good-natured slave, unwilling to work yet forgiven for his back-slidings and errant ways. The boss " playfully " kicks him in the rear, and Fetchit responds with a broad grin and a sly wink to the audience. Here is the typical screen " darkie," a picture distorted out of all serious reality. Black clown Fetchit follows in the Uncle Tom tradition : he is a " good nigger," he is lazy and shiftless, yet " all right at heart," and—most important of all—*he knows his place*. Paul Sloane's film contained no theme of any real significance ; he remained in the well-worked groove, he avoided controversy, perhaps did not admit that any existed. To sum up : " Hearts In Dixie " was an ambitious, probably well-meaning pioneer effort, chiefly known as the film responsible for bringing to the screen that gifted and wholly delightful actor Clarence Muse, who has stayed in Hollywood since that time. His charming performance, fine dignity, grand voice and noble bearing more than compensated for the appearance of Stepin Fetchit in one of his more nauseating " lazy but lovable vagabond " parts.

Discerning critic Henry Dobb wrote pungently of this film in *Close Up* : " Superficially we might have advanced since the mountebankery of Griffith's ' One Exciting Night,' though Stepin Fetchit's rôles in ' The Ghost Talks ' and ' Hearts In Dixie ' are directly in the traditions of the vaudeville stage and the black-face comics. The Negro, in short, for all his humanity, is still behind the bars of the cage, a cage flooded with the glare of publicity and intoned with ' the haunting strains of Negro spirituals.' It is obvious from ' Hearts In Dixie ' that director Paul Sloane has not yet emerged from that state of mind which conceives of the Negro film as leaning towards open-necked shirts, bandana hats and the melodic charms of ' Old Black Joe ' and ' The Lonesome Road.' The tragedy is not the tragedy in the film, but the tragedy of the film ; the tragedy of these untainted folk strutting their stuff to the required pattern, playing their parts as the white man likes to believe they do. The Negro and all his coloured brothers are not museum specimens. Nor are they mountebanks. If they are blessed with a more than human power of music and speech, of rhythm and colour, then they have it over us mere whites. But if ' Hearts In Dixie ' is a specimen of coloured expression under the ægis of Hollywood let us next time hand the whole process over to the Negroes themselves."

Hallelujah

At all events " Hearts In Dixie " almost started one of the well-known Hollywood cycles, for soon after its production was announced Metro-Goldwyn-Mayer assigned King Vidor to direct " Hallelujah " which, to quote a 1929 publicity blurb—" will be the ace of the all-Negro talking pictures." If it was hoped that a director as intelligent as Vidor, and Negro actors like Daniel Haynes and Nina Mae McKinney, would make " Hallelujah " memorable, then expectations were short-lived. The slight story, of a country boy who temporarily succumbs to the wiles of a bad woman, probably seemed at first to possess some dramatic power ; and Daniel Haynes as the boy gave a performance which was extremely moving in its simplicity and sincerity. But the central theme became swamped, inevitably perhaps, by the forty or so singing sequences of folk songs, spirituals, baptism wails, work songs and blues. " Hallelujah," written by novelist Wanda Tuchock, was, however, an interesting film, and certain parts of it indicated the undeniable power of the director. But how much King Vidor was influenced by Hollywood's attitude to Negroes generally, and how much the film was altered in the cutting room are questions which must forever remain unanswered. Suffice to say that, in spite of all its promise, M.-G.-M's. " all-Negro epic " made only a minor contribution to the Negro struggle for recognition on the screen.

The scene of " Hallelujah " was laid in the cotton fields of the South, and in some of the mean dives of a Southern State, and was concerned with the eternal struggle between good and evil, as symbolised naïvely by the religious, God-fearing Negro and a loose, sophisticated coloured woman of the town. Effective character drawing was swamped by a great deal of preaching, shouting, baptising, soul-saving, dancing, gambling, love-making, continual singing of spirituals and happy work songs. A general " hot " time was had by all, in the accustomed tradition of the " good-for-nothing black man." Writers in the Negro Press considered, however, that " Hallelujah " was something of a step forward in the struggle for Negro expression on the screen, and even such severe critics as W. E. B. Du Bois admitted that it was beautifully staged under severe limitations and possessed commonsense and real life without the exaggerated farce and usual horse-play. But, as usual, opinion was divided, and certain Negro film critics referred to " King Vidor's filthy hands reeking with prejudice," and to the film's " insulting niggerisms." Sections of the white Press seemed to find the characterisations quite *amusing*. As the critic of the *New York Times* remarked : " The audience was especially amused by the baptism scene with a host of white-clad Hallelujah-rousing blacks standing on the side of the water ready to go through the baptism but evidently fearful of the ducking !" Lawrence Reddick observes : " ' Hallelujah ' was significant in that it gave Negro actors important rôles and did not exhibit the crude insults which disturb Negro patrons ; however, it did not advance very far beyond the usual stereotypes and, as everyone could see, being all-Negro it was by that token a Jim Crow film."

Lewis Jacobs went even further. " In undertaking ' Hallelujah,' King Vidor also said he was primarily interested in showing the Southern Negro as he is," he wrote, and went on : " The deed fell short of the intent. The film turned out to be a melodramatic piece replete with all the conventionalities of the white man's conception of the spiritual-singing, crap-shooting Negro. But whatever its sociological faults, and it had many, its technique reflected a thinking director."

" Hallelujah " received, on the whole, a favourable Press, since at the time it was produced it was considered by Bohemians and so-called intellectuals as " the fashionable thing " to be pro-Negro. (In New York this cult reached fantastic proportions for a period and has been described in a number of books, including Carl van Vechten's famous novel *Nigger Heaven*.) But in all the reviews which praised the movie one could determine the basic deficiencies of the narrow outlook which characterised film critics and audiences at that time. Here is a typical review from *Theatre and Film Illustrated*, February, 1930 : " From the very first shot of the cotton fields, where the coloured workers are heard singing at their work, the atmosphere of ' Hallelujah ' takes hold of one and one lives amongst and understands the people King Vidor is depicting. It can well be described as a song of the American Negro, in which are skilfully blended humour, pathos, sentiment, fervent religious emotions and equally fervent passion. The film is imbued with the revivalist spirit which, as it were, demonstrates the characters and films the main motif against which is played the drama of a Negro's love and emotions. It is instinct with an irresistible childishness which is at once transparently sincere and wholly moving."

And again : " King Vidor shows us the fanatical expressions of grief in which Negroes indulge. All through this sequence there is rhythm and music just as there is when they are rejoicing in the cotton fields ; only the theme is changed. Zeke becomes a revivalist preacher and gives addresses which admit the humour and allusions that are so essential to the make up of his kind." And the reviewer finishes by saying, " Rarely has the spirit of the Negro people been so finely portrayed as in this picture."

Although one may admit King Vidor's sincerity, and recognise his inspired direction of the crowd scenes and of the revivalist meeting sequences, one is forced to the conclusion that his film continued the hackneyed tradition, and showed the Negro as a simple, often stupid, religious, superstitious creature. " The picture of Negro life presented by ' Hallelujah ' as it finally appeared was still romantic, still shadowed by traditional clichés of Negro character and action " ; so wrote Edith Isaacs in *Theatre Arts*, August, 1942. The author went to see the film again, when it was shown in London by the New London Film Society in 1946, and realised once more that the creatures on the screen were not really human beings. They were merely black dolts dancing at the end of a string held by King Vidor, a white man with no real insight into the mind of the Negro or a knowledge of his aspirations and ambitions. As film critic Robert Herring wrote some fifteen years ago : " Both ' Hallelujah ' and ' Hearts In Dixie ' perpetuate the ' way down South in the land of cotton ' idea, which by now ought really to be forgotten."

And as Paul Robeson commented, in *Film Weekly*, September 1st, 1933 : " The box office insistence that the Negro shall figure always as a clown has spoiled the two Negro films which have been made in Hollywood, ' Hallelujah ' and ' Hearts In Dixie.' In ' Hallelujah ' they took the Negro and his church services and made them funny. America may have found it amusing, but to English audiences the burlesquing of religious matters appeared sheer blasphemy."

In *Close Up*, August, 1929, the editor, Kenneth Macpherson, had some interesting things to say on the subject. Here is an extract : " Now take the Negro film and decide whether you think international cinema is going to mean a thing when a white man directs, no matter how charmingly, blacks so that they must always seem to be direfully dependent on white man's wisdom. For all the coal-black hearts in Dixie must beat to please—meekly Uncle Tom, pleasant, thankful, serf beats. Confronted with an instability (his own) which he calls a race problem, the white man is always going to portray the Negro as he likes to see him ; no matter how benevolently. Benevolence, indeed, is the danger. Apart from being the most tricky and unkind form of human selfishness, it is often more than humbugged and always less than seeing, and does to sugar-coat much that is not, so to speak, edible."

But some critics found things in Vidor's film to praise. For example, Helen Fletcher, film critic of the *Sunday Graphic* and *Time and Tide*, wrote recently : " I found myself unusually excited by this Negro film. It has a curious hypnotic quality. Other films stress Negro insouciance and charm ; King Vidor's film stresses Negro intensity and even agony. Above all the film treats Negroes with equality ; it seems to me a film which does not date but which is as shaking to smugness now as it was in 1929."

Between 1929 and 1933 certain anti-Negro productions, like R.K.O.-Radio's " Prestige " and " Secret Service," became popular with cinema audiences, and drove the stereotype conception deeper into the public mind. " Prestige," directed by Charles R. Rogers in 1932, was laid in a French penal colony. The theme of the film was the eternal superiority of the whites over the black prisoners, and the " prestige " of the title referred, in fact, to the prestige of the white man. An example from the script serves to indicate the film's message.

" ' Back you swine ! ' Verlaine cried fiercely.

The blacks drew back ; the prestige of the white race was being revived."

Clarence Muse, nevertheless, gave an excellent study of the faithful friend and servant of Captain Verlaine, the French officer, played by Adolphe Menjou, and managed to off-set some of the film's many reactionary sequences. A production like " Secret Service," directed by J. Walter Ruben in 1932, was typical of the kind of Civil War film popularised by Hollywood in the 1930's. The hero, Richard Dix, is a gallant Southern gentleman in the Confederate Army, while Gavin Gordon, inescapably villainous, played (inevitably) an officer in the Federal Army. Just as inevitably, Shirley Grey as a Northern beauty, forsook her creed to follow her Southern lover. " Secret Service " was not, perhaps in itself, an important film, but it serves as an example of the type of Hollywood motion picture so often met with, in which the hero is always a gentlemanly Southerner, usually surrounded by faithful Uncle Tom retainers, while the Yankees are always drawn in the most unfavourable light.

Musical productions such as " Gold Diggers Of Broadway," "Stand Up And Cheer," " Fox Movietone Follies " and others, continued to feature outstanding Negro personalities from the Broadway stage, and night-club singers like Ethel Waters, Mamie Smith and Nina Mae McKinney. But although most filmgoers were agreed that the Negro seemed to possess enormous filmic potentialities, Hollywood failed to do much about this. When coloured people were used in films they were cast in the familiar groove, or alternatively an attempt was made to camouflage their colour. Thus, actress Hazel Jones played a beautiful *Burmese* siren in the Walter Huston film " West Of Singapore," while Etta Moten danced and sang in R.K.O.-Radio's " Flying Down To Rio," as a dusky *South American.*

By 1931 Harry Alan Potamkin felt obliged to declare : " The Hollywood sound film is bringing the Negro in with a sort of Eastman Johnson-Stephen Foster-Kentucky Jubilee *genre;* or with the Octavus Roy Cohen-Hugh Wiley crowd satisfiers, where the Negro is still the nigger-clown, shrewd sometimes and butt always." He was right. Hollywood had failed ; and it was thus left to two idealistic men in New York to make the first really important movie giving a Negro a rôle he could, as it were, get his teeth into. The film was " The Emperor Jones," from the play by Eugene O'Neill, and the actor was Paul Robeson.

The Emperor Jones

O'Neill had concerned himself with Negro themes in several of his plays, including the above, " All God's Chillun Got Wings " and " The Dreamy Kid." He was among the few American playwrights who foresaw the rapidly growing part the Negro would play in the American scene and he is included in that small but important band of white dramatists who have written soberly and sincerely about Negroes. Two young men of the theatre, John Krimsky and Gifford Cochran, planned to make a series of films of O'Neill's plays and for their first independent effort they decided to produce " The Emperor Jones " in a small New York film studio. They chose for the leading part thirty-five year-old actor and singer Paul Robeson, who had previously made a great success on the stage as Brutus Jones, both in New York and London.

Robeson, like many other coloured actors and actresses, found his work appreciated more in England and on the Continent than it had been in the United States, and up to 1933 he had practically made his home in London. He returned to New York (after having made his first screen appearance in an English silent film called " Borderline "), making his début in sound films by playing one of his favourite stage rôles. To say that his screen performance as Jones was a *tour de force* is perhaps an understatement. The film itself was not entirely satisfactory but Robeson's work showed that he had reached maturity as an actor, and was potentially one of the greatest screen personalities. " The Emperor Jones " was remarkable in that it gave to a Negro actor a leading part in a film also featuring white actors, something never previously experienced (a possible exception being the case of James B. Lowe who played Uncle Tom in a silent version of " Uncle Tom's Cabin"). To have a black man playing the star part in a film in which the white actors were of lesser importance was indeed something of a filmic revolution. Indeed it was enough of a social revolution to make the film a financial failure ! Distribution difficulties were encountered, especially in the Southern States, and " The Emperor Jones " was seen only by a relatively small number of people, although it was warmly received by the critics. Nevertheless Krimsky and Cochran abandoned their project of making " All God's Chillun Got Wings " and other O'Neill plays, and so far as is known neither has produced a film since. Their names, however, will be remembered with gratitude by the millions of filmgoers who have since enjoyed the work of Robeson on the screen. It was their foresight and courage in starring a Negro actor, at a time when Hollywood was doing its best to kill all attempts by coloured actors and actresses to bring real characterisation to their meagre rôles, which started Paul Robeson on a brilliant film career. " The Emperor Jones " also gave encouragement to many independent Negro producers, who thereafter began to make their own films to be shown mainly to Negro audiences.

This O'Neill film was praised by most critics in the U.S.A. and Europe as one of the outstanding films of the year, with such notable exceptions as Robert Stebbins, who wrote in *New Theatre*, July, 1935 : " ' The Emperor Jones' maintained unbroken the chain of white chauvinism forged in the carbon-arc lights of the Hollywood studios. Paul Robeson is presented as a vainglorious braggart, a murderer, a tin-foil Napoleon who imposes upon and exploits heartlessly members of his own race. And when finally they rise against him his false front falls away. He is revealed for what he is, and by extension, what all Negroes are supposed to be, creatures who stand trembling in a murky land of shadow, peopled with the ghosts that rise up out of the swamps and jungles of the primitive mind."

Critics of the Negro newspapers were divided ; some believed that it was a significant gesture that a white man could be presented on the screen as the " lackey " of the Negro Brutus Jones, and as his intellectual and social inferior. Others, however, emphasised the scenes where Robeson was shown as a humble and servile Pullman porter, and afterwards as a convict in a chain gang. These sequences, asserted some critics, put Robeson in an unsympathetic light, and the final scene, when Brutus Jones is grovelling in superstitious fear in the jungle, was cited as a negation of all the film's good points (in that it indicated that a Negro servant who rose to fame as a black emperor would ultimately achieve only death and disgrace). There were many such criticisms, and even Robeson himself was not completely satisfied with the result of what must, however, be reckoned as a worthwhile and distinctly revolutionary venture. (It is interesting to note that in a review of this film appearing in the magazine *Film Art*, Summer, 1934, the word " nigger " appears twice, surely an indication of the derogatory attitude of some reviewers at that time to a dignified Negro personality, an attitude which persists in many quarters even today.) However, the film followed O'Neill's play religiously, and attacks on it for the above reasons constituted, in effect, an attack on the play itself (and were to a degree justified). Nevertheless, " The Emperor Jones " *was* a landmark in Negro films, and is still considered among the most original motion pictures of the past decade.

An early talking film which had given a fine part to a coloured man was " Arrowsmith," directed by John Ford, in 1932, in which Ronald Colman played a doctor and scientist and an excellent Negro actor, Clarence Brooks, played the part of a dignified doctor, who stood side by side with Arrowsmith in his experiments in the West Indian jungle and his struggles and triumphs in the cause of science. " Arrowsmith " was hailed everywhere as the best example of fair and tolerant film treatment of a Negro since the arrival of sound films, but it was, unfortunately, swamped by a mass of Hollywood efforts in which Negro characters behaved like half-wits. In films such as " The Ghost Talks," " Judge Priest," " The Littlest Rebel " and " In Old Kentucky " the coloured people were treated like animals, and behaved like them. Stepin Fetchit, for instance, was much to blame for popularising a characterisation which was to incur the bitter hatred of all

SHIRLEY TEMPLE and BILL ROBINSON in *The Little Colonel*

intelligent Negroes. As servants or as tap dancers he, and other coloured performers, grinned and gaped their way through both major and minor Hollywood productions, demolishing all the good work done by fine Negro stage players on Broadway and elsewhere. To most filmgoers Robeson was yet to come, Rex Ingram was unknown and the word " Negro " was inextricably interwoven in the minds of audiences with " Stepin Fetchit."

There were, of course, a number of early Hollywood musicals which starred well-known black-face comedians from the American vaudeville stage and radio. Among these were " Why Bring That Up ? " and " Two Black Crows In The A.E.F.," both featuring Moran and Mack, and " Check And Double Check," in which Amos and Andy, the famous radio act, were starred. These " nigger minstrel " movies were not, however, a great success, and in the past fifteen years there have been few pictures of this type made by Hollywood, exceptions being " Hypnotised " with Moran and Mack, " The Phantom President," in which George M. Cohan performed an obnoxious black-face act, and certain of Al Jolson's films.

Imitation Of Life

In 1934 Universal produced a film of Fannie Hurst's novel *Imitation Of Life* (re-issued in 1946), in which Louise Beavers appeared as the self-effacing, faithful, kind-hearted epitome of the worst type of " mammy " rôle. A widespread and bitter controversy arose on the showing of this production and Fannie Hurst and Sterling Brown, film critic of the magazine *Opportunity*, became involved in a clash of opinion concerning the effect of the film upon world audiences. Miss Hurst indignantly gave it as her opinion that Negroes should express " a little more gratitude " for the fact that she had featured them and their problems in her novel and screenplay. But Brown continued to attack the film, pointing out that the Negro character followed too closely so many others in a long line of stupid subservience. As an example, he drew attention to sequences of the film in which Louise Beavers tells her white mistress (Claudette Colbert) that she does not want to take her share of the profits from their

Above : *Bataan* **directed by Tay Garnett. Below :** *The Proud Valley* **directed by Pen Tennyson.**

joint pan-cake business, preferring to remain on the

premises and to serve her white ma'am with true Negro dog-like devotion. All she desired, it seemed, was to be able to serve her mistress well, and " to have a big funeral with white horses " when she died. And in spite of the part being played with great charm by Louise Beavers, who excels in this type of rôle, it was obvious that this study of abject servility was a reflection of the worst elements of Negro and white relations in American society.

As William Harrison pointed out in *Sight and Sound*, Spring, 1939, " Professor Brown of Howard University recorded his objection to a line uttered by a character in the film, played by Ned Sparks, who referring to the Negro cook's refusal to take a share in the profits, made the remark, ' Once a pan-cake, always a pan-cake,' for he held that this particular line, in its context, was a slur cast upon the Negro race. In rebuttal Miss Hurst countered that all her Negro characters were serious and so afforded scope for Negro actors and actresses wider than that previously enjoyed by them. She felt that Negroes owed her a debt of gratitude for this service, but her statement aroused even further resentment from a notoriously sensitive people, as her knowledge of the nuance of inter-racial relations in the United States was not equal to her sympathy." " Yet," added Harrison, " the Negro spokesman had to realise that without financial resources for large-scale production the Negro community is dependent, and will be so for a long time, upon the Hollywood industry."

" Imitation Of Life " was also important in that, in the sub-plot, attention was drawn to the Negro cook's mulatto daughter, a girl who could easily pass for white because of her extremely light skin. (This delicate subject has never been dealt with by Hollywood since that time.) Fredi Washington, a fine and sensitive New York stage actress, played this rôle with great intelligence, and brought sympathy, understanding and attention to what was originally quite a minor character in the film. As *Literary Digest*, December 8th, 1934, remarked about this : " The real story, the narrative which is merely hinted at, never really contemplated, is that of the beautiful and rebellious daughter of the loyal Negro friend. She is light-skinned, sensitive, tempestuous ; and grows bitterly indignant when she sees that the white girl with whom she has been reared is getting all the fine things of life while she is subjected to humiliation and unhappiness. Obviously she is the most interesting person in the cast. Her drama is the most poignant, but the producers not only confine her to a minor and carefully handled sub-plot, but appear to regard her with distaste. They appear to be fond of her mother, because she is of the meek type of old-fashioned Negro that, as they say, ' knows his place,' but the daughter is too bitter and lacking in resignation for them."

To return to Fetchit, " Snowball," " Sleep 'n' Eat," Louise Beavers, and the others, it is safe to say that all the films featuring such actors as these showed the black man in a contemptible light. Fetchit portrayed the lazy, ignorant, good-for-nothing coloured servant in dozens of films, including " Swing High," " Stand Up And Cheer," " Carolina," and others, and the American public lapped it up. In fact, so successful was his contemptible impersonation of this type of part that Fox Studios signed him to a fat contract, so that his long line of biased characterisations might be continued in films like " David Harum," " Helldorado," " The Country Chairman " and similar productions. It is not suggested that the studio deliberately " wrote in " anti-Negro parts in their films, but since Fetchit's popularity with mass movie audiences was founded upon these unfair portrayals, Hollywood, notorious for its system of type casting, continued to allot him similar rôles, especially in films dealing with the Southern States.

To an extent his position was taken over in the middle 'thirties by veteran dancer and actor Bill Robinson who, while remaining a pleasant and ingenuous figure, nevertheless began to portray a series of " Fetchit " characterisations after he had appeared with some success as Shirley Temple's good-natured servant in the Fox film " The Little Colonel " in 1935. Thenceforth Robinson danced and " mugged " his way through a number of " faithful servant " parts in such productions as " The Littlest Rebel," " Steamboat Round The Bend," " In Old Kentucky," " Rebecca Of Sunnybrook Farm " and " Road Demon." In each of these he was the same genial underling, quite charming, but contributing very little towards the encouraging of a more realistic attitude of world filmgoers to the thirteen million black Americans. Only once did he play a dignified rôle with distinction, and that was in the Fox film " One Mile From Heaven," produced in 1937 (and in which, incidentally, the beautiful Fredi Washington gave another extremely moving performance). It is not a condemnation of Bill Robinson that he was rarely seen in a part which reflected beneficially on the Negro race. Rather has it been the fault of the producers themselves, who never allow sympathetic coloured *characters* to find their way into pictures. Thus Robinson shares the same dilemma of all Negro players : either they appear in subservient parts and endow them with what sympathy they can, or else they boycott Hollywood altogether and try to earn a living in stage and radio productions. The difficulties and disadvantages of the latter course are fairly obvious. Most Negro actors feel that it is a step forward to play a speaking part in a film, providing it is not too maliciously overdrawn ; and this attitude is partially justified. The history of Negro film actors has shown that whereas twenty years ago coloured players were never given parts of even minor importance, today some dozens of Negroes appear regularly on the screen. And, of course, some coloured actors and actresses, like Paul Robeson, Eddie " Rochester " Anderson, Rex Ingram and Lena Horne, have become extremely popular " names " at the box office. This then must be considered something of a forward move. Obviously the next step is for those actors who have become important box office names to refuse rôles which reflect even by implication a derogatory attitude to coloured people generally. And, as we shall see later on, certain leading players have in fact done so.

So Red The Rose

In 1935 King Vidor, director of " Hallelujah " five years previously, directed the film version of Stark Young's best-selling anti-Negro novel of the old South, *So Red The Rose*, with Margaret Sullavan, Walter Connolly, Randolph Scott, Daniel Haynes and Clarence Muse. Like " The Birth Of A Nation," the film was concerned with the Civil War period in American history, and like Griffith's film it was a libellous presentation of the social conditions of the Southern slaves, picturing their revolt against their owners as based only upon laziness, greed and hysteria. Negro leaders were shown as opportunists, misleading a simple-minded people who were happy enough to be left in their lowly place in American society, and, in fact, were obstinately devoted to their white masters. This film was a colossal travesty in every possible way.

Paramount issued a number of publicity stories in connection with the making of the film. One such hand-out read : " Sociological experiments are by no means the purpose of film-making and the few daring souls who have invaded this most controversial of all fields have met with disastrous failures. Yet there is a tendency in 1935 to depart somewhat from the standardised forms of screen literature and to liberalise this media to conform to modern tolerance and thought."

This was a subtle and cynical method of drawing the sting of those liberal organisations which the studio knew would immediately attack the finished film for its misrepresentation of Negro efforts towards their own emancipation. The producers were already preening themselves for *having* coloured actors in their film ; this, seemingly, being their method of conforming to " modern tolerance and thought " (see above). In the same publicity release the studio stated : " There has been a marked decrease in that form of intolerance which specialises in the drawing of colour lines and your coloured performer of merit now shares marquee distinction with the whites." How true was this, then and now ? The Negro actor's salary is a great deal lower than the white actor's in the same category. Whether he is a small part or featured player he is discriminated against on the set and in the finished picture ; his photograph never appears in a newspaper advertisement of the film, nor are publicity photographs of coloured artists distributed to the Press. So much for Paramount's assertion.

To refer again to the general line of studio publicity : " King Vidor holds the opinion that the coloured race is the most difficult of all people to handle as a group in the making of motion pictures. *Fundamentally living only for the joy they get out of life* (author's italics) they are inclined to laugh at serious things and this native comedy is sometimes difficult to overcome when sheer drama is necessary."

Let us take a look at another publicity paragraph : " King Vidor took this day's work most seriously. He outlined his story to his coloured group and made some of them cry through a somewhat maudlin presentation of the evils which their ancestors were *supposed to have suffered* (author's italics). This had the effect of putting them in the proper mood and the rapid change from happiness to sullen anger was accomplished without delay."

This then was the line taken by the publicity department before the screening of " So Red The Rose." Now for the film itself. It tells the story of an old Southern family during the Civil War, whose treatment of its slaves is humane and understanding (at least from the white point of view). There is no reference to the deep feelings of bitterness due to the splitting-up of Negro families, the starvation of the slaves and general ill-treatment of the black workers which took place during the Civil War itself, treatment which became more vicious as the military situation worsened for the South. In Stark Young's film there is no apparent reason given for the revolt of the slaves on the plantation, except that Cato, a trouble-making slave, played by Clarence Muse, causes unrest by holding before his fellows a highly coloured picture of a life of greed, luxury and happiness, which should rightfully be theirs. And when the crazed Negroes, ugly with hate, turn against the gentle hand that has fed them for so many years, the audience is encouraged to feel only resentment at their efforts to become free. When William the faithful butler in true Uncle Tom tradition (played by that good Negro actor Daniel Haynes) tells the coachman to unhitch the horses, the man replies, " I've unhitched horses for the last time. Let the white folks unhitch their own horses. I'se gonna be free." And with an hysterical shout he runs towards the slave quarters in a frenzy of ecstasy and excitement, shouting " Free, free for true. I'se gonna be free." He arrives at the spot in the plantation where the slaves are gathered in rebellion, hatred and malignity transforming their faces. Cato, the ring-leader, now shown as a brutal hate-crazed slave, is haranguing the mob :

" You been slaves long enough, ain't yer ? " he cries.

" Yes, that's right," comes the answer.

" You want what belongs to you, don't yer ? "

" Yes, ain't it true ? "

" Thass right ! "

" Are yer gonna take what belongs to yer ? "

" Yes ! Yes ! We sho' is ! "

" Or wait until somebody else eats it up."

" No ! No ! No, we ain't."

" All this is yours ! Go and get it ! "

Following this the slaves rush hither and thither, greedily stealing pigs, chickens and horses, screaming and shouting " I got mine ! I got mine ! " And Cato declares : " Before long we'll all be sitting in the golden chairs in the big house. It all belongs to us now ! We're the kings ! No more ploughing, no more chopping cotton, no more planting, jest sittin' in the sun ! " Then the slaves work themselves up into a veritable frenzy, the while stealing and plundering and generally making merry on the plantation. " Lincoln has given us de land ! " they cry, " no more work for us ! "

But in the old Southern homestead sits the mistress of the house, a proud daughter of the Confederacy (Margaret Sullavan). She is worried in case the sound of the rebellion should reach to the manor house, where her father, the traditional Southern colonel, is dying. The girl knows that his heart will break if he realises that his devoted servants and slaves have turned upon him ; so with a heart-warming simplicity she strides fearlessly into the slave quarters, and breaks up the rebellion by slapping one of the ring-leaders in the face, and shaming the rest of the rioters with a reminder that they are all her dear, dear friends and they must continue to be " good " for the sake of her dying father. Confronted by the brave little woman whom they have loved since she was a child, the slaves break down and cry, chanting hymns and following her to the manor. And when their beloved colonel finally dies peacefully the slaves disperse quietly, and go about their work on the plantation. The revolt is crushed ; white supremacy, kindness and courage have won the day !

Many critics attacked the film. As Arthur Draper pointed out in an article, entitled " Uncle Tom, Will You Never Die ? " in *New Theatre*, January, 1936, " If ' So Red The Rose ' succeeds at the box office in the South it will be at the cost once again of provoking even sharper racial lines than exist in these States at the present time, of provoking an even greater hatred by the whites for the Negroes, of breaking the solidarity between workers of all races that is today beginning to change the Old South of infamous reputation into a New South built on workers' pride."

The movie had a fair success due mainly to the performance of Margaret Sullavan, but was heavily criticised by the Negro Press and by liberal organisations everywhere. Daniel Haynes was so hurt and disgusted with the finished film that he returned to New York and refused to appear in movies again unless he had the right to approve the theme, and then only if the part gave him an opportunity to show his race in a sympathetic light. He bitterly regretted the contribution he had made to race hatred in this film, and to my knowledge, like Charles Gilpin, he never went back to Hollywood.

The Negro in Films

The Green Pastures

Since the time of " Hearts In Dixie " and " Hallelujah " Hollywood had fought shy of making all-Negro movies. But in 1936 Warner Brothers decided to film the successful long-running " The Green Pastures " by Marc Connelly, with a well-known Broadway actor, Rex Ingram, as De Lawd. The play purported to be " a delightful and daring portrayal of Negro religion." As a publicity hand-out read : " The stories of childhood live again in the naïve beliefs of these coloured Christians. Humour, courage, love and forgiveness are inter-woven in this moving panorama of primitive life. Biblical incidents are transmuted into a living faith which plays on the humanity of God. One of the most original features is the symbolising of a religious development as God learning from experience." For censorship reasons Hollywood had never extensively tackled religious subjects but Warners decided that " The Green Pastures " was a play which deserved to be seen by a wider audience, and asked author Marc Connelly to co-direct the film (with William Keighley) in order to ensure that the sincerity of the original conception would not be lost in the film treatment.

The film of " The Green Pastures " was in the form of a flashback, with a prologue and an epilogue set in a Sunday school for coloured children. The preacher is reading from an early chapter, and endeavours to transpose explanations for the benefit of his pupils. The film then dissolves into a kind of juvenile Negro idea of Heaven in which the Lord (beautifully played by Rex Ingram) is shown as a kindly Negro parson. The story concerns itself with the creating of the world, from the Garden of Eden, to the murder of Abel and finally to the incident of Noah and the Ark. It is simple but effective. Felix Barker wrote of it in *World Film News*, September, 1936, as follows : " Rex Ingram's every feature is of purity and benign goodness. The measure of beauty which the film brings to the public consciousness ought certainly to outweigh ordinary rule and precedent."

But in the opinion of some critics, " The Green Pastures," adapted from Roark Bradford's sketches of Southern life, " Ole Man Adam And His Chillun," offered little that was new. Though delightfully written, with a nice sense of humour and some original touches, Connelly's play nevertheless did very little to enhance the status of coloured people in the public mind, and, for that matter, neither did the film. Well-intentioned, it merely gave filmgoers once more the happy, religious, hymn-singing black man, whose idea of Heaven seems to consist mainly of long white night-gowns, hymn-shouting and fish-fries. In fact, " quaint " was the word most used by reviewers to describe the acting of the all-coloured cast, although every critic was insistent that Rex Ingram, who gave a dignified and moving portrayal, deserved to be rewarded with important rôles in further films. Eddie Anderson's Noah and Ernest Whitman's Pharaoh were other outstanding studies which received critical praise in a well-acted film. Like " Hearts In Dixie " and " Hallelujah," " The Green Pastures " served to point once more to the high quality of much Negro talent in the field of filmic interpretation. As William Harrison asserted in *Sight and Sound*, Spring, 1939 : " It is universally recognised that the Negro possesses considerable and unusual histrionic ability." He went on to say, " This talent has imperfectly revealed itself in the cinema. The reason for this deficiency in utilising an admitted reservoir of talent must be sought in the fact that the rôles usually assigned to Negro actors have had only two stops : farce and pathos."

Ingram's performance in " The Green Pastures " managed in many ways to depart from the above, and his work, in particular, brought to the screen a new conception of Negro dignity, of the kind indicated previously by the acting of Paul Robeson, Fredi Washington, Daniel Haynes and some others. The film was generally well received. The critic of *Time* wrote : " One of the principal dangers of the cinema was that Heaven would either be improved beyond any Southern piccaninny's dreams, or else that the artfulness of its simplicity might seem condescending. The producers have avoided both these pitfalls. Heaven has been improved, but only slightly. God is still a shabby Negro preacher, calm, elderly and not too competent. He has notions what to do about the earth, but the notions do not often work, and he is still puzzling when the picture ends." Some interesting examples of the diversity of other critical opinion are given below :—

" Nothing will induce me to argue about whether this picture is what is called ' commercial ' or not. But with my last breath I will defend its beauty, its sincerity, its nobility, and its piety. If you are interested to see a film that unquestionably has these fine qualities, then see ' The Green Pastures.' Lack of commercial success of such a film could only be a criticism of the

public, not of the picture. It is beside the point to discuss ' acting ' and ' production ' of such a picture. Thanks to the nature of the coloured people, I can believe that the players lived their parts in a spirit of reverence. To suggest blasphemy or to say that the cinema is not the place for such a subject is to deny divine ubiquity and simplicity which are the roots of any faith worthy of the name."
Stephen Watts, *The Sunday Express.*

" If this film is allowed, the Divine Judgment cannot but fall upon this country."
Rev. F. L. Langton.

" The picture is too blasphemous and shocking to contemplate ! "
Admiral Sir George King-Hall.

Lawrence Reddick gives as his opinion that Hollywood turned a rather majestic and dignified play into a light and, for the most part, ridiculous travesty ; and sections of the Negro Press were inclined to agree with him. Nevertheless the film constituted a landmark in Negro progress on the screen. It gave rôles of importance to some well-known Broadway players who remained in the film city thereafter, actors such as Clinton Rosemond, Oscar Polk, Ernest Whitman, Eddie Anderson and others, many of them coming to screen prominence within the next few years. The film further revealed the potentialities of movies exclusively Negro, while pointing out the deficiencies in the unrealistic attitude which leads Hollywood to make them. However well-intentioned, they inevitably line themselves up on the Jim Crow side of the fence.

There are two schools of thought on this subject, both vigorously asserting their points of view and both carrying a measure of justification. This difference of opinion has been present since the coloured artist first appeared in Hollywood. On one side there are those who assert that a Negro playing *any* part on the screen is better than no Negroes on the screen at all, and on the other side those who believe that the Negro should appear only in films which show his correct relationship to a white community and not in fairy-tales, fantasies or films treating the subject lightly and unrealistically. Ultimately it would seem that the intelligent cinemagoer very naturally condemns all films which show the Negro in an unsympathetic light, while still applauding any production, all-Negro or otherwise, which gives a coloured actor an opportunity to show his talent, and to play his part towards wider recognition of the Negro's rôle both in the film and in society.

An example of the strong division of opinion is indicated in the following comments : " Because of the Negro movie many a prejudiced white who would not accept a Negro unless as a servant, will be compelled to admit that at least he can be something else ; many an indifferent white will be beguiled into a positive attitude of friendliness ; many a Negro will have his race consciousness and self-respect stimulated. In short, the Negro movie actor is a means of getting acquainted with Negroes." So wrote Geraldyn Dismond some ten years ago in *Close Up*. But as Robert Stebbins replied, in *New Theatre*, " It would be difficult to hit upon another such example as Dismond's of wishful prophecy so precisely unfulfilled ! "

Mervyn Le Roy and Fritz Lang

Mervyn Le Roy, a Hollywood director whose best work was done during his long and successful association with Warner Brothers, demonstrates in his films a keen sense of sympathy with the Negro. One remembers his treatment of the Negro prisoner, played by Everett Brown, in that superb movie, " I Am A Fugitive From A Chain Gang," dealing with Southern labour camps and produced in 1932. The Negro is shown in the early part of the film as one of Paul Muni's comrades. He reveals a good brain, a friendly nature and a clear philosophy. It is hinted that, like Muni, he also came into the chain gang as a result of circumstances almost amounting to a Southern States " frame up." Le Roy's sympathetic handling of the Negro rôle reached its climax in the scene where Muni, rebelling at the injustices of the labour camp system and realising that the bigoted Southern warders will see that he never gets his long-promised reprieve, decides to make his escape. He is helped by his black friend, who with his great strength, patience and selfless bravery aids Muni to make a getaway by breaking his chains with his sledge-hammer. The feeling which remained after seeing " I Am A Fugitive " was that the Negro is an ordinary human being, capable of great friendship, loyalty and courage.

One of the most effective attacks on the old American custom of lynching and therefore, by implication, an anti-discrimination

71

movie, was Fritz Lang's magnificent film, "Fury," made for M.-G.-M. in 1936, with Spencer Tracy and Sylvia Sidney. It was indeed significant that Lang, a foreigner, should choose for the subject of his first American film a story about mob violence, one of the most striking and least savoury aspects of the U.S.A. The details of the lynching in this film made it of unbearable horror, of a kind only equalled by the more recent "Strange Incident," directed by William A. Wellman. There was no Negro character in "Fury," but it was one of the most moving appeals for greater tolerance ever made in Hollywood and a really great motion picture. I do not think Lang has directed a better American film than "Fury," one of the landmarks of motion picture progress.

Warner Brothers made a film called "Black Legion" in the middle 1930's, which starred Humphrey Bogart and was an excellently produced attack on the Ku Klux Klan. Depicting how in the U.S.A. an ordinary worker with progressive views could be threatened, beaten and even murdered by anti-Jew, anti-Negro, anti-foreigner Fascist organisations such as the Klan, it was an intelligent and timely effort which lined up with such other notable Warners' productions as "I Am A Fugitive," "They Won't Forget" (and "In This Our Life" which came a few years later). "Black Legion" was a forthright critical examination of that dreaded terrorist organisation, the New Ku Klux Klan, which flourished in the Middle West between 1935 and 1937. It was, in effect, an indictment of the notorious Ku Klux Klan of the earlier period, that murderous group of fanatics glorified by Griffith in "The Birth Of A Nation," and reveals American brutality, stupidity and hypocrisy masquerading under the cloak of patriotism. A courageous production, extremely progressive in treatment and implication, it was, not unnaturally, widely boycotted by exhibitors in the Southern States.

They Won't Forget

Mervyn Le Roy again showed his deep interest in the colour problem of the South in his memorable film "They Won't Forget," which he directed for Warners in 1937. Adapted from Ward Greene's powerful novel *Death In The Deep South*, it was, broadly speaking, an indictment of Southern intolerance. Greene's book is the story of the rape and murder of a young girl in a Southern town, and the arrest of a new schoolteacher who, being a Northerner, has previously incurred disapproval from his fellow citizens in this prejudiced and bigoted little township of the Old South. Quickly the law gets to work in condemning the Northerner without evidence, and when a famous Liberal lawyer arrives from New York to defend the schoolteacher the issue soon becomes not so much the Law versus the Accused as the North versus the South. As Mervyn Le Roy stresses again and again in this grim and moving film—they won't forget ! Of it, *Cinema Arts*, July, 1937, said : " Warners have tackled a sociological problem regardless of possible hostile reaction from sectional audiences " (meaning the South).

And not for a long time has there been such a sane filmic assessment of Southern values. The picture attempts to portray with clarity, understatement, and no degree of bitterness, the continued existence below the Mason-Dixon line (in the 1930's at least) of a spiritual revival of the worst elements in Southern tradition. Symptomatic of this revival is the flaring up of an added ferocity in the treatment by the whites of their Negro fellow-citizens. Le Roy shows how every year, on the anniversary of the end of the Civil War, the bitterness of the white townsfolk towards their former slaves evinces itself in a number of outbreaks, not the least of which is a renewal of mob hooliganism, as well as major and minor persecutions—and occasional lynching. More vividly than any other Hollywood film " They Won't Forget " points to the tragedy of some backward Southern communities, still living in their feudal past, still refusing to acknowledge that the Civil War brought with it a revolution in the American scene. It takes its place alongside the significant social documents of the screen.

Giving many acting opportunities to such first-rate players as Claude Rains, Allyn Joslyn, Gloria Dickson and Edward Norris, the film also saw a memorable performance from that fine actor Clinton Rosemond, who played the coloured janitor. Naturally, being black, and having worked near the scene of the crime, this quiet, kindly and harmless old menial is suspected of the murder and, in a particularly brutal scene, is third-degreed by some semi-Fascist Southern police officers. The Negro is black-jacked, brutally beaten and finally thrown back into his cell, with clothes torn and head bleeding. His poignant cry, " I didn't do it. So help me. I didn't do it," as he lies moaning in his cell, will remain long in the memory of those who saw the film. Inevitably the drama ends in a lynching, though in this case the victim is the white Northerner.

In her book *America At The Movies*, Margaret Farrand Thorp writes : " 'They Won't Forget,' which concerned a Southern town's lynching of a schoolteacher suspected of murder chiefly because he was a Northerner, could not be shown in theatres below Washington. The director, Mervyn Le Roy, was, the report goes, surprised ; he did not expect the South to take it personally. The North, on the other hand, has so forgotten the emotions of the war between the States that a New England audience is no more insulted by the sight of Yankee troops burning a Mississippi mansion ('So Red The Rose,' 'Gone With The Wind') than by the spectacle of the hordes at the gates of Pekin."

The film was indeed attacked bitterly by the Southern States, but critics in all parts of the world acclaimed it as a great American film. Howard Barnes wrote in the *New York Herald Tribune* : " 'They Won't Forget' takes its place naturally with 'Fury' and 'Black Legion' as one of Hollywood's infrequent but exciting excursions into the more sinister expressions of our social system. In my opinion it is finer than either of them. The film is much more than the screen record of a specific mob murder. There is a dispassionate perspective in the script and in Mr. Le Roy's consummate direction that makes this a universal and abiding arraignment of intolerance and crowd fury." Richard Kerr described "They Won't Forget" as "a truly great picture." In Britain, too, the film received high praise. Basil Wright, in *World Film News*, December, 1937, stated : " 'They Won't Forget' is a savage, terrible, horrifying, cynical and unequivocable exposé of the backwardness and degeneration of the small-time towns of the Southern States, which have, with their lynchings and their Scottsboro' Trials, made American justice stink to Heaven."

"They Won't Forget" occupies an honoured position in the annals of serious movie-making. It reflects great credit on Mervyn Le Roy and Warner Brothers, a studio which has never hesitated to make films on controversial themes. For that praiseworthy pre-war series of hard-hitting motion pictures which began with "I Am A Fugitive" and ended with "Confessions Of A Nazi

Spy " in 1939, Warner Brothers deserves a permanent place in the Honour Roll of the Hollywood industry.

Gone With The Wind

And so we come to " Gone With The Wind." Like Griffith's historic film, it dealt with the South, the Civil War and the efforts of the Negro to free himself from slavery, and, as Lawrence Reddick remarks, these films possess interesting similarities. Both were extraordinary from an artistic and technical point of view, both were heralded with almost fantastic publicity, both were remarkably long (" Gone With The Wind " lasted nearly four hours) and both were huge financial successes. Nevertheless it could be seen that the American film itself and film audiences generally had grown up considerably. No longer was it possible, as Griffith had done, to lay stress upon inflammatory appeal. Director Victor Fleming concentrated instead on the characters of Scarlett O'Hara and Rhett Butler, the " romantic leads," and his attitude to the black characters in the film was notable for its subtlety. Whether this was the subtlety of unconscious discrimination or that of a fully conscious desire to follow, a little more carefully, in the footsteps of Griffith, one cannot say. At any rate many critics felt that where Griffith's film ended Fleming's film began.

The novel is probably well-known to most people. Apart from its rather florid central theme, it succeeds in eradicating from the mind of the reader any liberal consciousness which may have resulted from knowing that the Northern States won a victory over intolerance when they achieved the larger political and military victory in the Civil War. The film succeeded admirably in continuing the popular Southern myth that the South had in fact won an ideological war, that, indeed, although the Negroes had been set free they still remained inescapably fettered as historic inferiors to the white race, socially, politically and economically. " Gone With The Wind " marked a high point in the Hollywood move to show that so far as the Negro was concerned United States opinion had reverted to the " Southern Mammy and Uncle Tom tradition." Hollywood's apparent obsession with films on Southern themes, especially films which " put the Negro in his place," cannot always have been a mere accident. Surely it is not unreasonable to suggest that those who make these films possess pre-conceived notions on this subject, with the result that literally millions of filmgoers are yearly doped with a subtle—and sometimes extremely unsubtle —form of harmful propaganda. As an indication that I do not under-estimate the potential audience of an anti-Negro film I should like to point out that by 1944 David O. Selznick, the producer of " Gone With The Wind," estimated that nearly sixty-four *million* people in the United States and Canada had seen his film !* Add to that the audiences in the United Kingdom, the British Empire and in other parts of the world and you have a startling indication of the very real menace of a film which propagates anti-social ideas and around which is wrapped the pill of " star-studded entertainment."

During the making of " Gone With The Wind " the National Association For The Advancement of Coloured People (N.A.A.C.P.) instituted a vigorous fight to have some of the most offensive scenes eliminated or, at least, softened ; as a result, the film, when finally shown, was not by any means as vicious as the novel.   And bodies like the National Negro Congress, the Negro magazine *Opportunity*, other Negro newspapers, and certain Left and Liberal political groups, continued to denounce the film in the Press. The magazine *Socialist Appeal* described it as " a distorted glorification of the Old South."   Both the *Daily Worker* and *New Masses* carried on a vigorous blast against the film's showing, describing it as Fascist, reactionary, an incitement to race hatred, a monstrous slander of the Negro people, and going on to assert that the film justified the existence of the Ku Klux Klan.

The New York State Committee of the American Communist Party went further and issued the following statement : " ' Gone With The Wind ' revives every foul slander against the Negro people, every stock-in-trade lie of the Southern lynchers.   Well-dressed in a slick package of sentimentality for the old ' noble ' traditions of the South, this movie is a rabid incitement against the Negro people. The historical struggle for democracy in this country which we have come to cherish so dearly is vilified and condemned.   The great

DOOLEY WILSON, HUMPHREY BOGART and INGRID BERGMAN in *Casablanca*, directed by Michael Curtiz.

The film was also re-issued with considerable success in the U.S.A. and Britain in 1947 and 1948.

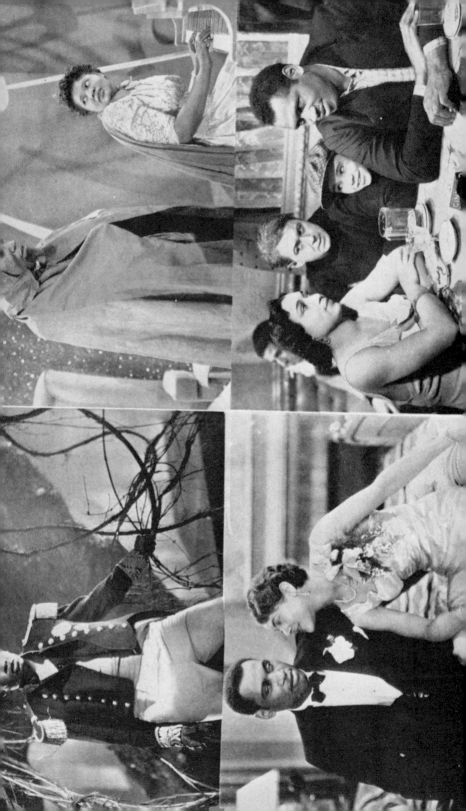

liberator, Abraham Lincoln, is pictured as a tyrant and a coward. Not only is this vicious picture calculated to provoke race riots, but also to cause sectional strife between the North and the South just when the growth of the labour and progressive movement has made possible the increasing unity of Negro and white, on behalf of the common interests of both."

Negro leaders, lecturers, educationists, public figures, artists, actors, and many others condemned the film, and some trade unions supported moves to picket cinemas where " Gone With The Wind " was showing. Their combined efforts, however, to have it banned or to have the offending passages removed were not successful. Nevertheless such was the interest aroused by mass demonstrations against this famous film that it served to educate the public to a further awareness, firstly of the fact that there *were* anti-Negro elements in certain Hollywood films, and secondly of the dangerous power of the movie for developing reactionary social attitudes. For, as Lawrence Reddick says, " The net effect of such a film on the public mind can only be guessed."

Walter White, Secretary of the N.A.A.C.P., stated, " Whatever sentiment there was in the South for Federal anti-lynch law evaporated during the ' Gone With The Wind ' vogue." And, in his pamphlet examining race relations in motion pictures, Reddick records that at least one Southern child who had seen the film is reported to have told his Negro nursemaid that she would still be a slave and his daddy would not have to pay her if it had not been for the Yankees ! Dalton Trumbo, speaking at the Hollywood Writers Congress in 1943, said : " The most gigantic milestones of Hollywood's appeal to public patronage have been the anti-Negro pictures like ' The Birth Of A Nation ' and ' Gone With The Wind.' "

Hattie McDaniel was given an Academy Award for the best acting of the year in a supporting rôle for her work in " Gone With The Wind." This was the first time that a Negro had ever received such an award from the Academy of Motion Picture Arts and Sciences, but the fact that she was given an " Oscar " for her work as a stereotyped " Mammy " in this highly controversial film caused a great deal of further dissension. Indeed many Negroes

Above left *Song Of Freedom*
Above right : *Harlem On Parade*
Below left : *The Emperor Jones*
Below right : *Big Fella*

felt that Miss McDaniel should have refused to take the award as a protest against her part.

To sum up : " Gone With The Wind " convinced millions of Southerners that the war had been for them an ideological victory, and that the place for the black man was in the lowest stratum of society. It stirred up further feeling against the " damned Yankees," and as a prime example of how a moving picture can incite intense racial hatred Victor Fleming's film of the Margaret Mitchell novel lines up worthily alongside Griffith's film of *The Clansman.*

CHAPTER FIVE

SONG AND DANCE

" In almost every instance where a Negro artist, dancer or singer has been used on the screen, he has been introduced either in an ' all-Negro film ' or in a segregated sequence, which amounts to the same thing."

" *Negro Digest,*" *June, 1946.*

Song

The Negro as musician is widely known in films. Since the coming of talking pictures he has been featured regularly in the rôle of jazz instrumentalist, singer, performer, and what-have-you. Indeed many coloured entertainers and personalities have come to the fore in the sphere of the musical film, earning huge sums of money and becoming box office names. Thus we encounter people like Cab Calloway, Duke Ellington, Fats Waller, Louis Armstrong, Louis Jordan, Count Basie and many other instrumentalists and band-leaders prominently featured in the cast-lists of numerous Hollywood musicals. (In this connection it is somewhat ironic to note that whereas such " personalities " as Calloway, Ellington and Armstrong are paid large sums of money to make what may be termed " star " appearances, Negro actors, infinitely more distinguished in their own particular field, have to suffer continually from indifferent casting and billing.) Since 1929, producers have been only too eager to employ well-known coloured stage and radio musical comedy stars and dance-band leaders. The long, sad trail of Negro appearance in films thus follows a certain set routine : from savage to servant and finally from servant to performer. Here and there along the trail, as I have endeavoured to show, there have been divergencies from the usual pattern, isolated instances where talented Negroes have risen above their rôles and played their parts with compelling, though occasionally pathetic, dignity.

In the minds of many filmgoers Negroes are inextricably inter-woven with jazz trumpeters, due principally to the way in which Hollywood has relentlessly utilised the considerable Negro talent in the field of jazz and popular music. In many kinds of musicals a black jazz band is featured, though one never sees a " mixed " band on the screen, i.e., an orchestra consisting of both white and coloured musicians, for since Hollywood does not wish to antagonise Southern audiences the Jim Crow ruling prevails even in song and dance movies. An instance of how this operates was provided by the film " Sweet And Lowdown," made a few years ago, and featuring Benny Goodman and his Orchestra. It is well known that Benny Goodman has long made a practice of using certain coloured musicians in his otherwise white groups. He has carried out this progressive policy for some time, and in the famous small contingents like his Quartet and Sextet well-known Negro musicians, such as pianist Teddy Wilson and vibraphonist Lionel Hampton, are featured along with the white musicians. (Both these Negro instrumentalists were included in the Goodman Quartet in the Warners film " Hollywood Hotel," made in 1938.)

So popular has the Benny Goodman Orchestra been with American audiences over a long period that he has successfully managed to incorporate his " no colour bar " ruling into his stage shows, and by now thousands of American audiences have learned to accept " mixed " orchestras. Goodman was the pioneer in this field, and his example has since been followed by many famous and popular American orchestras. However, when he went to Hollywood to make " Sweet and Lowdown," the band-leader immediately encountered opposition to his well-known policy. It is on record that he made a strong resistance, but apparently he was finally defeated, for in the finished film, when the famous Goodman Quartet was given prominence, the Negro Teddy Wilson was replaced at the piano by an eminent white pianist Jess Stacey. And the same happened in Goodman's other recent films, " The Girls He Left Behind " and " Stage Door Canteen " ; thus Hollywood makes sure that though it may offend Negroes it does not offend the susceptibilities of Negro-baiters. More ironic instances could surely not be given of how the colour bar penetrates even into the field of filmic jazz.

The magazine, *The Melody Maker*, reported an incident as follows in the issue June 28th, 1947 : " As the director was about to give the go-ahead signal for a sequence featuring Charlie Barnet and his ' mixed ' orchestra on the set of ' Freddie Steps Out,' being made at Monogram Studios, in rushed the top men from Monogram's sales department. ' Stop the film ! ' they cried, ' Get those Negro boys off the band-stand. We cannot have coloured musicians playing in a white orchestra.' Barnet protested, so did producer Sam Katzman, but the money boys, their eyes on the film's Southern exposure, were adamant. The Negro musicians had to leave the set."

It is, however, encouraging to note that Universal has often included in its musical productions the orchestra of Freddy Slack, a white group which prominently features an internationally known Negro clarinet player, Barney Bigard. It is true, however, that Bigard is very light-skinned, and thus would not photograph as too obviously Negroid. (Therefore it would appear that *light-skinned* Negroes still have a chance to be seen on the screen playing in the same bands with white musicians.)

Duke Ellington, eminent Negro composer and orchestra leader, has made several appearances with his band, in such films as " Murder At The Vanities " and " She Gets Her Man." His most recent movie appearance was in " Cabin In The Sky," in which he was featured prominently in the exciting night club sequences. Ellington has a good personality, is handsome and well-dressed. All his screen appearances have been markedly successful, and it is likely that he will soon appear in a prominent rôle in a full-length film dealing with the progress of jazz, to be produced and directed by Orson Welles. Another leading Hollywood director, Edward Dmytryk, has also announced that he will make a jazz film featuring Ellington, which seems an exciting prospect.

Cab Calloway, more essentially a showman than a musician, is a popular film personality who has been featured in half a dozen Hollywood musicals, the first being " The Big Broadcast," the most recent being the all-Negro production " Stormy Weather." His more important appearances, however, have been in non-Negro films, and so popular and attractive are his personality and general orchestral ensemble that Calloway has managed often to infuse considerable significance into what otherwise might have been unimportant and stereotyped band-leader appearances.

There is, for example, his work in the Warners production " The Singing Kid," which starred Al Jolson and in which Calloway was allowed to joke with Jolson, who treated him with genuine affection, to exchange wisecracks with Al and generally to behave in an un-selfconscious and un-raceconscious manner. In fact, " The Singing Kid " deserves a place in the short but important list of films which have presented members of the Negro race to good effect, since in this production the fact that Calloway was a Negro was never stressed, which is in itself a significant point. It must be admitted, however, that Cab has made a number of concessions to popular taste, and has clowned and sung his way in traditional rolling-eyed manner through half a dozen other musical movies. But he is an interesting personality, with a clear insight into the complexities of anti-Negroism, and an earnest desire to play his part, no matter how small, in obtaining a square deal for his race.

Born in 1907 in New York, young Cabell, after a boyhood in Baltimore, went to law school in preparation for entering the same profession as his father. But later, when his sister Blanche who had become a vocalist and band-leader opened in a Chicago revue, the boy decided to join her. And since his first appearance on the stage in " Plantation Days " Calloway has had phenomenal success. He first came into prominence when he sang in a New York revue, " Connie's Hot Chocolates," and afterwards Cab Calloway and his orchestra zoomed to popularity and became famous in Europe as well as in the States. Calloway is now one of America's foremost show business personalities, and exercises a great deal of influence on the " teen-agers " of the U.S.A. On the stage he is an impressive figure, dancing, gyrating, singing, giving an outstanding performance of rhythmic Negro music and dance. Off-stage he is quite a serious person, and confesses to possessing something of a dual personality. " In the theatre it is difficult," Cab says, " to exercise much influence on the great American public with regard to racial questions, except in an indirect way. But if, in creating a large body of followers and friends for my orchestra and my whole entertainment organisation, I have perhaps managed to convince a few doubters that the Negro is a human being who deserves human treatment, then I have played my admittedly minor part in helping towards greater racial understanding."

Another well-known Negro band-leader is Louis Armstrong, who has been seen in such musicals as " Pennies From Heaven," " Jam Session," " Atlantic City " and, more recently, Warners' " Pillow To Post." Because of his outstanding personality Armstrong is often given acting rôles in films, though it must be recorded that he has so far failed to distinguish himself in this direction. Louis falls quite naturally into the Stepin Fetchit-Willie Best-Mantan Moreland category of " movie mugging," and in every publicity still he appears always to assume the startled and slightly inane expression which is conventionally regarded as " typically Negroid." Nevertheless Armstrong is acknowledged to be one of the most brilliant trumpeters in the history of jazz and his playing has been heard to good advantage in some dozen films. In " Pillow To Post " his screen personality proved to be attractive and in his duets with that lovely Negro singer Dorothy Dandridge he managed to be extremely entertaining (though the scenes were cut out by the Memphis Censor). In " Cabin In The Sky " Louis was given a non-musical part, playing one of the satellites of The Evil One, which he handled quite adequately. His newest film is " New Orleans," in which he has a prominent rôle. Both Hollywood producers and filmgoers generally seem to like him and it is likely that Louis Armstrong has an interesting film future, and one not limited only to musicals.

Fats Waller, who died a few years ago, was a great screen favourite who, since making his film début in 1935 in " The King Of Burlesque," was successfully featured in many prominent Hollywood musicals. The atmosphere of a New Orleans " dive " in the film " Stormy Weather " really became authentic when Waller and his small group of coloured jazzmen commenced to play real heart-felt blues as an accompaniment to the throaty singing of Ada Brown ; and Fats Waller has brought similar authenticity to other productions with a jazz background. Waller, one of the most kindly and genial of all entertainers, always brought a whiff of good humour into his screen appearances. He was admired, one might even say beloved, by millions, and his sudden death as a result of a heart attack on a train going to New York, in 1944, was mourned in all parts of the world. His death was certainly a great loss to filmgoers everywhere.

Count Basie and his Orchestra were seen in " Hit Parade Of 1943 " for Republic and also in " Stage Door Canteen " for Sol Lesser, while their particular brand of swing music has been heard to good effect recently in a series of Universal musicals. In " Follow The Boys," a new Negro band-leader came to the fore, namely saxophonist and vocalist Louis Jordan, who after making several Hollywood appearances—his most recent were Monogram's " Swing Parade Of 1946 " and Columbia's " Meet Miss Bobby Socks "—went to New York, to star in some all-Negro films. He has an easy, charming personality, and many of the songs which he first featured with his orchestra have become widely successful on the radio. According to *Ebony*, the Negro magazine, the first two Negro films in which he appeared—" Caldonia " and " Beware," both produced by Astor, and directed by Bud Pollard—were quite innocuous, even if they did not represent much of a step forward. (The cast of " Beware " included such well-known coloured players as Frank Wilson, Valerie Black and Milton Woods.)

Dorothy Dandridge, wife of dancer Harold Nicholas, was seen singing with Count Basie in " Hit Parade Of 1943 " and in 1946 had a considerable success in Warners' " Pillow To Post." She is a very beautiful girl with a most attractive singing style ; more will certainly be heard of her. At present, the most renowned of all coloured singers in Hollywood is of course Lena Horne. Since she appeared in " Panama Hattie " in 1942, Lena has been kept continually busy by her studio, Metro-Goldwyn-Mayer, who regard her as one of their leading stars. Today she is the most famous coloured film actress in the world and exerts a considerable influence on Negro opinion, for she is well-known as a militant and fearless artist.

In " Sensations Of 1945 " Dorothy Donegan and Gene Rodgers scored something of a success in an exciting piano interlude (deleted by the Memphis Censor for Southern audiences), while Maurice Rocco, a musician who has become famous during the last few years as " the boogie-woogie pianist who never sits down to play," was seen to good advantage in Paramount's " Incendiary

Blonde," and other films. It is Hazel Scott, however, who has undoubtedly achieved the highest pinnacles of musical fame on the screen. Hazel is considered among the leading jazz pianists in the world today, and her film appearances have been markedly successful. Making no concessions to Hollywood, she will never appear in the parts of " piano-playing maids " or similar parts, but is seen always just as " Hazel Scott." Many times reported as saying that she would rather play herself on the screen than " another coloured servant rôle," Hazel feels very strongly on the subject. Indeed it is said that her film contract is one of the most amazing documents ever drawn up between a Negro and a film company. By virtue of her beauty, personality, courage and talent, Hazel Scott has achieved a considerable position of prominence in the story of the progress of her race.

Hazel, who is married to politician and author Adam Clayton Powell, was born in Trinidad, where her mother was a concert pianist. Taught to play from the age of three, Hazel went with her family to live in New York City and by the time she was eight she had won a scholarship to the Julliard School of Music. When she was twelve she appeared as a soloist in Carnegie Hall, playing Tschaikowsky's Piano Concerto. In her teens, however, Hazel began to have an interest in jazz, and finally she became well-known as a jazz pianist at the Café Society. In 1940 she opened at the Café Society Uptown, where she was for some years afterwards the principal attraction. Her popularity is amazing ; it is said that she gets more than seven hundred and fifty letters a week, which is remarkable for a Negro artist. She went to Hollywood first in 1943 to appear in Columbia's " Something To Shout About," and her subsequent films have included M.-G.-M.'s " Thousands Cheer " and " By Hook Or By Crook," and Warners' " Rhapsody In Blue," in which she scored a resounding success both as pianist and vocalist. In each of her films Hazel plays the part of herself, but some day she would like, she declares " to do some real acting."

" I could play some of the great Negro characters of history, like Sojourner Truth, the Civil War abolitionist, or maybe I could play the part of a Negro W.A.C. of today," Hazel once said. She refuses, however, to play any parts which she considers do not reflect credit on coloured people. " I have turned down four singing-maid rôles in movies during the past year or so," she stated recently, and added, " Some producers want you to come on the set, dust off a piano and then sit down and play. But I will not do anything like that ! "

Her film contract says that Hazel Scott will not wear a handkerchief round her head nor dirty clothes in a film ; all coloured performers in her show must portray " respectable rôles," and she herself must always be presented as an intelligent female artist. Hazel is militant and courageous. To give a small, but significant incident : in a recent Hollywood production she refused to appear in a sequence with eight Negro girls because they were wearing soiled aprons. Finally the coloured star won her point and the girls appeared in new, white, starched dresses. She has often expressed the hope that the Negro performer who represents the handkerchief-headed, corn-cob pipe-smoking, continually-grinning old school of stereotype will fast disappear from the screens. Hazel feels also that a coloured player can work many benefits in the sphere of artistry. As she says, " I am certain that my work both on the screen, on the stage and in the many hospital and army camp tours that I have made is beneficial to race relations." Hazel Scott goes on to point out : " We Negroes may go further in acting and entertaining than in any other fields because we are permitted to express ourselves. And we could do the same in aviation, industry or anything else, if there were fewer obstacles against us. Be that as it may, America loves its performers, and those of us who do perform have a distinct duty—we must show ourselves to the best advantage."

Warner Brothers made an excellent short film in 1946 called " Jammin' The Blues," photographed and directed by Gjon Mili. The film portrays in stark, realistic photography the pure undiluted music of a small jazz group. Jazz knows no colour bar, and in most of these " jam sessions " in various restaurants and night clubs the musicians consist of both white and coloured players. In the film a white musician was included as the guitarist in an otherwise all-Negro group, since director Mili felt that a film about jazz music should not be made on Jim Crow lines. (But Max Jones, reviewing the film in the magazine *Melody Maker*, October 19th, 1946, writes : " An incidental point—and one that may be attributed to Hollywood's immense colour phobia—is that Barney Kessel, the only white member of the group, has been skilfully avoided by the lens save for one brief glimpse in an angle shot. Thus the band appears all-coloured and will presumably not offend anti-Negro opinion.") " Jammin' The Blues " is, however, among the most exciting and authentic jazz films ever made, and takes its place with that small and exclusive group of movies with jazz themes which includes Michael Curtiz's " Blues In The Night," Robert Siodmak's " Phantom Lady " and William Dieterle's " Syncopation."

The latter, made some five years ago by R.K.O.-Radio, was particularly interesting in that the well-known Negro actor Todd Duncan, who had previously refused many Hollywood offers, was brought from New York to play an important featured part as a New Orleans trumpet player who teaches a white girl the fundamentals of jazz. Duncan, an intelligent and dignified player, made his rôle stand out ; many of his scenes with Bonita Granville, who played the jazz-minded white girl, are among the most sympathetically handled inter-racial scenes on record. Directed by ex-actor Dieterle, " Syncopation " was an extremely interesting film, and it is to be regretted that Todd Duncan has made only very rare screen appearances since this production. It is said that he has refused so many servile parts that Hollywood has become tired of asking him. This may well be so, for it is doubtful if many such rôles as sympathetic as the one Duncan played in " Syncopation " have come his way since that time.

In many musical films since 1929 there have been *special* sequences devoted exclusively to Negroes, who, one notes, are never allowed to sing, play or dance with white performers, but are always confined to a special section of the production. Since coloured dancers were segregated in the early talking film, " Movietone Follies Of 1929," Hollywood musicals have followed the same pattern. Typical of the modern kind of musical was Warners' " Thank Your Lucky Stars," which had a special Negro section featuring Hattie McDaniel and Willie Best. Paramount's " Star Spangled Rhythm " also featured a Jim Crow sequence with " Rochester " and Katherine Dunham, and there are dozens of similar instances of Hollywood's emphatic use of a colour bar. (There has, for example, never been a film in which a white girl danced or sang with a Negro or a coloured girl with a white man. Ludicrous maybe, but true nevertheless. Lena Horne's numbers in M.-G.-M.'s " Ziegfeld Follies " were strictly Jim Crow with coloured leading man, chorus girls and extras.)

A seven-year-old pianistic prodigy, Frank Isaac Robinson, known as " Sugar Chile," has been signed to a contract by M.-G.-M. making his first appearance in " No Leave, No Love." This amazing Negro child has been playing jazz piano since he was three years old, and graduated from playing hymn tunes to blues and boogie-woogie. Saxophonist Coleman Hawkins and blues-singer Josh White appeared in Universal's " The Crimson Canary." Ann Jenkins, singer and pianist, was heard to advantage in Paramount's " People Are Funny," while various vocal and instrumental groups such as The Mills Brothers, The Ink Spots, The Charioteers, The Delta Rhythm Boys and The King Cole Trio have made regular film appearances since the coming of sound. In Warners' " Rhapsody In Blue," the story of George Gershwin, part of this composer's famous Negro operetta " Porgy and Bess " was re-staged with Ann Brown in her original stage rôle. But in the same film an entire sequence conceived for coloured dancers was done by whites with *blacked-up* faces. (Incidentally, in " Saratoga Trunk," also produced by Warners, Flora Robson was blacked-up in burned-cork to play the rôle of Angelique, a French Negro servant, one of the most important parts in the entire picture. Presumably Warners felt that the public would not take too well to a film in which an actual Negro woman exercised such a powerful influence over the heroine, Cleo Dulane, played by Ingrid Bergman. Negro opinion was strongly incensed by this retrogressive step ; it had been more than thirty years since D. W. Griffith, noted for his anti-Negro bias, had regularly used blacked-up whites for coloured rôles. Since Griffith's time the practice had dropped ; now Warners had revived it, though luckily it was an isolated case.)

The Hall Johnson Choir has been in existence for nearly twenty years. It is a unique group, which has gained immense prominence in its versions of Negro spirituals, for Johnson himself has a deep love of spirituals dating back to his birth-place in Athens, Georgia. He studied music from the age of eight, and later he taught music in New York. Sitting in the orchestra pits of the various orchestras in which he played the viola, Johnson often thought how he would like to train a group of Negro singers to sing the spirituals in the soulful manner in which he had heard them sung as a child. Eventually in 1925 he formed a group of eight singers, who after their début in various Harlem churches began to be well-known on the radio throughout the United States.

The choir has been heard on the stage in such productions as
" The Green Pastures," and in Hall Johnson's own play " Run
Lil' Chillun." They have also been heard as a background
to a number of Hollywood films, including the screen version of
" The Green Pastures," and others like Columbia's " Meet John
Doe " and " Lost Horizon." The Hall Johnson Choir is one of
the most famous choirs in the world, and a number of films have
been enlivened by the beautiful background singing of this Negro
group. They are certainly unique, since there is no other body of
singers who are used so consistently in stage and film productions
which are not themselves essentially Negro in character. They
have succeeded to some degree in breaking down racial barriers,
at least *behind* the scenes of film-making.

Most musical films feature coloured personalities in some capacity
or other ; indeed it is difficult to recall a film of this type in which
Negro singers, instrumentalists and dancers did not appear.
Hollywood accedes to public demand by giving " feature spots " and
billing to nationally-known coloured artists, but the Jim Crow
ruling still persists. Thus one encounters either all-Negro musical
films, or all-Negro sequences in otherwise white films, but never
under any circumstances are black and white performers allowed
to " mix " in front of the camera. And, although Negro players
are daily becoming more popular and powerful, Jim Crow has
not been relaxed in any way. Hollywood's colour bar still holds
good in musical films.

Dance

Some of the greatest dancers in the world have been Negroes,
and in recent years a large proportion of them have been seen
on the screen. The most outstanding acrobatic dancers are, of
course, the internationally-known Harold and Fayard Nicholas,
whose superb dancing has been seen in many films, principally
in " The Great American Broadcast," " Carolina Blues," and
" Stormy Weather." Both were seen in London as child
prodigies in Lew Leslie's " Blackbirds Revue Of 1935," and since
their return to America they have been kept continually busy
on the New York stage and in Hollywood. To watch the deft
agility of Fayard and the fantastic body twirlings and acrobatics
of Harold, the younger brother, is an extraordinary experience.
Their dancing is a sheer joy to watch and constitutes perfect

modern ballet. There have been long sections devoted to their dancing in many musical films, and indeed a great deal of trouble appears to be taken with the setting, lighting, photography and direction of these sequences. In their own field the Nicholas Brothers have no equal.

But probably no Negro dancer has become as famous as Bill Robinson, that wonderful veteran of tap dancing, who, as " Bojangles," has tapped his way through a score of films in the past ten years. It was in a Shirley Temple film that one first became conscious of Robinson's extraordinary ability, though he had been delighting American audiences for forty years previously in numberless musical shows and Broadway revues. In his day, Robinson was peerless and even at the present time he has few rivals in his particular field. A superb sense of rhythm and an easy nonchalance are his two main assets and one can hardly believe, when watching him effortlessly perform the most intricate steps, that he is nearly seventy. Among his films are " The Little Colonel," " In Old Kentucky," " The Littlest Rebel," " One Mile From Heaven " and the more recent " Stormy Weather," in which he danced and played the leading rôle opposite Lena Horne. Eddie " Rochester " Anderson is also a considerable dancer, and in many films, from Columbia's " The Music Goes Round " to Paramount's " Man About Town," he has excited admiration with his beautifully executed dance routines in his highly inimitable style. In " Star Spangled Rhythm " he danced with Katherine Dunham in a specially devised sequence.

In the lengthy gallery of Negro rhythm one remembers the dancing in " Hallelujah " : the gyrating bodies of the Negro couples in the night club, and especially the crude but exciting tap-dancing and shimmying of Nina Mae McKinney. And one recollects in the earliest days of talking films, the many all-coloured dancing sequences in films like " Fox Movietone Follies Of 1929." In nearly every American musical film there is a section in which Negro dancers appear, always to good effect, for they are naturally at home in the dance medium.

Katherine Dunham

An indication of how the Negro lends himself particularly to the more serious forms of the dance was given by the Katherine Dunham Ballet in some fascinating sequences in " Stormy

Weather," and again in the short film " Carnival In Rhythm."
Katherine Dunham is one of the leading exponents of modern
dancing in America. Her justly-famous Negro Ballet Company
has been seen on Broadway and in Hollywood films, and of her
work Walter Terry wrote in the *New York Herald Tribune :* " Miss
Dunham is laying the ground-work for a great Negro dance."
She has, in fact, evolved a new style of dancing, and due to her
efforts a serious Negro group has been acclaimed, for the first
time, as representative of the finest ballet in America. Katherine
began dancing when she was a child. Born in 1910, in Joliet,
Illinois, where her father owned a dry-cleaning establishment
and her mother was a school teacher, Katherine, at the age of
eight, organised a cabaret at the local Methodist church. She
succeeded in shocking the congregation but raised a considerable
amount for the church fund and began a career which has been
largely concerned with the dance since that time. When she was
ten years old she learned to play the piano and afterwards developed
an extraordinary sense of rhythm ; later she studied dancing under
Ludmila Speranzeva, and then followed her brother Albert to
Chicago University, where she earned a Bachelor of Arts degree
and organised a School of the Dance. Kathleen studied here
for three years and soon learned that dancing is one of the earliest
expressions of man's impulses, emotions and reactions to the world
about him and that the forms of the dance persisted long after the
circumstances which inspired it have vanished. " Dancing,"
she once said, " is a living record of a people's history. You can
learn more about people, what they are, what they have been,
from their dances than from almost anything about them."

Among the audience at one of her early dance recitals was Mrs.
Alfred Rosenwald Stern, who was impressed with Katherine's
work and subsequently offered her a fellowship of the Rosenwald
Foundation, so that the girl could study dancing at her leisure.
As a result of this fellowship Katherine left the United States and
travelled extensively in Jamaica, Cuba, Trinidad, Martinique
and Haiti ; and it was in Haiti that she learned a great deal
about primitive dancing and anthropology, now one of her favourite
subjects. (Indeed she is known in America as " the dancing
anthropologist.")

After returning from Jamaica, the young Negro girl wrote
scores of articles and various academic theses on her findings,

and with the dance material which she brought back she began to organise her now extensive library. In 1931 she had given a first performance of a Negro Ballet in Chicago and her small experimental dance group had also been seen in recitals in other large towns. Following Katherine's return from her travels she was asked to do the choreography of her first important work, a ballet for the Federal Theatre in Chicago and at length she arrived in New York as the choreographer of the famous Left Wing musical " Pins and Needles."

Her first solo dancing appearance in New York was at the Windsor Theatre, where she gave a performance of her own show, " Tropics And Le Jazz Hot." This was soon followed by the famous " Cabin In The Sky " in which Katherine Dunham and her Ballet Company came into nation-wide prominence ; her success really dates from this production. Nowadays her company gives performances as a separate entity ; like the American Ballet Theatre, it has a place of importance in the world of the dance in the U.S.A. She has been seen in such Hollywood films as " Star Spangled Rhythm" dancing with Eddie Anderson, while the Dunham Group danced in " Stormy Weather " and also in a short film for Warners (devoted entirely to Katherine and her company) called " Carnival In Rhythm." Her recent New York shows have included " Carib Song " and " Tropical Revue," both of which have successfully established Katherine Dunham as pre-eminent in her own style of dancing and dance creation.

Katherine's work in " Star Spangled Rhythm " and " Stormy Weather " reveals that she is particularly suited to the film medium, but although she has many plans for making extensive screen appearances with her company in the future, the dancer has also refused a number of film offers for reasons stated below. An interesting personality, she is highly intelligent, vital, versatile, talented, social-conscious. For Paramount she acted as dance director on such films as " Pardon My Sarong " ; now she concentrates on her own pupils. At her famous dance school both the instructors and the students are of all races ; they work in harmony without any thought of colour, and are intent only on creating something worth while to contribute to the American dance theatre. Situated in the heart of Broadway, the Dunham School of Dance provides a centre of racial harmony. As Katherine herself says : " Complete inter-racial justice must ultimately be achieved if American culture is to be finally and truly democratic."

On the question of racial discrimination on the screen, Miss Dunham has certain definite and long-held views. She wrote to the author as follows : " I feel that not only the American Negro but every minority group has been in an extremely unfortunate position in pictures in America. Hollywood is controlled by a very small group of people who have an extremely far-reaching influence on the entire body of American thinking, in some cases even extending to an international scope. Contrary to human progress, these people have not heretofore had a very liberal attitude toward minority groups and in every case Orientals, and American Negroes particularly, have been treated with as little dignity as possible."

Katherine went on : " During the war a great effort was made to relieve this situation. Responsible groups of Negroes went to some lengths to try to discourage Negro performers from accepting rôles which were discriminatory and stereotyped. It was not easy, because the economic situation played such a very heavy part, actors often accepting unpalatable work because of their need for remuneration. The efforts on the part of such organisations as the National Association for the Advancement of Coloured People and the International Film and Radio Guild have, however, had some very positive results—for instance, Negroes are now being shown as a part of the general street scene, both in feature films and in news reels. And the Negro servant type has in some cases been permitted to drop his loathsome dialect. Also, of course, great strides forward have been made by such personalities as Lena Horne, Duke Ellington and Paul Robeson and also by the character parts portrayed by Rex Ingram, Leigh Whipper and others.

" As for myself, I can only say that in many cases I have had to reject offers for film employment because of my firm belief that this important form of propaganda must be controlled at any cost. Hollywood still doesn't consider Negroes as people. Why don't the movies move with the times?

I might add that there are great hopes among the more progressive Negro peoples that film-makers in Mexico and Europe

GEORGE BRENT, ERNEST ANDERSON and BETTE DAVIS in *In This Our Life* directed by John Huston.

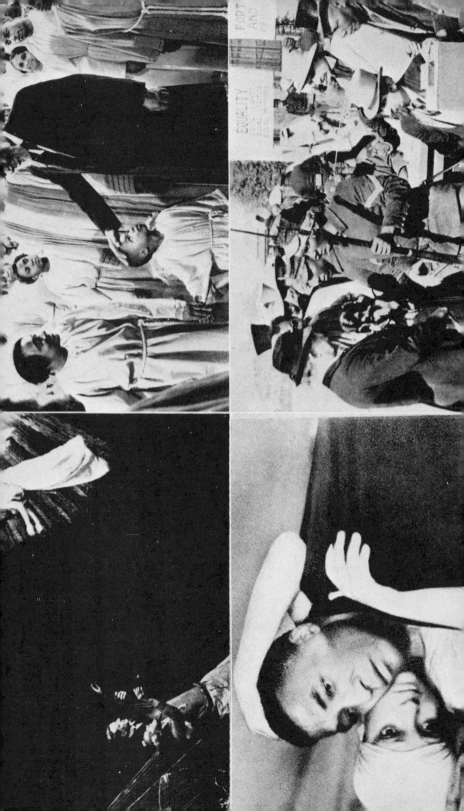

will have the foresight to make use of the great quantity of Negro talent in their countries, and that once this has been done the resultant films are somehow released in the United States. For on this matter, Hollywood can certainly take a leaf out of Europe's book."

" Katherine Dunham, Ph.B., lecturer, scholar, and authoritative interpreter of primitive dance rhythms," (to quote from *Collier's Magazine*) is an outstanding personality in the American scene. Intelligent and outspoken, she commands immense respect, both as a person and as an artist. Her dancing was recently described by John Martin in the *New York Times* as " lively, colourful, humorous, endlessly entertaining and beautifully racial." And, not only as an artist but as a fearless spokeswoman for her race, like Lena Horne, Katherine Dunham has achieved world prominence. Indeed her particular contribution to the serious dance has opened up an avenue of artistic endeavour for Negroes in a medium which is peculiarly their own.

Above left : *Uncle Tom's Cabin*
Above right: *The Green Pastures*
Below left : *Hallelujah*
Below right : *The Birth Of A Nation*

CHAPTER SIX

INDEPENDENT AND GOVERNMENT FILMS

" Then is the hope for Negroes to be in films made by Negroes ? That would be a hope, if the American Negro had given evidence of caring for and understanding his own experience sufficiently to create works of art in the other medium. But the American Negro as graphic artist has shown very little awareness of this experience ; as writer he is imitative, respectable, blunt, ulterior, and when he pretends to follow Negro materials, he does little more than duplicate them."

HARRY ALAN POTAMKIN, *in " Close Up," August, 1929.*

" The idea of the Negro and the film is no mental funfare for the epigrammatical and perverse, and cannot be countenanced because of slack enthusiasms and unfounded wishes. Either the Negro is or is not capable of taking into his hands and using well and thoroughly for his own good and the good of all civilizations a weapon of which Lenin said, ' For us the cinema is the most important of the arts '—or he despises it and is not equipped to take control. It will rest almost entirely with him, and what it would lead to anybody can foretell. But that is relatively unimportant today when anybody can foretell anything. Ultimately it should not but mark a big step forward in the humanisation of the human race."

KENNETH MACPHERSON, *in " Negro," edited by Nancy Cunard (Wishart, 1934).*

Independent Films

From time to time in the past twenty years various Negro producers, and some white producers, have made independent films with all-coloured casts designed to appeal mainly to coloured audiences. It is a regrettable fact, however, that none of these has been outstanding ; indeed most of them have been mediocre. In any case, because of their all-Negro casts, they come into the much-despised category of Jim Crow films. They are usually very cheaply made. And, as William Harrison remarks in *Sight and Sound*, Spring, 1939 : " The Negro spokesman had to realise that without financial resources for large-scale production the Negro community is dependent, and will be so for a long time, upon the Hollywood industry. Numerous independent productions have borne out the fact of the Negro's dependency upon Hollywood."

The main rôle played by independent Negro film producers is that of supplying the Negro cinemas. There are some four hundred of these in the United States* catering either exclusively or predominantly for Negroes, depending upon the region of the country. As Margaret Farrand Thorp writes in her *America At the Movies* : " The fourteen million American Negroes seem to be the only considerable section of the population who cannot go to a movie whenever they have the price. Some Southern cinemas reserve special sections for Negroes. Others do not admit them at all. There are few Negro cinemas. About one for every twenty-one thousand Negroes."

These cinemas are listed in the *Negro Handbook 1944* as follows :—

State	Towns	Total Theatres	Negro Theatres
Alabama	179	229	18
Arizona	64	99	—
Arkansas	192	299	6
California	413	1,179	8
Colorado	134	254	—
Connecticut	89	213	—
Delaware	20	36	1
Dist. of Columbia	1	65	13
Florida	142	335	40
Georgia	186	353	20
Idaho	138	200	—
Illinois	474	1,123	21
Indiana	235	537	6
Iowa	512	703	—
Kansas	309	461	4
Kentucky	204	348	4
Louisiana	181	383	22
Maine	133	206	—
Maryland	94	245	17
Massachusetts	185	454	—
Michigan	297	728	7
Minnesota	349	446	—

*This is the figure given by the " Film Daily Yearbook," but the " Motion Picture Herald," August 2nd, 1947, gives the number as 684, and points out that the number has increased by 287 Negro theatres since 1940.

State			Towns	Total Theatres	Negro Theatres
Mississippi	..	..	131	242	18
Missouri	..	..	387	701	14
Montana	..	..	141	198	—
Nebraska	..	..	267	384	1
Nevada	..	..	31	47	—
New Hampshire	..		70	111	—
New Jersey ..	..		194	542	9
New Mexico	..		65	113	—
New York ..	..		464	1,433	39
North Carolina	..		232	452	20
North Dakota	..		171	200	—
Ohio ..	..	..	360	1,015	17
Oklahoma	..	..	229	492	6
Oregon	..	..	138	253	—
Pennsylvania	..		561	1,313	19
Rhode Island	..		29	65	—
South Carolina	..		120	200	9
South Dakota	..		162	205	—
Tennessee	..	..	138	292	17
Texas ..	..	..	564	1,322	30
Utah ..	..	..	127	200	—
Vermont	..	..	45	68	—
Virginia	..	..	183	246	20
Washington ..	..		173	333	—
West Virginia	..		219	345	4
Wisconsin	..	..	259	474	—
Wyoming	..	..	49	65	—

Among the early Negro companies were Oscar Micheaux Pictures, of New York, who made such films as " The Wages Of Sin " and " The Broken Violin," featuring famous coloured actors ; and the Coloured Players Film Corporation, which had its headquarters in Philadelphia and made such melodramas as " Ten Nights In A Bar-room," starring Charles Gilpin. Most of the pictures made by these early Negro concerns in the first years of the talking film were inferior even to the usual type of Hollywood second features. They were shown largely in Negro cinemas and their only usefulness was in putting before the public some indications of the possibilities of the Negro in films.

Octavius Roy Cohen was concerned with the production of a series of shorts, known as the " Florian Slappey " comedies, full of repugnant " black-face " humour of the lowest type. In 1929 Cohen himself wrote and directed " Melancholy Dame," with Evelyn Preer, Eddie Thompson, Spencer Williams and other Negro actors, but soon afterwards he retired from film production. However, the tradition of Octavius Roy Cohen has, unfortunately, continued both in Hollywood films and, perversely enough, in most independent Negro films.

Negro producers work with a very small capital and are consequently unable to produce films of wide entertainment or social value (not that the latter is often attempted—on the contrary). Some ten years ago Joe Louis, the world heavyweight boxing champion, co-starred with Clarence Muse in a film called " Spirit of Youth," a typical success story of the poor coloured boy who becomes a boxer and fights his way to the top of the commercial tree. Henry Armstrong also starred in a similar production, " Keep Punching." These, like such other Negro films as " Dark Manhattan," " Bargain With Bullets," " Life Goes On " and others, demonstrated that even Negro producers themselves did not seem able to break the Hollywood stereotype. Admittedly, in these films Negroes played leading rôles, but most of the films were so bad, so inexpertly acted, so shoddily produced that it is likely that they did more harm than good.

Mamie Smith, the well-known Harlem blues singer, starred in a number of these " quickies," most of which were directed by white directors. Typical of this kind of movie was " Sunday Sinners " which, to quote from its publicity sheet, " is the story of a courageous minister who rallies his flock to fight the riff-raff of a great city. Racketeers prey upon him from all sides and in the darkest hour of gloom his followers, aided and abetted by the taunts of enemies, enrol in the army of righteousness and drive to the wall those who flaunt his greatest wish of Sunday observance." (In this, as in most cases, the blurb was distinctly better than the film.) Similar productions were " Murder On Lenox Avenue," described as " the story of a man who summons all his courage in the face of gravest danger to fight in the glory of his race," and " Mystery In Swing," concerned with the murder of a famous jazz band-leader. Arthur Dreifuss, now working in Hollywood for Columbia, directed several of these films, and other white directors served their " apprenticeship " in the Negro independent field. Some white directors specialise in the production of all-coloured movies. One such is Bud Pollard, whose first Negro film was " The Black King," made in 1932, and whose more recent efforts include a series of Louis Jordan comedies made in New York.

Clarence Muse often played leading rôles in Negro films made in New York, Hollywood, Chicago and elsewhere. One of the best of these was " Broken Strings," directed by Bernard Ray, with a screenplay by Muse himself, which told the story of a celebrated Negro violinist who through an accident is never able to play again, but who finds his outlet in teaching his son to play. " Broken Strings " was a modest little film which may, however, be counted as one of the best of a mediocre batch, certainly one of the least " sensational " of these cheaply produced movies. More recently independent Negro producers have made considerably fewer films but certainly better films, of which an example is " Double Deal," directed by Arthur Dreifuss, with a cast including Monte Hawley, Jeni Le Gon, Florence O'Brien and a popular Harlem actor, Maceo B. Sheffield. But the majority of these contain the same faults, and veer only very occasionally from the usual stereotyped groove. It would appear that even Negroes themselves are unable to break new ground in the majority of their " independent " productions, although it must be agreed that the reasons for this are mainly economical.

Jed Buell, who claims to have made the first all-Negro Western film, " Harlem On The Prairie," in 1939, produced a comedy a few years ago called, " Mr. Washington Goes To Town," finished in six days for less than £3,000. This effort, a typical Negro comedy, which had a wide showing in the Negro cinemas, contained all the familiar stock situations of a typical Hollywood " quickie." Indicative of the general level of this production was an example of the dialogue given to the leading character, rolling-eyed Mantan Moreland, " Pork chops is the fondest thing I is of ! " This film, and its successor, " Lucky Ghost " also starring Mantan Moreland, like the majority of these all-coloured movies, was fairly well received in the Negro cinemas, but obtained little showing elsewhere. Apparently most of the small companies engaged in producing these kinds of comedies anticipate a very limited exhibition and budget their films accordingly. The actors and actresses are, without exception, coloured, but most of the producers and directors are white. For example, Jack and Dave Goldberg, the founders of a company called " Negro Marches On," are white producers who have been successfully making short all-Negro films for more than ten years. Their most recent features include " Harlem On Parade," a revue starring Lena Horne, and " We've Come A Long, Long Way," a more serious effort, described as " an amazing human document—a cavalcade of a race."

Jack Goldberg, one of the pioneers in the field of Negro entertainment, began producing all-coloured stage shows in New York in 1925. His many theatrical productions include " Put And Take," " Deep Harlem," " Rosanne" (which featured Charles Gilpin, and afterwards Paul Robeson), and "The Emperor Jones," with Jules Bledsoe. In 1937 he produced the first all-Negro newsreel ; this is still functioning today. (There are other newsreels of this kind. For two years or more there has existed a popular Negro newsreel, produced in Chicago by the All-American Newsreel Company, which deals with Negro celebrities of the sport and entertainment world and also with social events in Chicago's coloured quarter. The newsreel is shown not only in Chicago's Negro theatres but is exhibited also in other big cities like New York, Baltimore and Los Angeles.)

In 1938 the Goldbergs featured Josephine Baker in their film " Siren Of The Tropics " and followed this by starring Bill Robinson in a short film, " Harlem In Heaven," after which they went to Hollywood, opening their own studios for the exclusive production of Negro motion pictures. Recently they have made such movies as " Mystery In Swing," " Double Deal," " Paradise In Harlem," and at their new studios in Florida they have produced some better-class feature-length films, such as " Sunday Sinners " and " Murder On Lenox Avenue."

In 1945 Jack Goldberg produced " We've Come A Long, Long Way," the story of the American Negro, and the film was subsequently shown not only in cinemas but in schools, colleges, churches and educational establishments all over the U.S.A. In an interview on the radio with film actress Adrienne Ames in 1946, Goldberg stated that in his Florida studios he intended to make a minimum of eight all-Negro films every year. The first of these features, he said, would be " Negro Boys' Town," described as a dramatic story of a municipality entirely governed by boys (based on an actual institution of this kind just outside Pittsburgh.)

The producer further declared that in his Florida studios every employee would be a member of the Negro race, including authors, directors, actors and technicians. His revolutionary plan sounds exciting, and it remains to be seen whether the films made as a result of Goldberg's policy will be any better than those independent Negro productions already seen. Certainly coloured workers have not been generally employed in Hollywood studios. As Phil Carter pointed out in an article in *The Crisis*, February, 1946 : " There are very few Negroes working on the technical and production sides of film-making. There have been one or two Negro writers, a few musicians and a handful of dance directors, but that is about the sum total of Negro effort behind the Hollywood scenes. It seems that on the whole Negroes have not concerned themselves largely with the less glamorous phases of movie-making and have concentrated specifically on acting." In the same article, Mr. Carter drew attention tó the fact that Negroes have not fully realised that they represent a considerable percentage of audience attendance. As he says : " During the war, film attendance in the United States realised the astonishing figure of one hundred million per week. Assuming that about ten million of these patrons were Negroes, it is safe to say that they were spending on an average as much as three million dollars each week at the box office. This is surely a rebuttal to some who have claimed that Negroes have no right to question what goes into their screen entertainment."

As Carter remarked, very few Negroes are employed as technicians by the film studios ; one of these, however, is a noted composer and band-leader, Phil Moore, who works in the music department of a Hollywood studio, and has written a considerable amount of film music. He is a noted leader of those Hollywood Negroes who are daily demanding more recognition for their talents, but was recently quoted, in the magazine *Ebony*, as saying : " I think it is a foolish thing to demand something just because we are one tenth of the nation. We need to get our feet on solid economic ground. A solution towards the race problem for Negroes is— individual efficiency. If a white man goes to get a job he does it because he can do a job, not because his skin is brown or otherwise.

The longer they are able to patronise us, the longer they'll look down on us."

Moore continues : " Hollywood's handling of the Negro is grossly unfair. Admittedly when film producers show Negroes as maids and servants it is a true picture, but it is also true that there are Negro doctors and lawyers and soldiers, and I would like to see them on the screen once in a while too. Many better film parts have been written for Negroes but have subsequently been struck out because the producers do not think it is a commercial proposition to give Negroes good rôles."

He also points out that Southern States censors have intimidated film directors into submission. He instances the action of screenwriter Bradbury Foote who submitted a film script on the Negro composer James Bland to the Memphis Censor in advance of production because he was told by the studio that they would only buy his script subject to Dixie approval !

Is the solution then to be independent efforts made by Negroes themselves ? Often they are criticised. Goldberg's film " We've Come A Long, Long Way," purported to be an account of the progress of the Negro race in the past seventy-five years. It is described as " radiating a sense of gratitude for opportunities for advancement, in the greatest strides made by the Negro race since its emancipation. The film's most outstanding quality is its emphasis on continued progress."

That may have been so, but nevertheless the film earned many bitter comments from the Negro Press, who claimed that it concentrated on showing that in the United States of America the Negro is getting a fair deal (which could not be farther from the truth). Goldberg describes the film as " one which demonstrates the achievements of the Negro under a democratic government which continues to open doors to further opportunities and achievements." Most Negroes would, however, contest this statement, and it is unlikely that a producer with such a belief, however sincerely held, will ever succeed in producing films which, in the long run, are beneficial to the Negro's *continued* struggle. This, as many affirm, is now only just commencing, with the return of thousands of Negro soldiers from Europe to their former ghettoes in the Southern States and elsewhere. Goldberg's plans are interesting but his avowed production policy will possibly clash even further with enlightened Negro opinion.

Scheduled to go into production in 1948 at Fox Movietone Studios in New York was " Boy ! What A Girl," the first of twelve Negro features to be produced by Herald Pictures, the president of which is Goldberg. Another independent company, the Toddy Picture Company of New York, have announced their programme for 1948. They intend to make eight full-length Negro features, including Lena Horne in " Bronze Venus," Pigmeat Markham in " House Rent Party," Eddie Greene in " Eddie's Laugh Jamboree," Louise Beavers in " Prison Paid," Nina Mae McKinney in " Gun Moll," Mantan Moreland in " Mantan Messes Up," Ralph Cooper in " Gangsters On The Loose " and Jeni Le Gon in " Murder Rap."

To quote Ted Toddy, president of Toddy Pictures, reported in *Motion Picture Herald*, April 12th, 1947 : " Negro audiences do not care for the heavy emotional dramas. Their choice in film enter- tainment is the picture which features light comedy, outdoor adventures, musical comedies with an abundance of singing and dancing, and comedy-romances."

Considering the above, one feels inclined to agree with William Harrison, who wrote in *Sight and Sound*, Spring, 1939 : " The conclusion is inescapable that independent Negro producers have lacked the social vision needed if the Negro is to be represented fully and truly in the cinema today, and if the stereotypes in which he is cast are to be discarded. The dramatic possibilities of Negro life, which is so rich and varied, and the potentialities of the Negro actor, already demonstrated in even the poor media accessible to him now, will reveal themselves fully when this social vision arrives."

Government and Documentary Productions

In 1942 the American Department of Agriculture made a short film called " Henry Browne, Farmer," which depicts a small American farmer, a Negro, at work in the fields and at home, emphasising his contribution to the war effort. It shows the farmer's family working in the fields with him, and finally we see them all going into the nearest town to visit the eldest son, a soldier-mechanic in the American Air Force. As Iris Barry notes in a letter to the author, " This film is effective because these people ' simply happen ' to be Negroes, and no particular point is made of this." Other interesting films on similar themes made during the war include one called " Negro Colleges In Wartime," produced by the Office of War Information, and one entitled " Jazz," which was beautifully photographed and contained many authentic shots of Negro jazz performers. In addition the American Film Centre, a progressive organisation of documentary groups, corresponding to our own Film Centre in London, produced a film in 1940 called " One Tenth Of Our Nation," which dealt with the miserable living conditions of the majority of the United States' fourteen million coloured citizens.

This excellent documentary, directed by Henwar Rodakiewicz, set out to show the inadequate conditions of education among the Southern Negroes. Poor schooling facilities were illustrated and the shortage of school buildings was also made clear. In contrast to this condition several examples were presented of experimentation along the lines of better education of rural Negroes. Scenes from the Campas Tuskegee Institute were shown, along with a variety of vocational courses which had been made available at a limited number of schools. Finally it was made clear, however, that these examples were rare and that a great job had still to be done in the field of educating rural Negroes. It indicated some bright spots such as the opportunities, few though they might be, of obtaining professional and technical training. The treatment of the subject was downright, progressive and sympathetic. A film on a similar theme was " As Our Boyhood Is," which interested itself mainly with the problems of rural education among the Southern Negroes. Another worthy documentary production was " A Place To Live," directed by Irving Lerner for the Philadelphia Housing Association, which told more in two reels about the lives of urban Negroes than dozens of Hollywood films.

Among recent and worth-while semi-documentary productions was a short film " Dr. George Washington Carver," produced by Metro-Goldwyn-Mayer, and written around the life and work of the famous scientist. This was a first-rate piece of cinema, and propaganda of the most valuable nature in the fight to present a tolerant viewpoint to the cinema-going masses. (It is likely that a Hollywood studio may soon produce a full-length feature on Carver's highly interesting life.)

The United States Government, like the British Government, entered the motion picture field extensively during the Second World War and sponsored, and itself produced, some scores of films. One of its features was "The Negro Soldier," produced, written and narrated by Carleton Moss, and directed by Frank Capra under the auspices of the U.S. War Department, which told the story of the Negro's part in the wars of the United States. However, it apparently minimised the rôle played by nearly a quarter of a million coloured soldiers who fought on the side of the Union during the Civil War and for this it was severely criticised. Nevertheless, the film must be considered an important step forward, for it did attempt to point out the dignity and courage of the many thousands of Negro soldiers who have fought in recent years for the United States, and more especially during the Second World War.

Some interesting facts reveal themselves about "The Negro Soldier." More than three hundred cinemas in New York alone showed the film, and two hundred and fifty cinemas in Detroit. Thousands of requests came from the South to show the film in white cinemas. Of it Leon Hardwick wrote, "This film is one of the greatest ever made from a Negro standpoint, telling the story of the Negro Serviceman's contribution to American defence brilliantly and interestingly." Henry Lieven directed another in the series, "The Negro Sailor," with Joel Fluellyn and Leigh Whipper in the leading rôles, though this did not have the same wide success as "The Negro Soldier."

The Negro Serviceman's part in the war received prominence in three short film subjects, made by the War Department. These were "Teamwork," produced by the United States Signal Corps, "Call To Duty" and "The Highest Tradition." It is to be hoped that many more documentaries will be made by the War Department and by other government production units. There is much ignorance and prejudice in the world concerning the Negro race and it is certainly the duty of the U.S. Government to dispel this lack of knowledge and thus help to fight the continued existence of that organised hatred and prejudice which is a blot upon the U.S.A. and its way of life.

CHAPTER SEVEN

THE NEGRO IN EUROPEAN FILMS

The British Film : 1930-1940

The history of the Negro in British films is largely the story of two actors : an American, Paul Robeson, who has been a great favourite with British film audiences during the past dozen years, and Robert Adams, of British Guiana, who recently scored a success in " Men Of Two Worlds." Between them they have appeared in about a dozen interesting films, though, unfortunately, opportunities for Negro screen acting occur all too rarely in British studios. There is, in fact, very little comparison between the social scene in Britain and the United States in so far as the Negro problem is concerned, since there are many millions of coloured citizens in the United States, while the number of Negroes living in Great Britain amounts only to a few thousands. However, the effect of Hollywood's anti-Negro bias may be felt on this side of the Atlantic also, though the results are perhaps not quite so important. Whereas continual prejudice on the screen can lead—as it has done in the United States—to race riots and heightened racial tension, the net result in Great Britain does not amount to anything so drastic. In this matter the ordinary British cinemagoer approximates in his reactions to the average American living in a Northern town where contact with Negroes is slight, an attitude which may be summed up as one of good-natured contempt for those " unfortunates " who possess a skin darker than their own, an attitude which only becomes even slightly vehement on, for instance, the question of inter- marriage. It is more than likely that the average Englishman, while holding no particular prejudice against the Negro as an individual, might have certain qualms about allowing a coloured man to marry into his family, and this attitude has been engendered to a great extent by the films he goes to see. And because more than eighty per cent. of these films are of Hollywood origin, it may be generally agreed that his prejudices are a result of the anti-Negro bias reflected in American movies.

In Britain there are perhaps some twenty thousand coloured people, who came originally from such places as Sierra Leone, Nigeria, the West Indies, Aden, Malaya and the United States of America (though many are born in England). A large number of these " immigrants," mainly African seamen, have settled permanently over here, and with their English, Welsh and Scottish wives and families they live in Liverpool, Cardiff, London and other sea-ports of Great Britain. As the leader of an Empire consisting mostly of coloured people, Britain " officially " adopts a policy of complete racial equality but even well-informed English people are sometimes unaware of the wide gap which exists between politics and reality. Economic and social discrimination against the coloured man does indeed exist in Great Britain, though obviously to a far less degree than in the United States. Among Negroes themselves there is a saying " In the States the Negro is the last to be hired and the first to be fired ; in Britain he is not even hired," and to some extent this is harsh but nevertheless true.

I quote from the report of a committee set up in Cardiff in 1929 to examine the racial problem here : " Little difficulty in their school-days is experienced as the coloured children mix quite freely with the white children. It is when they leave school and desire to enter industry that the difficulties arise. The industrial problem is much more acute in relation to girls, for though the boys are not so easily placed as white boys, there is not the same prejudice shown to the coloured by male workers as by female workers. It is a very sad commentary on the Christian spirit shown, and indicates that the colour bar is in existence in this country."

That was nearly twenty years ago, and happily the situation has greatly improved since then, considerably during the past ten years and more especially during the wartime period. In this respect Great Britain is similar to the U.S.A. As K. L. Little writes in his pamphlet on *The Relations Of White People And Coloured People In Great Britain* (Le Play House Press, 1946) : " Despite all the difficulties of the present situation there is also another side of this picture. Close friendship based on mutual confidence and respect exists in a number of individual instances between white and coloured people in this country. In some educational circles in particular, as well as among other sections of society, there is considerable and practical interest shown in present problems. Some of the staunchest allies of the coloured folk of

Cardiff and other cities are the white people who live alongside them. In the universities, too, although there are exceptions to the rule, English students mix quite well with Indian, African and other non-European undergraduates, and relationships there labour as much, possibly, under mutual shyness as any other factor. A West Indian was recently President of the Oxford Union, and that position in Cambridge as well as Oxford has been held by other non-Europeans."

Mr. Little hits the nail on the head with a bang, however, when he goes on to point out the following : " Colour prejudice in Britain must be put down to no small extent as an important social and educational lag. Relatively very few English people have ever met an educated coloured person and for the great majority secondhand representations as afforded by books, the cinema and so on, provide the nearest approach to reality. Many such representations, and the cinema in particular, are distinctly prejudicial in character. For example, in the stereotype of the American Negro—screened at a rough estimation in at least two out of every seven separate programmes—the audience is shown a person who is good-humoured, but whose status and occupation are *always* servile and menial. The audience sees, as the representative of a whole race, someone who has a peculiar and foolish fear of ghosts, and who possesses, in addition, an optical mannerism— a trick of bulging the eyeball—which is suggestive of hyperthyroidism."

But in spite of the fact that many British cinemagoers regard the Negro as a buffoon and clown, and think of coloured actors usually in terms of " Rochester," " Sleep 'n' Eat," " Rastus," Bill Robinson, Stepin Fetchit, " Sambo," and " Alexander and Mose," the general attitude in this country reflects a greater tolerance than exists in the U.S.A. Certain British movies have helped to spread this more enlightened attitude and one actor in particular, Paul Robeson, has made great contributions here to a new understanding of the life and problems of coloured people everywhere.

Robeson is held in such high esteem in this country that he made his second home in London for a number of years. He discovered, like many American Negroes, that the European way of life gave more opportunities to coloured artists, and indeed his career is a reflection of this fact. His greatest successes have been in British films, although during the war years he confined his appearances to the stage in New York and elsewhere. As a concert singer, Robeson achieved extraordinary popularity in Britain, and the same may be said of the films which he made here between 1935 and 1939. Each of these portrayed a Negro as the dignified, intelligent central character, and each showed Robeson against the background of normal British social life, as an accepted part of an English community, making a truly memorable series of British films.

Sanders Of The River

The main exception to the above was the Alexander Korda film made from Edgar Wallace's story " Sanders Of The River," in which Robeson played his most unfortunate part, that of Bosambo, a native tool employed by the white district commissioner to keep the African tribes under British dominance. " Sanders Of The River," directed by Zoltan Korda, in 1935, is a justification of colonial imperialism, and therefore follows a set pattern. Robeson was the star of the film, and since he saves the life of District Commissioner Sanders, he is shown in the final reel in an heroic light. But neither Robeson nor certain of the critics were happy about this film. As the American film critic Robert Stebbins remarks, in *New Theatre*, July, 1935 : " Here we have the pathetic spectacle of one of the most gifted and distinguished members of his race placed in a position where in actuality he is forced into caricatures of his people." And there could perhaps be no more fitting comment on the anti-Negro direction of " Sanders Of The River " than the enthusiastic remarks of the reviewer in the London *Times*, who stated, " This film if shown abroad will bring no discredit on Imperial authority." The London *Daily Herald* went to the extent of suggesting that if " we could only give every subject race a native king with Mr. Robeson's superb physique, dominant personality, infectious smile and noble voice, problems of native self-government might be largely solved." Was this intended irony ?

" Sanders Of The River " marked Robeson's début in British pictures (apart from the silent experimental film "Borderline," which he had made in 1930 and which was only seen by a handful of people) and Paul **Right : PAUL ROBESON and NINA MAE MCKINNEY in *Sanders Of The River*. Below : *Pillow To Post*, a typical U.S. musical film.**

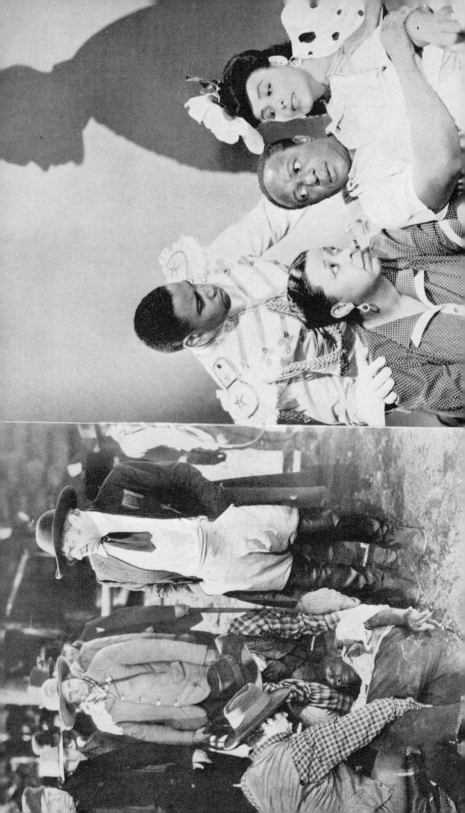

was not by any means satisfied. He expressed his disappointment with the final film and announced his intention not to make further movies of this kind. In 1936 he went back to the United States and, during this time, appeared as Jim in Universal's " Show Boat," made in Hollywood, but within a few months he once more returned to England, where he began a series of films destined to hold an important place in the history of Negroes on the screen. The first of these was " Song Of Freedom," produced in 1936.

Song Of Freedom

This film, directed by J. Elder Wills, tells the story of a young Negro stevedore whose wonderful bass voice is heard at an amateur concert in a public house by an impresario who signs him up and sends him on a successful concert tour. The Negro is a great success, but his happiness is marred when he learns by accident that he is the descendant of a famous line of African kings and that his tribe is in need of a leader. Torn between his natural desire for fame and success in England and the urge to return to his people in Africa, the singer becomes unhappy and finally he decides to return to his own people. This is the plot in bare outline.

In an article in *World Film News*, June, 1936, Harry Watt wrote : " Robeson, who is now working on his new film 'Song Of Freedom,' feels that in it he is representing the Negro race and overcoming colour prejudice. He feels this not because he is conceited, but because he realises that he is the most publicised Negro in the world. It was only because the film presents Negroes as ordinary human beings, and not the caricatures that are invariably shown in American films, that Robeson consented to make it. He has turned down many offers because he felt they did not show the Negro in a sympathetic light."

The story of "Song Of Freedom" is based on an African legend told to Robeson by Major Claude Wallace when they were working together on " Sanders Of The River." Major Wallace and Dorothy Holloway wrote the screenplay, which, in more detail, tells of an African queen who was in the pay of the Portuguese in the slaving days. Her tribe find out and kill her, but her son and his wife escape and fly

Right : *Cabin In The Sky* **directed by Vincente Minelli. Left :** *Stand Up And Fight* **directed by W. S. Van Dyke.**

up to the Portuguese, taking with them the carved disc worn only by the chief of the tribe or his descendants.   The traders callously sell them into slavery, but their descendants always hand down the disc, not, however, knowing its true signifi- cance.   Robeson is discovered as Zinga, the last descendant, a labourer in the London docks, still in possession of the royal disc and a snatch of song which has haunted him from birth ; both are legacies from Africa.   He is heard one day singing in a pub by an impresario and later becomes a famous singer, but he learns the story of the disc from an anthropologist when at the height of his success, and giving up everything goes to Africa to join his people.   Here, however, he experiences many difficulties since the Africans are loath to accept a stranger as their king, and the witch doctor incites the people against him.   Finally, when he and his wife are in danger of losing their lives, Zinga remembers the song.   It is revealed that this is the secret song of kingship, and when he sings this in his deep powerful voice the enraged tribe realise that he is indeed their rightful king.   The film ends with Zinga returning to Europe to undertake his concert commitments, the proceeds going towards the benefiting of his people with new social and educational amenities.   Each year he leaves his African island home to give a concert season, afterwards returning to his own people.

That is the story of a film which, though modestly made, was extremely popular in this country and had a wide showing.   It atoned, in some ways, for Robeson's first British film, " Sanders Of The River," for both the Negro singer and his wife (delightfully played by Elizabeth Welch) were beautifully drawn and sym- pathetic characters.   Robeson showed himself once more to be an actor possessed of many attributes : intelligence, a really splendid singing voice and a fine screen presence.   His best friend in the film, a fellow stevedore who shares his good fortune, was well played by Robert Adams, now a leading British film actor, while the other members of the cast included such well-known players as Esme Percy, Joan Fred-Emney, Ronald Simpson, George Mozart, Orlando Martins, Connie Smith and James Solomon.

The film dealt largely with an English dockland town which might have been Liverpool, Cardiff—or even London's East End—it was in fact London.   The Negro stevedore, his wife and coloured friends are seen drinking in the same bars, dining at the same tables and mingling freely with the white dock workers. There is no hint of discrimination, which in any case does not in fact exist in everyday life in Britain's docklands, and no trace of a suggestion is made throughout that the Negro characters are in any way inferior to the whites. On the contrary, Robeson is shown as a natural aristocrat, the king of an African tribe, a splendid figure of a man, while his wife is a soft-spoken, intelligent and utterly charming character. In all, " Song Of Freedom " provided an antidote to the mass of Hollywood poison being pumped out yearly at the time of its release. The film was not only a London success but was seen all over the British Isles and on the Continent (incidentally it was successfully re-issued in 1946). The name Robeson served to attract large audiences, who could not help but be affected by its tolerance and by the sympathetic treatment of the coloured people in the film.

Robeson, in *Film Weekly*, September 19th, 1936, was reported as declaring : " ' Song Of Freedom ' is a kind of test piece. It gives me a *real* part for the first time. I have always been up against two difficulties on the screen. The first, and less important, is that my reputation as a singer has misled producers into refusing to try me out as an actor. The second is the difficulty which confronts all coloured artists. Film producers take the attitude that a Negro must be a romanticised puppet (usually comic) or else be of no interest to filmgoers at all. You saw the result in ' Show Boat.' I was given a sentimental ' bit ' which did little more than feature me in a couple of songs. I feel that I can do much more on the screen than that. I made ' Song Of Freedom' to prove my point. In this film I play the part of a coloured stevedore who wins operatic fame and then returns to his own people in Africa. The story presents me as a real man— no more romanticised than a white man would be in a similar rôle. It is the first step in my effort to break down the prejudice that somehow Negroes must always be ' different ' on the screen."

Of it Graham Green, film critic of *The Spectator*, wrote : " The direction of ' Song Of Freedom ' is distinguished but not above reproach, the story is sentimental and absurd and yet a sense stays in the memory of an unsophisticated mind fumbling on the edge of simple and popular poetry. The best scenes are the dockland scenes, the men returning from work, black and white in easy companionship free from any colour bar, the public-house interiors, dark faces pausing at tenement windows to listen to Zinga's songs, a sense of nostalgia.   There are plenty of faults even here, sentiment too close to sentimentality, a touch of quaintness and patronage, but one is made aware all the time of what Thomas Mann calls ' that gnawing surreptitious hankering for the bliss of the common-place,' the general exile of our class as well as the particular exile of the African."   " Song Of Freedom " was the first important Negro film to be made in Britain, and it still remains as one of the best.

Robert Adams, who played the comedy rôle of Monty in J. Elder Wills' film, was also seen as the faithful friend of the boy Easy in Carol Reed's version of " Midshipman Easy," produced by British Lion in 1936.   It was an important featured rôle and the Negro was outstanding as the stout-hearted cook who would defend the white boy with his very life.   Later on, Adams was featured in a comedy, " Old Bones Of The River," in which he played a comic Bosambo to Will Hay's District Commissioner.   This film, made at Sound City, contained parts for a number of coloured actors, and Adams gave an excellent performance.   It was by no means a good movie, being a poor burlesque of the Korda film " Sanders Of The River," but Adams had a much better part in his next film, " Song Of Freedom," which re-united him with Paul Robeson.   And Robeson, who had had a comparative failure with " Sanders Of The River," but an unqualified success with " Song Of Freedom," made his third British talking film at Shepherd's Bush Studios in 1937.

King Solomon's Mines

He was starred with Sir Cedric Hardwicke, Roland Young, Anna Lee and John Loder in the Gaumont British production of " King Solomon's Mines," directed by Robert Stevenson.   This proved to be an uninspired film version of the famous Rider Haggard story which gave Robeson the part of the friendly African, Umbopa, who accompanies Alan Quartermaine and the others on their perilous journey to find the gold mines of King Solomon.   There was little opportunity for characterisation in the part of this strong, simple giant, but Robeson infused it with as much personality as he could possibly get into the rôle of a huge, almost-naked African.   A really fine touch of character was contributed by Robert Adams, as a villainous chieftain who seeks to guard the treasure from the white interlopers. With a hideous make-up, and with one eye partially closed by a kind of thick white glaze skilfully fixed over it by the make-up man, Adams presented a fearsome figure and with its many intriguing mannerisms his performance certainly captured interest, if not sympathy. " King Solomon's Mines " may be classed in the same category as " Sanders Of The River," and although Robeson's Umbopa was not the same servile creature as Edgar Wallace's Bosambo, this production was, to many filmgoers, frankly disappointing.

Jericho

Paul fared much happier, however, in his next film, " Jericho," produced by Walter Futter, in North Africa, in 1938, and directed by American Thornton Freeland. Here Robeson was co-starred with Hollywood actors Henry Wilcoxon and Wallace Ford, and given a rôle of heroic proportions as the soldier under sentence of death who escapes from war-time France to Africa, there to live as a desert sheikh. He carried the whole film on his broad shoulders, saved his white comrades from disaster and generally behaved in an almost " Superman " fashion. Paul was partnered by a beautiful African girl, Princess Kouka, whose first English-speaking film this was (and, incidentally, her last). " Jericho " was shown in America under the title " Dark Sands," and due to Robeson's international reputation it had a fair success. How American audiences in the South must have reacted to a Negro hero, who was twice as intelligent, attractive and heroic as the white characters in the film, one can only hazard a guess (if the film was ever released in the Southern States, which is doubtful). It must, at any rate, have been something of a surprise to all filmgoers for years fed on the conventional stereotypes.

Big Fella

Hammer-British Lion Productions, who had previously made " The Song Of Freedom " at Beaconsfield Studios, made another film starring Paul Robeson, in 1938. This was called " Big Fella," and differed from the previous film in that the central Negro character was not, at first, shown in an altogether sympathetic light. This was not a bad thing, since I feel that the continual depiction of a Negro as a kind of " Superman " (e.g., " Jericho ") might lead to incredulity, disbelief and finally antagonism on the part of white audiences, even in Great Britain and Europe. They would not be too happy in any case, to stomach too often the screened exploits of heroic Negro giants, and their attitude, in such instances, might be envy probably followed by antipathy. Rather should the Negro character be indistinguishable from the whites, excepting of course by his natural colour and personality. In other words, the really ideal film would be one in which Negroes and whites are shown working together and living together in complete harmony, as neighbours, with only the occasional discords arising from any normal human relationships. Thus any films which show the Negro continually as an inferior, or alternatively always as a superior being, must inevitably be considered unrealistic. That was why—to return to " Big Fella "—it was a pleasurable surprise to find Paul Robeson playing in a film as a character who at first seems not altogether pleasant. He is shown in the beginning of the film as a shiftless dock-side worker, unable to keep a job for any length of time, always moving on to the next town. One day, however, he meets an orphan, a little white boy who at once takes a liking to the tall, good-humoured, lazy Negro, and persists in following him around from saloon to saloon. Finally the man is intimidated by the child's persistence, and at length decides to take charge of the orphan. Later he grows very fond of the little boy and obtains a steady job in order to look after him properly. A real affection develops between the child and the Negro, an affection which is dealt with sympathetically and intelligently by the director, J. Elder Wills. " Big Fella " was a charming film and a step forward in Paul's film progress.

Robeson's friend, his chum throughout the film's length, is a fellow dock-worker, a white man. The two men and the boy are inseparable, and nowhere in the film does the Negro appear to suffer because of his colour. On the contrary, due to his immense strength he is, if anything, admired and respected by the other stevedores. There are many scenes of conviviality in which the coloured workers share the same pleasures as the white workers and, throughout, not the smallest sign of discrimination. Yet " Big Fella " suffered certain attacks by Negro papers, especially in Africa, where some film critics of the African Press asserted that Robeson should have refused to appear, as he did in the first part of the film, in the inevitable coloured rôle of a lazy good-for-nothing. Robeson answered his critics by pointing out that the film was the story of a Negro's regeneration, and that he subsequently became a sympathetic character in the final reels of the movie. Certainly, " Big Fella " was well received by audiences everywhere, and was generally considered to be an excellent follow-up to " Song Of Freedom." And just as one can never assess the harm done by an " Imitation Of Life," a " So Red The Rose " or a " Gone With The Wind," so it is difficult to assess the immense amount of goodwill and international understanding engendered by films like " Song Of Freedom " and " Big Fella," both of which are landmarks in Robeson's progress.

The Proud Valley

In 1939 Paul appeared in the most important film he has ever made, either in Britain or Hollywood. This was Ealing's " The Proud Valley," produced by Michael Balcon and directed by Pen Tennyson (a brilliant young British director who was unfortunately killed in a flying accident while serving with the Royal Navy in 1940). The story, written by Herbert Marshall and Fredda Brilliant, was originally entitled *David Goliath*. Marshall, a well-known London theatrical producer, had produced Paul Robeson in the play " Plant In The Sun " by Ben Bengal at Unity Theatre in 1938. (As I have noted elsewhere, Robeson gave up the chance of West End stardom to appear with this progressive theatre group in a small theatre in King's Cross.) Marshall and Robeson had worked so well together that the former had written his story (in collaboration with his wife) with Paul in view as the character David. Novelist Louis Golding worked on the final screenplay, and the film went into production at Ealing in the summer of 1939, with Herbert Marshall as associate producer.

The story, which I shall deal with in some detail, is of David Goliath, a young Negro dock-worker from Cardiff, who travels to a Welsh valley in search of a job. During his wanderings he joins up with an old street busker and the two sing at street corners and outside the public house in Blaendy, a small Welsh mining town. David's resonant voice is heard by Dick Parry, the choirmaster of the local chapel, who is so keen to get the young Negro into his miners' choir that he persuades the manager of the mine to give David a job as a miner. Soon after this David goes to live in the house of Dick and his wife, a pleasant Welsh woman affectionately known as Mam, and quickly becomes one of the family. The two children of the house take to him almost immediately, although at first they are a little intimidated by his colour, until their mother explains, " Aren't Dad and brother Emlyn black too when they come up from the pit ? " David learns his job as a miner, becomes an accepted part of the village life, and sings regularly in the choir, though not without some opposition. Tremolo, an old miner, complains that it's a shame that this big black stranger should get a job in the pits just because he happens to have a good voice. But Dick, who has supported David from the beginning and given him a place in his own home, argues that to win at the coming Festival they need a voice like David's. His argument succeeds when he adds that Blaendy had lost at the Festival a year or two before because of a certain Irish tenor who had mysteriously appeared in one of the rival choirs ! Finally he convinces Tremolo and the minority opposition, and at length David is accepted by all his fellow-workers as a much-needed singer, a fine worker and a good comrade.

After the Negro has been in the village for a few months there occurs a disaster of the kind which is experienced in mining communities only too often. A fall of rock in one of the workings kills three men and imprisons half a dozen other miners, including Dick and David. When a rescue team is sent down to dig out the imprisoned men they find David supporting a mass of rock on his back, in an attempt to save Dick, lying underneath him, and badly injured. The Negro picks up his wounded friend and staggers out through the flame and smoke, past the burning gallery and up to the pit-head. But it is too late, for the choirmaster dies in his arms. Dick's son Emlyn is stunned by his father's sudden death, and with a helpless look on his face he asks David to break the news to Mam. The Negro presses the boy's shoulder sympathetically and promises to do it.

It was Dick's last wish that his choir should still enter for the Eisteddfod, and David carries on in his place, but bad times have come to the valley and after the disaster the coal owners close the Blaendy mine. The men find some solace in singing, but each day the situation worsens. David is a tower of strength at the Parry house but Emlyn is worried, and tells his friends that the village of Blaendy is doomed, and that David should go back to Cardiff and find another ship. " The whole world is open to you David," the boy says. But the Negro remonstrates with him. " You welcomed me here in good times," he says, " and I'm going to stay with you through the bad times."

The men finally decide on action, and the next sequence of the film shows a group of Blaendy miners setting out on a hunger march to London, there to demand from the coal owners that their mine be re-opened. The marchers, a long, weary, straggling group of men, with banners bravely flying, begin the long and difficult journey from Wales through England to the capital ; but the going is difficult, and the small stock of food soon runs out. Then David, who has accompanied his Welsh comrades on the march, has an idea. " Why can't we *sing* our way to London ? " he cries. And, with this, the whole body of miners begin singing, their voices bursting out in glorious unison as they sing the well-known melodies which have made Wales famous for a hundred years. As they pass through towns and villages, nearing London with each step, their singing brings them coins and food from the people and householders on the way who sympathise with the hunger march and the men's right to work for their families.

At length the miners reach London, and a deputation goes to see the coal owners. After a long and heated discussion, the owners agree to let the miners attempt to work the pit which had been closed since the disaster ; insisting, however, that this is a dangerous procedure and that the men can do it only at their own risk. The men are willing to try anything, believing that no risk could possibly be worse than years of enforced idleness and hunger. Triumphantly they return to Blaendy, and a dozen of the strongest and most experienced of them, including David and Emlyn, make a desperate attempt to hack their way through the damage left by the previous explosion in the pit workings. The rest of the village waits anxiously at the pit-head.

Eventually the men succeed in forcing their way through a wall of tumbled rock, when suddenly some loaded coal trams begin to move, gathering momentum in a few seconds. Smashing into a pile of rock they cause an enormous fall which corners the men in a small section of the pit. Like rats in a trap the seven survivors carefully examine the section of the gallery in which they are confined. There is very little air, and as it becomes fouler every minute the older men begin to gasp and fall to the ground. Finally the only one left standing upright is the giant Negro, David, frantically trying to use a mandrel on the rock-face. But at last the boy Emlyn has an idea, and suggests that the only possible way to get out is to blast a way through the solid rock, a dangerous procedure, since the blast might conceivably kill all the imprisoned men.

The miners decide, however, that as it is their only chance they must take it. They find a small piece of cable, but it is only four feet long, meaning that whoever fires the fuse to cause the explosion will probably be killed immediately, since the cable is not long enough for him to protect himself behind a wall or a pile of rock while plunging the fuse. Realising the implication of this, the men draw lots, and it falls to Emlyn to set off the fuse. David and Emlyn go forward and prepare the powder and cable. As they stand at the rock-face the Negro looks into the boy's eyes. " Let me do this son," he says. " This doesn't mean only your life. It means the life of your young wife, your mother and the kids. They've got nobody but you." Emlyn protests but David goes on : " Don't you see ? I'm alone. If you go it means so many. But if I go there's only me to consider."

Nevertheless Emlyn is adamant, but while his back is turned, David quickly smashes the lamp. And, as the boy goes far back into the gallery to get another lamp, David, with a last glance in Emlyn's direction, creeps forward, hesitates for a second, then drives down the plunger of the battery. There is a blinding flash, followed by a terrible roar. The mass of fallen rock is shattered and a current of fresh air disperses the smoke, revealing a clear way back to the coal-face. Emlyn is lying unconscious, but David has been killed by the blast. The men take off their caps ; they realise that David has sacrificed himself for them. And as they find their way back to the pit-head they softly sing the Welsh national anthem " Land of My Fathers." The film fades out on their coal-smeared faces as they clamber into the lift and rise up to the pit-head ; David's sacrifice has not only saved their lives, but their expedition has been successful. The workings are now re-opened, Blaendy once more will have life, and the name of David Goliath, the Negro stevedore from Cardiff, will live long in the memories of the Welsh people whom he loved and who loved him.

"The Proud Valley" is a film which cannot be too highly praised. It is a first-rate social document, an account of life in a mining village told realistically and imaginatively. The coming of the Negro from Cardiff's dockland to the mining town, his eventual acceptance by the miners and their families, the exciting mining sequences—all the incidents in the film are brought vividly to life. The character drawing was superb throughout. Edward Chapman gave a performance as Dick which ranks among the best acting seen in British films, while Clifford Evans, Simon Lack, Jack Jones and the others were all authentic Welsh types, each character being given life and realism. Paul Robeson was a magnificent David, but although he was the central character, he was nowhere allowed to obtrude to the detriment of the other figures in this day-by-day drama of a mine and those who work in it. Director Pen Tennyson did not concentrate all the subtleties into the character of David, and allowed the film to follow its own shape and form, becoming the story of a town and its people rather than the story of a Negro. In the choir sequences Robeson's splendid voice was heard as the soloist of the group, while as a miner, Paul certainly looked and acted the part. With his impressive body, stripped to the waist, he was a tower of strength in the mine, while around him stood his comrades at the coal-face, begrimed with black dust. And, as one of the miners remarks : "Down here in the mine we all look as black as one another. Down here race or colour does not matter ; we are all the same, all workers and friends together."

And that sums up the message of the film. David's heroism is made no more apparent than that of the dozens of other Welshmen who sacrifice themselves in the mines, and whose bravery is a constant lesson to those mine-owners who allow dangerous workings to be exploited for their shareholders. "The Proud Valley" is the finest British film dealing with a Negro theme, and marked the highest peak in Robeson's cinema progress. It was also to be his last British film, for shortly after it was completed he returned to the United States. It is obvious that English producers have shown more justice in their dealings with coloured actors, and as Robeson has declared that Hollywood no longer interests him, it is to be hoped that he will be able to make further British films in the post-war years.

The Negro in Films

The Wartime Period: 1940-1947

" The Proud Valley " was still on the studio floor at the outbreak of war, and was released early in 1940 ; it therefore enters the list of improved wartime productions from British studios.   During the war our films increased in quality, and our industry secured a firm footing in the affection of British audiences.   Indeed, we have made some of the finest films in the world during the past few years, and although Robeson is no longer with us, we still have coloured players of the calibre of Robert Adams, Orlando Martins and Elizabeth Welch, each of whom has made a number of successful film appearances.   Robert Adams, who was so good in earlier productions like " Midshipman Easy " and " King Solomon's Mines," concentrated during the war on stage appearances, but he also appeared in such films as " Dreaming " and " It Happened One Sunday," while he received featured billing in both " Caesar And Cleopatra " and " Men Of Two Worlds." In " It Happened One Sunday," directed by Karel Lamac for Associated British, Adams played the part of a wrestler who is injured in the ring and finishes up in a hospital bed alongside the hero of the film, played by Robert Beatty.   Adams and Beatty become good friends, and there are one or two amusing sequences in the hospital, in which the Negro actor is allowed to demonstrate a nice sense of comedy.   In Gabriel Pascal's " Caesar And Cleopatra " Adams played a featured rôle as the Nubian Slave, and his performance and physique so impressed Thorold Dickinson who was then preparing to direct a semi-documentary, " Men Of Two Worlds," that he cast the Negro actor as Kisenga, one of the principal characters in a film which proved to be a major British production of 1946.

I have described Thorold Dickinson's film as a *semi*-documentary ; there have been a number of " pure " documentary films made by British producers on various aspects of the Empire, both before and during the war.   In the middle 1930's, Publicity Films produced half a dozen short films for Cadbury's dealing with Africa and the West Indies.   One of these, " Trinidad," photographed in Technicolor, was of particular interest, giving fascinating glimpses of the Trinidadians, who vary in colour from ebony to the lightest of light brown.   Some of these productions were widely shown in British schools.

126

Irene Nicholson and Brian Montagu made a film in 1937 for the *Trinidad Guardian* called " Callaloo," a documentary of the island, with a thin story acted by Trinidadians of whom one, Ursula Johnson, a worker in Port of Spain, proved to be quite outstanding. Some of the music for the film was written by Edric Connor, the well-known Negro baritone, now living and working in England, who also sang several songs on the film's sound track. During the war the Ministry of Information sponsored some films about the Empire, including " An African In London," directed by George Pearson, for the Colonial Film Unit, in which Robert Adams played the central character, a cultured African. (But generally it is the documentary producers of the United States who have been responsible for the most interesting factual films dealing with Negroes, especially in the war period.)

A fine Negro actor who has been appearing in British films for nearly twenty years is Orlando Martins, so magnificent as Magole in " Men Of Two Worlds," and who also scored a personal success previously in " The Man From Morocco," directed by Max Greene for Associated British. The latter was a story of the men of all nationalities in the International Brigade, and Martins, as Jeremiah, represented an African fighter for freedom, who joined the Brigade in 1937 and fought against Franco and Fascism in Spain. The Negro was shown to be a courageous fighter, an intelligent speaker and a good friend ; he has a number of important scenes with the Czech captain, played by Anton Walbrook, and in every way is treated as an honoured member of a gallant body. Nowhere is there any reference to his colour, or any sort of discrimination indicated. The film itself was inclined to be romantic and novelettish, and obviously the subject of the International Brigade has still to be treated with the seriousness it deserves, but for its delineation of the Negro soldier, Greene's " The Man From Morocco " deserves recognition.

Elizabeth Welch, an American, has been acting in London for many years in cabaret, revue and straight plays. She entered British films in 1936 when she played the part of Paul Robeson's wife in " Song Of Freedom," and she also appeared opposite Robeson later on in " Big Fella." During the war Elizabeth was seen in Warners' " This Was Paris " and British Lion's " Alibi," in both of which she played the rôle of a good-hearted night-club entertainer. In the Tommy Trinder film " Fiddlers Three," directed by Harry Watt for Ealing, she played the part of Frances Day's faithful attendant, and had a number of amusing lines. But it was in " Dead Of Night " made by Ealing in 1945, that Elizabeth played her most interesting film rôle since the two Robeson pictures. Here she acted as a popular Parisian night club owner who sang the blues, joked with the customers, was a good friend to everyone and was altogether an attractive personality. She played an important part in the development of the plot, and was featured in the film's billing with such eminent players as Michael Redgrave, Googie Withers, Mervyn Johns, Hartley Power, Ralph Michael and Frederick Valk. (More recently Elizabeth has been successfully appearing on the London stage.)

Apart from Paul Robeson, Robert Adams, Orlando Martins and Elizabeth Welch, the number of prominent coloured actors and actresses in British films is quite small. Eslanda Robeson, who appeared with her husband Paul in " Borderline " in 1930, also acted in the Robeson film " Big Fella " in 1937, playing the part of a coloured café-keeper. She later appeared as the Arab chief's wife in the Capitol film " Jericho," which was made in Cairo and the North African desert. (Also well-known as a writer, she published a biography of Robeson, titled *Paul Robeson, Negro,* in 1930 and a book of travel, *African Journey,* in 1946.)

Other notable players who have appeared with success in British films of the past few years include Uriel Porter, Sam Blake, Rudolph Evans, and Viola Thompson. They played their most important rôles in the historic " Men Of Two Worlds."

Men Of Two Worlds

In 1943 Thorold Dickinson, a young director who had been responsible for such excellent wartime films as " Gaslight " and " Next Of Kin," began work on a production designed to show Africa as it is today. Three years later the film was shown in London and received praise from the critics as being a worthy and courageous attempt to make a serious film on an important social theme. The three years' work had been worth it, for " Men Of Two Worlds " must be reckoned as something of a triumph for its producer, director, writers and leading actors.

The most significant feature of this film was that it told the story of two men, one European, the other African, who in coming together jointly solve an urgent modern problem which neither can tackle separately. The idea of a contemporary coloured man standing, as it were, between two worlds, between the ages, a human being gifted and developed and yet punished by circumstances as they are, made an instant appeal to Dickinson and his colleagues. The film was conceived and carried through carefully, painstakingly and above all authentically.

The story is of Kisenga, an African composer and pianist, who after fifteen years in Europe gives up his concert tours in order to return to his own country. His people, the Litu, are involved in the move of the District Commissioner to uproot whole villages and move them away from the large area infested by the tsetse fly, carrier of the dreaded sleeping sickness. District Commissioner Randall is, however, having some difficulty in moving the people to the newly cleared land, for the Litu are under the influence of their witch-doctor, Magole, who does not wish the people to obey the white man. When Kisenga arrives in Tanganyika he is regarded with suspicion by his own people, and his efforts to convince his chief that the tribe should, for their own good, move away from the infested bush meet with no success. The Europeanised African is frankly contemptuous of Magole, who keeps his position of power by appealing to the superstition and backwardness of the people, but the Litu are more influenced by the witch-doctor than they are by the educated young composer who had left their village many years before. When Dr. Catherine Munro, a white doctor working with Randall and Kisenga, demonstrates a blood test on Kisenga's father, Magole prophesies that the old man will shortly die, for the white woman has taken his blood and will surely kill him. Kisenga naturally does not take this seriously, nor do the white people, but in fact his father is suddenly smitten with malaria and, within a few days, dies.

This unexpected development has the effect of making Magole seem more powerful than ever, and under his leadership the Litu strongly resist all efforts to move them from their village. The tsetse fly is coming nearer every day and the District Commissioner has resigned himself to watching the Litu die off one by one, but Kisenga, moved by his people's danger, challenges Magole's authority by daring him to take his blood and put him under a curse. The witch-doctor does so, and promises that Kisenga will also die as his father did. Then begins a struggle between

the two men. In spite of his European outlook Kisenga finds
that " the thousand years of Africa in his blood " make him
susceptible to the evil power of suggestion. Night after night
he sits in his hut, working and composing. The drums beat
steadily and monotonously all night and under the influence of
the heat, a touch of malaria and the evil power of Magole, Kisenga
in spite of himself finds that he is succumbing. It is a silent battle
of good against evil ; slowly Kisenga becomes weaker and finally
takes to his bed, eventually becoming delirious.

In his mind there is a constant struggle, the struggle between
his background of primitive African superstition and the new
awareness made possible by his contact with European civilisation.
For Kisenga a step backward into the dark abyss of belief in witch-
craft and superstition would mean that his progress in the new
world has been as nothing. But if he succeeds in triumphing over
the malignant power of suggestion wielded by Magole, he reasons
that then there might still be hope for himself and all the educated
Africans in the world. Randall and Dr. Munro are desperate,
for they are quick to realise the implications of Kisenga's collapse.
In one last dramatic sequence Randall sits at Kisenga's bedside
trying desperately to convince him of Magole's machinations,
trying to give him back the will to live. And outside the hut the
children of the village, who love the composer and his music,
begin to sing the choral sequences of one of his African symphonies,
which Kisenga has previously been teaching them. The impact
of his beloved music, the quiet insistence of Randall's voice, the
awareness of his own position, all these succeed in bringing Kisenga
through the crisis. He lives, and with his recovery Magole is
discredited ; his power broken, the witch-doctor leaves the village
and the Litu are saved from his evil influence. On his recovery
Kisenga realises that his work as a Negro consists of bringing
truth and progress into the lives of his own tribe, and instead of
returning to the concert platform in Europe, he decides to stay in
Africa to teach and work and help his people progress to a better
future.

The above is a bare outline
of an historic production. The
background of the film is remote
and primitive Africa, the implications of the theme are

Above : WILLIE BEST, typical
Negro comedian, with BOB HOPE
in *The Ghost Breakers* Below :
A censored scene from *Brewster's
Millions*

far-reaching ; for the first time in film history a production deals with the lives, hopes and triumphs of intelligent coloured people. Kisenga, played by Robert Adams, is featured with white actors of the prominence of Eric Portman as District Commissioner Randall and Phyllis Calvert as Dr. Catherine Munro. Other Negro players who appear in the film include Orlando Martins, who scored a great triumph as Magole, Eseza Makumbi (who was brought to England from her native Uganda especially to play the part of Saburi), and Tunji Williams.

The film was made under the greatest difficulties. As Thorold Dickinson writes, " First we wrote the story and screenplay (the story was by Joyce Cary from an idea by E. Arnot Robertson, the screenplay was by Herbert Victor and myself), chose the locations and designed the settings. This occupied some eight months, four of which were spent travelling. On the way out to West Africa a U-boat sank our cameras and stock. When we were put ashore a thousand miles from Lagos, the Customs took away our only still camera against our flight to East Africa, and mislaid it until we were on our way home again ! We had to carry out colour tests using a borrowed Leica.

" In the winter of 1943-44 a unit returned to Moshi to photograph the exteriors. The rest of the unit travelled with the equipment by slow convoy to Cape Town and thence overland to East Africa. This took more than three months, while we watched fine weather pass and five months of monsoon rain come nearer. Fresh colour film had to be sent by air from Hollywood, where the exposed film had also to be flown for processing. By the autumn of 1944 we managed to get sufficient material for our bare requirements.

" Chapter three began with a further delay of four months, while we waited for scarce Technicolor equipment to be sent to us. In February, 1945, when we finally began work at Denham we had lost one year owing to war conditions. We completed the studio work by August, 1945, and by the time we had begun to edit the film the last of our location work came back to us from Hollywood, where it had been sent for processing. In November, 1945, we recorded the magnificent score by Arthur Bliss, and in January, 1946, the film passed into the studio

Above : **An *Our Gang* comedy.**
Below: *So Red The Rose* **directed by King Vidor.**

laboratory. So ended three years of immense difficulty. But I am glad to have worked on the making of such a film."

" Men Of Two Worlds " was indeed a long time in the making, but it was eminently worth it. It was a revolution in film-production. As Ethel Fisher writes in *Film Quarterly*, Autumn, 1946 : " The film is unique in that for the first time one is given a picture of Africa as it is today and because it shows the African as he is. For once we do not see the Negro as bell-hop, shoe-shine boy or figure of fun ; instead one is shown the modern, educated young African turning to the service of his race the best of two civilisations. Perhaps the most outstanding feature of the film is the fact that for the first time a Negro player is featured with a British star. Kisenga (Robert Adams) and Randall (Eric Portman) share almost equal honours in the unfolding of the story. One is the complement of the other : neither character would mean anything without the other."

Robert Adams' own views on the film are interesting : " For myself," he states, " it has been a privilege to be the pioneer of serious dramatic acting in films, for such I consider the opportunity in ' Men Of Two Worlds.' The past, the much deservedly criticised past where my people were shown as traditional inferiors has, I believe, gone for good. We must look to the future with the hope that as a better understanding dawns, greater opportunities to show the constructive contribution of the Negro will be afforded. Bitterness and resentment will do we Negroes no good. We must forgive and forget. But while I look forward to a permanent change for the better in our artistic and professional status, I would hate to feel that all the sordid aspects of my people were kept off the screen. Perhaps by showing them, filmgoers will begin to think that some effort should be made to remove these conditions permanently, thereby ending an apparent acceptance of the conception in certain white people's minds that such is the natural environment of the Negro. Progress and understanding are here and, I believe, have come to stay permanently."

The film had a good critical reception on the whole. Dilys Powell of the *Sunday Times* considered it " highly intelligent and interesting " ; Paul Holt of the *Daily Express* wrote that it was " superb, exciting and satisfying " ; while P. L. Mannock of the *Daily Herald* described it as " a remarkable British achievement." Both *The Times* and the *Daily Mail* pointed out that the film not only dealt with a serious problem, a subject of real importance, but dealt with it intelligently, while the general opinion of the majority of the Press was that " Men Of Two Worlds " was a landmark in British film production.

Joan Lester, film critic of *Reynolds News*, summed up the general opinion when she wrote : " Easily the most interesting and the most ambitious film of the week is Two Cities' ' Men Of Two Worlds,' directed by Thorold Dickinson. . . . One feels a sense of gratitude for a director who brings ideas into his work, and if the picture just misses the poetic rhythm of ' The Forgotten Village,' which has a similar theme, it has a wider sweep of canvas. More-over, it is good to see coloured people introduced into a film other than as comic relief. Robert Adams, as the successful musician who abandons his career after fifteen years among white people in order to go back and help his own people, Orlando Martins as the witch-doctor, Eseza Makumbi as the musician's sister, Tunji Williams, Viola Thompson and a host of other coloured actors bring a fine poise and dignity to the screen."

Perhaps the final word on the subject may be contributed by a writer in *Ebony*, January, 1946, who remarks : " Never in an American film has an attempt been made to portray Africans as other than ferocious savages prancing about the jungle in grass skirts. But, Hollywood to the contrary, most Africans wear pants rather than loin cloths, most Africans behave like human beings rather than animals, most Africans think like adults rather than children. It has taken the British, colonial-conscious as they are, to recognise the coming of age of Africa and to attempt to portray in a popular movie the dramatic story of the Dark Continent without the corny, stereotyped conception of the Frank Buck school. ' Men Of Two Worlds ' marks the first break with past tradition, and pictures Africans with sympathy and respect."

Thorold Dickinson, long known as a young director with pro-gressive views, has been waiting many years to make this film. He believes that it is a potent weapon against discrimination, and it was his original intention to have the film widely exhibited in the United States, as well as other countries throughout the world. However, the London *Evening Standard* of August 12th, 1946, evidently thought the possibilities of this happening were extremely small, for in the Londoner's Diary a paragraph appears as follows : " ' Men Of Two Worlds,' produced by Two Cities, cost more than six hundred thousand pounds. There is little likelihood that it will be shown in the United States of America, however, *because of its subject.*" (Author's italics.) This may only have been an opinion as expressed by a leading London newspaper, but there is more than a grain of clear thinking in it. Hollywood, which has consistently refused to recognise that coloured people are human beings for fear of antagonising anti-Negro communities in the South, is hardly likely to want a film such as " Men Of Two Worlds " shown in the U.S.A., for it is the type of production which Hollywood itself is afraid to tackle. The more credit should then go to the British producers who made this outstanding contribution to racial understanding.

The Continental Cinema

Negroes, since there are comparatively few living in Europe, do not appear very regularly in films made on the Continent, but where they do figure it has been noticeable that they are treated without any form of racial intolerance. In a number of French films the coloured characters are merely shown as Frenchmen, and the fact that they are black is never stressed. A good example of this treatment occurred in the film " Toni," made by Jean Renoir in 1935, which dealt with quarry workers in the Riviera. Dick, a Negro character, appeared here as one of the Frenchmen ; he lived in a communal household with his fellows, ate with them, drank with them, talked with them, worked with them. In short, he was treated as an ordinary human being, no reference to his colour being made throughout the film.

In Jacques Feyder's " Le Grand Jeu," made in 1935, there were scenes in the Foreign Legion, where the hero (Pierre-Richard Willm) goes after having disgraced himself in Paris. Here all men are equal and the Negro members of the Legion mix freely with the whites. Feyder's film is like all French films in this respect ; whenever coloured characters appear they fit naturally into the picture and there is never even the slightest suggestion of discrimination. Thus in the café scenes of Jean Vigo's " L'Atalante " one saw coloured people drinking and dancing with the whites in perfect harmony, something never witnessed in Hollywood films.

In the famous ballet film " La Mort Du Cygne," directed by Jean Benoit-Levy, a coloured child is a member of the school attached to the Paris Opera (and what an enchanting little child she is). No discrimination is apparent here. The French have long been notable for their civilised attitude in this matter, and representative films like " Toni," " Le Grand Jeu," and " La Mort Du Cygne " are a sufficient demonstration of the non-existence of a colour bar either in France or in French films.

Among the few German films in which coloured actors have appeared, one in particular springs to mind. This is " War Is Hell," directed by Victor Trivas in 1933. (Trivas is now in Holly-wood, and recently collaborated on the screenplay of the R.K.O. International film, " The Stranger," directed by Orson Welles.) The film dealt with a group of soldiers of all nationalities during the First World War, concentrating its attention upon five main characters, one of whom was a Negro. Not only was this character treated with sympathy, but what is more important he appeared in the film as just another soldier, who shared the dangers of the trenches with his comrades, demonstrating the same fortitude, the same courage, the same humanity. A Frenchman, a German, a wounded English officer, a Jew, and the Negro are together in a devastated ruin between two trench-lines. Dependent on one another they get into difficulties, not understanding each other's language. Only the Negro, a cabaret artist who mangles all languages indiscriminately, laughs cheerfully and makes peace between them, until they are all bombed to death—by the bombs of both sides, an ironic Trivas touch. " War Is Hell " may be classed as the German counterpart to the French film " Toni," and each is the best example of an intelligent handling of an inter-racial theme. There were, however, a number of other films made in Berlin before Hitler became Chancellor, which revealed a similarly wide outlook. (It is, of course, interesting to note that following Hitler's rise to power the standard of the German cinema deteriorated considerably. One facet of an artistic descent into " Nazi culture " was that no Negro actors were ever allowed to appear in German films, since Hitler followed in the footsteps of fascist opinion in the Southern States of America in classing the Negro as an animal of the lowest order.)

In the Soviet Union a distinguished film was made a few years ago on the life of the celebrated mulatto Alexander Pushkin, the Russian poet whose parentage was partly Russian and partly Negro. And in other films Soviet film-makers have demonstrated that their belief in the equality of all races is not only a theory. Among those which included racial themes was " The Circus," directed by Alexandrov for Mosfilm, which tells the story of a boy in love with a girl who is an American circus star, hounded from her own country and pathetically bewildered by the villainous circus master, whom she has rebuffed. The *denouement* of the film comes when the villain revengefully discloses the heroine's secret —a Negro child—the reason she had left the United States—during the circus show. Holding the black child up in his arms the ringmaster points at the mother and waits for scorn and abuse. It does not come, however ; instead the little coloured boy is taken from him and passed lovingly from group to group. As Louise Watt wrote in *World Film News*, February, 1937 : "The child's gradual change from fear and subjection to confidence and freedom said more for racial equality than might months of oratorical propaganda." " The Circus," like most Soviet films, dealt intelligently with a social problem, and although the rest of the film was an unsuccessful attempt to make a musical on Hollywood lines, the film is notable for that one beautifully directed sequence of the sub-plot.

The film demonstrated the reasonable and realistic attitude of Soviet Russia to its citizens of every colour and creed. " Pushkin," " The Circus " and other Soviet films rank with Trivas's " War Is Hell," Renoir's " Toni," Wills's " Song Of Freedom," Tennyson's " The Proud Valley," and Dickinson's " Men Of Two Worlds " among the most significant contributions of the European cinema to international tolerance and understanding. They are all landmarks in the Negro's struggle for a just depiction on the screen.

CHAPTER EIGHT

SOME NEGRO PLAYERS

" The Negro must be conscious of himself and yet, internationally, linked with the nations which are culturally alien
to him."

PAUL ROBESON *in " New Theatre," July, 1935.*

Paul Robeson

In the annals of the Negro in art during the past twenty years
one name stands out above all others—Paul Robeson, actor,
singer, personality, lecturer and Socialist. The son of the
Reverend William D. Robeson, and the grandson of Negro slaves,
Paul was born in Princeton on April 9th, 1898. Paul's mother
died when he was six years old and soon afterwards the Reverend
Robeson moved to Westfield, taking his youngest child with him.
Later on the Robesons moved to Somerville, where for ten years
father and son lived together and learned to respect and love
each other. The elder Robeson was a busy, sincere, likeable
man, whose life's work was in establishing the church. His
son attended school in Somerville and showed a remarkable
aptitude for learning. When he was a little older he became
superintendent of the Sunday School, and often helped his father
with the services, leading the singing in church with his impressive
and beautiful bass voice.

In High School at Somerville Paul was not only a brilliant
scholar but conspicuous also in all-round athletics. It was a
mixed school and soon he became not only the most popular
Negro boy but also the most popular boy in the school. He went
freely and easily back and forth from both white and Negro homes.
To everyone this large, handsome Negro boy was " Paul " ;
everybody in Somerville knew him, everyone liked him.

In 1915 the boy won a State scholarship to Rutgers University,
and thus became the third Negro to enter this historic seat of
learning. Paul soon settled down to his studies, but later on he
tried out for the University football team. There had never
previously been a coloured player in a Rutgers team, but such
was his skill, great agility and speed that the giant Negro soon

became a tower of strength, and during the four years of his college life football fans all over the country spoke of him affectionately as " Robeson of Rutgers." In 1918 his beloved father died, but the fine spirit of the Reverend Robeson lived on in his son ; when Paul returned for his last year at Rutgers he worked harder than ever, graduating in 1919 with high honours. On leaving the University he was chosen with three others as the most representative men in scholarship, athletics and personality for his term at Rutgers. Paul delivered his first speech at this time on " Interracial Relations," and thus began a long and distinguished career of untiring work for the betterment of understanding between the races. When " Robey " finally left the university, the town of New Brunswick was as proud of him as Somerville had been. His record of popularity and prestige could hardly be bettered by a white boy, let alone a Negro.

Following his graduation, Paul went to New York to Columbia University Law School, and here he settled down in Harlem. At Columbia he was at home among his white classmates as he had been at Rutgers, while in Harlem he was just as much at home with his Negro friends. Robeson possessed the power to intermingle freely and without embarrassment on either side, and it is doubtful whether any other Negro has had access to so many white homes and been the honoured guest at so many exclusively white gatherings. In 1923 Paul obtained his degree in law and soon afterwards a successful New York lawyer invited him to join his firm. However, after many months of solid work in the law business, the boy encountered his first experience of race prejudice, for other members of the firm made their objections to the constant presence of a Negro in their office. Reluctantly Paul left law, having begun to formulate his own definite ideas about the position of the Negro in American society. He realised that he could fit in only with great difficulty as a professional man, and that for coloured lawyers there were remarkably few opportunities, since there were no big Negro estates, Negro institutions, banks or railroads. Thus in 1924 Paul Robeson found himself at the crossroads of his career.

Luckily for him, and for us, the stage beckoned. The Provincetown Players, one of the most intelligent and sincere theatre groups in America, invited him to play leading Negro rôles in " All God's Chillun Got Wings " and " The Emperor Jones," both by a new

140

playwright, Eugene O'Neill, a discovery of this group, which operated from a little theatre in McDougall Street, New York. The Provincetown Players, now occupying an important place in the history of the American stage, established and maintained a theatre where playwrights of sincere poetic, literary and dramatic purpose might see their plays in action and superintend their production without submitting to the commercial theatre's interpretation of public taste. The greatest single contribution of this playhouse to American drama was, of course, Eugene O'Neill. This alone justified its existence, but it also gave Paul Robeson to the American theatre and to the world, which makes the Provincetown Playhouse doubly significant in modern theatre annals.

The young Negro became a great friend of O'Neill, and week after week they discussed the meaning of the plays, discovering how similar were their interests in the theatre, in people, in social conditions. At the age of twenty-six P. Robeson, lawyer, became Paul Robeson, actor ; and subsequently a remarkably fine and successful actor. As George Jean Nathan, writing of his performance in " All God's Chillun Got Wings," remarked in the *American Mercury*, July, 1924 : " Robeson, with relatively little experience and with no training to speak of, is one of the most thoroughly eloquent, impressive and convincing actors that I have looked at and listened to in almost twenty years of professional theatregoing. He gains his effects with means that not only seem natural, but that *are* natural. He does things beautifully, with his voice, his features, his hands, his whole somewhat ungainly body, yet I doubt that he knows how he does them. As in the leading rôle of 'The Emperor Jones,' in which he is fully worthy successor to his Negro colleague Charles Gilpin, he here acts with all the unrestraint and terrible sincerity of which the white actor, save on rare occasions, is by virtue of his shellac of civilisation just a trifle ashamed. The effect is that of a soul bombarded by thunder and torn by lightning."

And Lawrence Stallings, writing in *The New York World*, was as enthusiastic as Mr. Nathan : " In ' All God's Chillun Got Wings ' there is no doubt of Robeson's ability," he stated, and went on : " The man brings a genius to the piece. What other player on the American stage has his great taut body—the singing grace and litheness of the man who with a football under his arm side-stepped half the broken fields of the East ? And who has a better voice for tragedy than this actor, whose tone and resonance suggest nothing so much as the dusky, poetic quality of a Negro spiritual, certainly the most tragic utterances in American life ? "

And O'Neill himself stated at the time : " In Paul Robeson's interpretation of Brutus Jones I have found the most complete satisfaction an author can get—that of seeing his creation born into the flesh and blood ; in his creation of Jim Harris in my ' All God's Chillun Got Wings ' I found not only complete fidelity to my intent under trying circumstances, but, beyond that, true understanding and racial integrity."

Paul's great successes in these two plays caused his interest in the theatre to grow. He realised that he could be happy doing this kind of work ; it was serious, worthwhile, important work, and he loved it. An idealist, he was a wonderful speaker who talked eagerly of his hopes and ambitions, declaring passionately, " If I can build up the great tragic figure of Brutus Jones so that he becomes the basis of tragic importance for the audience—make him a human figure—then tear him down in the subsequent scene ; if the audience, moved by his degeneration, his struggles, his fate, by his emotions—a Negro's emotions—admire and then pity this Negro—they must know then that he is human, that they are human, that we are all human beings together."

On another occasion he said : " If I can make people realise fully the pitiful struggle of Jim Harris in ' All God's Chillun ' and reduce them to tears for him at the end—weeping because a Negro has suffered—I will have done something to make them realise, even if only sub-consciously and for a few moments, that Negroes are the same kind of people they themselves are, suffer as they suffer, weep as they weep, that all this arbitrary separation because of colour is unimportant. If some day I can play Othello as Shakespeare wrote it, bring to the stage the nobility, sympathy and understanding Shakespeare put into the play, I will make the audience know that he was not just a dark, foreign brute of three hundred years ago in far off Venice who murdered a beautiful, innocent white girl, but that he was a fine, noble, tragic human figure, ruined by the very human weakness of jealousy."

Later on in London, and again in New York two years ago, Paul was able to realise his ambitions to play Othello. Indeed his performance as the Moor in Margaret Webster's recent Broadway production was enough to establish him for all time as one of the outstanding personalities of the American stage, a man with many great and wonderful gifts. One of these has been the gift of song. It is doubtful if anywhere in the world there are civilised people who have never heard Paul Robeson, in person, on the radio or on records and in films. He has created many world-famous songs, and his beautiful bass voice has been heard on countless gramophone records made in America and in Europe.

In 1924 he is reported as saying : " If with my music I can re-create for an audience the great sadness of the Negro slave in, for instance, ' Sometimes I Feel Like a Motherless Child,' or if I make them know the strong, gallant convict of the chain gang, make them feel his thirst, understand his naïve boasting about his strength, feel the brave gaiety and sadness in ' Water Boy,' or if I can explain to them the simple divine faith of the Negro in ' Weepin' Mary '—then I shall increase their knowledge and understanding of my people. They will sense that we are moved by the same emotions, have the same beliefs, the same longings, that in fact, we are all human together. That will be something to work for, something worth doing."

In 1925 Paul was invited to give a concert in New York of Negro music, in conjunction with pianist Lawrence Brown. He assented with eagerness and thus on April 18th of that year began the long and distinguished series of concerts which Paul has since given in all the big cities of the world. The first one, like all the succeeding hundreds of memorable concerts, was an enormous success. The music critic of the *New York Times* summed up the general feeling when he wrote : " Mr. Robeson is a singer of genuine power. His Negro spirituals have the ring of the revivalist, they hold in them a world of religious experience, it is a cry from the depths, this rich humanism that touches the heart. Sung by one man they voiced the sorrows and hopes of a people."

Paul began another phase of his career in the same year. He came to Europe, where at the Ambassadors Theatre, he duplicated his New York stage success in " The Emperor Jones." He loved England, and felt more at home in London than he had in America. As Eslanda Goode Robeson, his wife, writes in her book *Paul Robeson, Negro* (Gollancz, 1930) : " There were few inconveniences for him as a Negro in London. He did not have to live in a segregated district. He leased a charming flat in Chelsea near his friends ; he ate at many restaurants in town with his wife or

143

coloured friends without fear of the discrimination which all Negroes encounter in America. All this was important for his general well-being."

From 1926 until 1928 Paul and his wife travelled on concert tours in America, but in that year he returned to London where he played in the stage version of Edna Ferber's " Show Boat." Once again Robeson's beautiful voice and quality of greatness made him an outstanding success in England ; his acting in " Show Boat," and his singing at various concerts in London, caused the *Daily Express* to refer to him in a large headline as " A Negro Genius," and many other critics and writers agreed. Most of 1929 was taken up with a European concert tour ; it was in the following year, when he was in London, that Robeson was persuaded to make his first film appearance.

This was in an experimental silent film, " Borderline," produced in Switzerland, for Pool, by Kenneth Macpherson, editor of the well-known cinema journal *Close Up*, and an enthusiastic theoretician of film production and technique. Paul played a leading part in this film (in which Eslanda, his wife, also appeared), as Pete, a half-vagrant, young giant Negro. He enacted the leading rôle in a mixed cast ; director Macpherson allowed no distinction to be drawn between the Negro and the white characters. In fact he was so deliberate about this that one film reviewer at the time remarked, " The white folk of necessity, in this film, take subsidiary value. Macpherson has decreed this with delicate irony and ferocity." " Borderline " was about two Negroes who come in their wanderings to a small mid-European town. For a time they cross the backwater of small-town vice and malice, and leave it cleansed and hallowed when they depart. It was delicately played and directed. Macpherson will probably be the last to claim for his film any great importance, since on many occasions he declared himself to be far more interested in abstract film values than in concrete social realities. However, that he wrote, produced and directed " Borderline," which not only gave prominent rôles to Negroes but depicted them in an heroic light, must be accounted a considerable, and certainly an historic, achievement. This Pool film is important not so much in itself as for the fact that firstly it marked the film début of Paul Robeson, and secondly it was the first of the lamentably short list of motion pictures which have treated the Negro and his problems with sympathy. It is likely that this modest production has now been forgotten ; at any event it was not widely shown, for it was a silent film made during the period when talkies had become a craze. As a kind of defiant gesture, Kenneth Macpherson in 1930 decided to make this contribution to film art, which he considered had come to the end of its greatest phase with the advent of the sound film ; in any study of the Negro on the screen his gesture, " Borderline," will not only *not* be forgotten but will always have a place of primary importance.

In 1933 Robeson made his first talking film, this time in New York, where he was invited by two young independent producers, John Krimsky and Gifford Cochran, to repeat his stage triumph of Brutus Jones in a film version of Eugene O'Neill's masterpiece directed by Dudley Murphy, a Hollywood screenwriter and director. This production of "The Emperor Jones " was an artistic success, and Robeson was outstanding in the name rôle, although neither the play nor the film were well liked by Negro critics who claimed that, to an extent, the plot trod the well-worn path. As they were quick to point out, it showed Robeson as a servile Pullman porter in the first scenes ; then later as the swaggering, brutal but cowardly emperor of the jungle, while the final scene showed him reverting to type as a frightened superstitious, broken black man. Nevertheless "The Emperor Jones " was a triumph, a revolutionary film, and by sheer force of his personality Robeson was responsible for making it a great success with intelligent moviegoers at least, although not unnaturally it later on encountered certain difficulties of distribution, especially in the South.

Robeson soon came back to Europe where he starred (as it proved later, unfortunately) in the British film of Edgar Wallace's " Sanders Of The River," made by Alexander Korda. Paul became very unhappy about his part in this film, which revealed itself to be thinly disguised Imperialist propaganda and although his performance was highly praised, he resolved to pay more attention to the scripts and treatment of his succeeding films. 1935 found him on a concert tour of the Soviet Union, where later his son Paul was educated. He visited many film studios, and in an interview in Moscow he stated : " In Soviet Russia I breathe freely for the first time in my life. It is clear that, whether a Negro is politically a Communist or not, of all the nations in the world the modern Russians are our best friends." Paul went on to say,

" The most important development in Soviet culture I have seen is in the moving picture field." And, indeed, there was some talk at one period of his making a film with the great Soviet director Eisenstein, though, unfortunately, nothing came of it, due to Paul's concert commitments elsewhere.

Robeson's wonderful physique and personality in " Sanders Of The River " so impressed film producers that he received many overtures from Hollywood, as well as from British film-makers. He decided that the stories offered to him by the latter were of more interest to him as a Negro, in that they gave him worthwhile parts as distinct from the servile posturings of Hollywood's screen Negroes, and he accepted an offer to appear in Hammer's " Song Of Freedom." After this he made a trip to Hollywood to play Jim and sing the immortal " Ole Man River " in the new Universal film version of Ferber-Kern's " Show Boat." By 1937 Paul was back again in Europe, and working in London, Cairo and Morocco, making " Jericho " for Walter Futter and Capitol. It gave him an excellent part and following this he appeared in " King Solomon's Mines " and " Big Fella." To an undistinguished rôle in the Gaumont British version of the Rider Haggard story Paul brought his great power and intelligence, but the film was only fair and it was later on, in Hammer's " Big Fella," that he was given another outstanding part in an excellent, though modest, production, in which he played a Negro worker who brings up a white boy, a dock-yard waif. Here Paul was given opportunities to display his tremendous charm to the full and to portray with sincerity the character of a complex but lovable person. This production was, in its way, admirable but it was his next British film, made at Ealing Studios just before the outbreak of the Second World War, which was undoubtedly Robeson's most important excursion into the motion picture field.

This was the momentous " The Proud Valley," in which Paul appeared as a miner in a Welsh village, working, singing, suffering and triumphing with his fellows. Never had Paul been seen to better advantage than in this fine film, which gave him an important, realistic rôle and a real cinematic opportunity of the kind he had long been awaiting. The film was a triumph for Robeson, director Tennyson, and producer Michael Balcon, and it is to be regretted that " The Proud Valley " was the last motion picture he was to make in England.

Since 1940 he has been acting in America, and indeed his long and distinguished career reached a peak with his magnificent performance as Othello in Margaret Webster's production in New York a year or two ago, a revolutionary staging, and the first time a Negro had played this part on the Broadway stage. In 1942 Paul was persuaded by Hollywood to make a film, the unwieldy " Tales Of Manhattan," in which he appeared as a stereotype " darky " with Ethel Waters as his ignorant, superstitious wife. Again Paul was extremely disappointed with Hollywood. At first he thought that he might make something out of his rôle, but when the film was shown and Robeson realised how his scenes appeared, he declared that he would never again make an American film until he played characters of prominence and sympathy of the kind which he had portrayed in British studios. Thus it is likely that it will be a long time before Hollywood can entice Paul back to make further films, for Robeson has become extremely sensitive on this question and wary of the types of parts now offered him. He sang, and also spoke the commentary, in a documentary, " Native Land," directed by Leo Hurwitz and Paul Strand in 1942, but he has not made an appearance on the screen since the unhappy " Tales Of Manhattan." Perhaps he may decide to take up his film career again here in England, where he left off in 1939 ? Certainly in British studios Paul Robeson has come nearer to real achievement in the cinema, and we would certainly welcome him back.

Rex Ingram

Some ten or more years ago, in the Warners' film version of " The Green Pastures," Rex Ingram first came into the public eye with his moving, sincere and highly praised performance as De Lawd. Actually Ingram is a youthful veteran of the screen, for it was in a silent film featuring Elmo Lincoln as Tarzan that this tall, broad-shouldered, handsome Negro first made his appearance. He also played in many silents and quite a few talkies before " The Green Pastures " made him a screen name. Today this fine actor is as well-known on the Broadway stage as he is in Hollywood. He graduated several years ago from North-western University with a degree in medicine, but shortly afterwards decided that his natural bent was towards the theatre. Twenty-six years ago the young doctor made his first appearance in a small part in a play running in Los Angeles. Since that time he has risen to an enviable position, being acclaimed as one of the foremost actors in the history of the Negro race.

Rex was born in 1895 on a river-boat, the glorious " Robert E. Lee," famed in song and saga ; his father was a fireman on the boat and the boy's early years were spent travelling up and down the Mississippi. When he was seven years old his family decided to settle down and moved to Los Angeles, where later on the boy attended the Urban Military Academy. Afterwards, at North-western University, Rex Ingram, like Paul Robeson, became a noted athlete, and when he finally graduated as a doctor he was extremely well-known in university circles for his activities in basketball, football, baseball and track athletics.

After Ingram had decided that he wanted to be an actor he returned to his hometown, Los Angeles, and began to make daily visits to the film studios. At last he " crashed the movies," his first film job being in an early version of " Tarzan Of The Apes," produced in 1920. This was followed by a number of minor screen parts, after which the young actor was given a rôle in David Belasco's production of the stage play " Lulu Belle," which opened in Los Angeles and was afterwards seen on tour all over the United States. In the next few years Ingram's reputation grew rapidly, following his much-praised performances in such Broadway plays as " Porgy," " Once In A Lifetime," and " Goin' Home." His other theatre successes included " Stevedore," " Beale Street," " Drums Of The Bayou " and more recently, " Marching Song."

Among his silent films were " The Ten Commandments," " The King Of Kings," " The Four Feathers " and " The Big Parade," while he was also seen in such talking films as " King Kong," " Sign Of The Cross," and " Trader Horn." He played a small part in Paul Robeson's first American film, "The Emperor Jones," made in New York, and has since been seen in Hollywood in " Captain Blood," " The Green Pastures," " Huckleberry Finn," " The Talk Of The Town," " Cabin In The Sky," " A Thousand And One Nights " and many others.

Ingram was brought to England by Sir Alexander Korda in 1939 to play the important rôle of the Genie of the Lamp in the film " The Thief Of Bagdad," and all those who

Above : *Mildred Pierce* directed by Michael Curtiz. Below : *Lifeboat*, directed by Alfred Hitchcock.

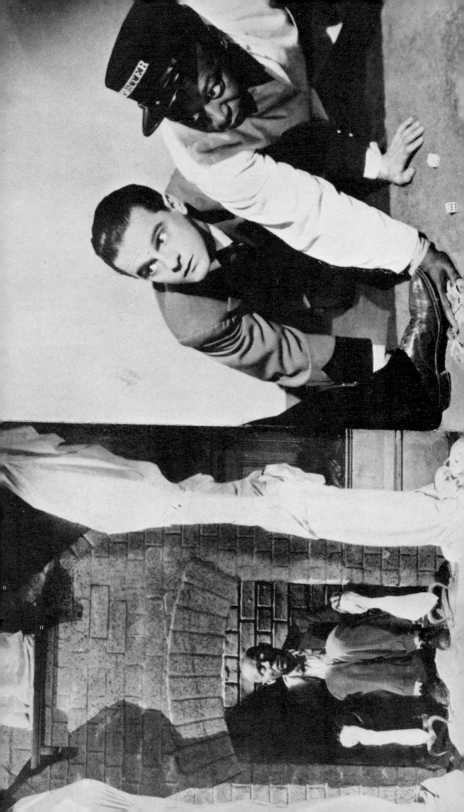

met him over here were entirely won over by his intelligence, charm, striking appearance and engaging personality. I often had long talks with Rex at Denham Studios, while he was waiting to appear in front of the camera, and found him to be a sincere person with progressive and outspoken views. He impressed upon me that his main task throughout his entire professional career has been to try to raise the intellectual and cultural standards of his people, and his work and writings indicate this to be true. Rex believes firmly that recognition for a single Negro is, in effect, recognition for all Negroes, and that is why it is important for individual coloured artists to be conscious of their responsibilities. He is a good talker, politically conscious and an untiring and militant worker in the theatre. In New York for many years Rex has always been associated with the progressive elements of the American stage and, like Robeson, he has the respect and admiration of all with whom he comes into contact.

Korda was impressed with Ingram's work with Sabu in " The Thief Of Bagdad," one of his most ambitious Technicolor productions, and made plans to co-star Ingram and Sabu in further films. Unfortunately the outbreak of the European War disorganised Korda's production plans and Rex had to return to New York. He greatly enjoyed working in England, however, and expressed his intention of returning as soon as conditions would permit. It is a fact that Paul Robeson received on the whole excellent treatment from British film producers during his many years in England, and it is likely that if Ingram were to return he, too, would be given rôles of greater significance and importance than he would in Hollywood. Many of us here in England hope that it will indeed be possible in the post-war years for Rex to alternate between London and the U.S.A.

Rex is an actor of extreme versatility. In " The Green Pastures " his study of De Lawd was deeply moving, bringing a wealth of dignity and faith to a beautifully written part. More recently, in " Cabin In The Sky " he went to the other extreme, playing the rôle of The Evil One, Lucifer, Jr., who is forever trying to entice Little Joe into the evil ways of

Left: *Chasing Trouble* directed by Howard Bretherton. Right : *One Exciting Night* directed by D. W. Griffith, the first of the stereotyped Negro comedies.

drinking, gambling and loose-living ; and both as De Lawd and as The Evil One, Ingram was superb. Occasionally he has played the types of parts which most Negroes have to play at some time or other in their professional lives— coloured servants and such-like. But it is true to say that when Ingram has accepted such a part it is only because he feels that he can make something of it, build it up, imbue it with his own personality. And certainly one must agree that sometimes, arising out of the intelligent acting of a Negro in a servile part, can come a further understanding of his people, a greater tolerance for all coloured races. In Columbia's " The Talk Of The Town," for example, Rex played Ronald Colman's valet, but the way that he acted this part left no doubt in the minds of all filmgoers that this kindly, dignified, beautifully spoken and intelligent valet was in fact more than a servant— he was a good counsellor and trusted friend of his employer. Throughout the film light-hearted badinage is exchanged between Colman and Ingram, leaving a pleasant impression of good relations between black and white in American social life. And although this rosy picture is largely false, and bears but little relation to reality in the American scene, it does not alter the fact that Ingram's performance and personality made the conception of the white-black relationship in " The Talk Of The Town " a step in the right direction.

Rex Ingram is one of the busiest Negro actors in Hollywood, but he rejects as many rôles as he accepts, for obvious reasons. Recently he played once more the rôle of the Genie of the Lamp, this time in a Hollywood film, Columbia's " A Thousand And One Nights," and since then he has been seen in Universal's " Fired Wife," Columbia's " Sahara," and Benedict Bogeaus' " Dark Waters." (He has also found time to make successful Broadway appearances in such plays as " Freedom Road " and " St. Louis Woman.") For his work in the film " Sahara," Ingram was awarded a special citation by the Motion Picture Committee for Unity, for the most outstanding contribution for the year by a Negro actor. I have dealt elsewhere with the important social and political significance of this film and the Negro character. In addition to its being an extraordinarily well-conceived and well-written part, there is no doubt that this character came to life principally because it was played by the impeccable Ingram.

Even in minor rôles this actor has always been noteworthy, and it was therefore not surprising to find that in a part of real importance he should be so outstanding. " Sahara " marks a peak in Ingram's long and distinguished career.

It is interesting to recall how the part was originally cast. Some time ago, when Zoltan Korda, who directed " Sahara," was travelling in North Africa he became acquainted with a fascinating Negro called Tambul, the son of a native chieftain. Tambul had recently returned from a United States university in order to live and work among his people, and was spending unlimited time and energy opening up a new world for his race. Korda was impressed by this work and by the man himself, and later he became extremely friendly with Tambul. In Hollywood, a year afterwards, when he was casting " Sahara," Korda remembered his African friend, for the script called for a Sudanese soldier, and he visualised the rôle as Tambul. The character was a strong one, a leader among his own people, a man of great integrity, and Korda immediately realised that the person who could best portray this rôle was Rex Ingram, whom he had worked with so well in England on the film " The Thief Of Bagdad." Ingram's success when the film was shown justified Korda's belief in his ability.

Among his considerable gallery of film portraits one can call to mind his playing of Jim, the Negro servant, in the M.-G.-M. version of Mark Twain's immortal " Huckleberry Finn," made in Hollywood some years ago. In this film Rex acted the part of a kind of big brother to Huck Finn (Mickey Rooney), and Huck and Jim went through a number of adventures together, both as equal protagonists in boyhood delights. Ingram's likeable personality was an outstanding feature of this film and even in competition with such an acknowledged scene stealer as Mickey Rooney, he managed to hold his own.

One can see how much Ingram can influence a part by noting his recent work in the film " Dark Waters." What originally was probably a very ordinary rôle of a Negro plantation worker in Florida was transformed in his capable hands into a sympathetic rendition of a devoted friend, who tries to help the heroine (played by Merle Oberon) out of danger, and for this pays with his own life. A lesser actor would have made a fair success from this. Not so Ingram. His performance in " Dark Waters " was penetrating, sincere ; he made a real character from the Negro labourer, and received a great deal of favourable notice from the many critics who realised that a large amount of thought and care had gone into his creation.

A year or two ago Ingram purchased an estate in Warm Springs Canyon, fifty miles from Los Angeles. Here he intends to form a permanent residence and training centre for young Negro men and women who wish to enter the theatrical profession, thus founding on the West Coast an American Negro Academy of Dramatic Art, with teachers of experience and reputation. All his life Rex has dreamed of the time when coloured people may be given the same opportunities in life as whites, and in this way he feels he can make his own special kind of contribution to a realisation of his ideals. " Good actors," he says, " can be of far more value towards greater tolerance for Negroes than possibly any other form of art. It is on film actors specifically that the spot-light falls more heavily, and if filmgoers see more good coloured actors playing bigger and better screen rôles then this can do nothing but create goodwill for our people. I have tried to play my own personal and minor part towards this end, and I intend to help all young Negroes who wish to become adept in the acting profession to achieve their object, and so take the struggle one step nearer our common ideal."

These are sensible words from a man whose reputation has been based on constant sincerity and considerable talent. Rex Ingram takes his place alongside Robeson, Marian Anderson, Richard Wright, Canada Lee, Langston Hughes and the many other Negroes in art who have helped to bring honour to their race in the past thirty years.

Lena Horne

The rise of the coloured actress and singer Lena Horne to her present cinematic prominence is a phenomenon not previously experienced in Hollywood. This beautiful girl is Negro America's leading film star ; she gets more than two hundred fan letters every day at M.-G.-M. Studios, where she is under a long-term contract, and photographs of Lena are plastered on walls in homes in every part of the world. She is light-skinned enough to pass for a South American ; in fact when she first went to Hollywood attempts were made to persuade her to pass herself off as a *Mexican* actress.

Lena refused hotly. She is proud to be coloured, and is known as one of the most militant members of her race and a fearless upholder of Negro dignity and basic democratic rights.

Born in Brooklyn twenty-eight years ago, she made her stage début at the age of six in Philadelphia in the play " Madame X." Her mother, Edna Scotchron, was a member of the Lafayette Stock Players, the famous Negro group from New York who were then visiting Philadelphia on an extended tour. Lena substituted for the child, who appears in a cot during one of the scenes in this well-loved melodrama, and during the rest of the tour she acted on the stage as often as she was allowed. Already she had decided to become an actress. Her mother, however, decided that her daughter should first be given a good education and sent her to a boarding school in Fort Valley, Georgia, where Lena's uncle was the dean. When she was fourteen the young girl returned to New York, and graduated from high school there.

Still determined to go on the stage, Lena, at the age of sixteen, managed to get a job in the chorus at the famous Cotton Club in Harlem. The show in which she first appeared starred Adelaide Hall, Cab Calloway and the Nicholas Brothers, but after two years Lena was herself featured in the shows, as a singer, and also with Avon Long as a dancing team. She left the Cotton Club to become the featured singer in Noble Sissle's Band for a year, and soon afterwards was featured in Lew Leslie's " Blackbirds of 1940." Lena first came into the limelight when she became the vocalist with Charlie Barnet's Orchestra, thus being the first Negro girl to be featured with a white dance band. Afterwards other white orchestras followed Barnet's example and engaged Negro girls as vocalists, but Lena Horne was the pioneer. Then followed successful engagements as a singer at the Café Society in New York, and at the Mocambo in Hollywood where Lena was seen by a film executive and offered her first major screen rôle as a Caribbean singer in Metro-Goldwyn-Mayer's " Panama Hattie " in 1942 ; (she had previously appeared in some short films and also in an independent Negro film, " The Duke Is Tops ").

At that time, Metro-Goldwyn-Mayer were planning to make a film version of the successful Broadway all-Negro show " Cabin In The Sky " and Lena Horne appeared to be the obvious choice for the part of the vivacious Georgia Brown. Her subsequent test showed that she was a screen find and her appearance in this film resulted in her being awarded a seven year contract by M.-G.-M. (in itself an innovation since coloured players invariably work as free-lances). Lena was loaned to Twentieth-Century Fox to play the lead in the all-Negro musical " Stormy Weather," and since then has been seen in a number of musical films for M.-G.-M., including " By Hook Or By Crook," " Thousands Cheer," " Broadway Rhythm," " Two Girls And A Sailor " and " Ziegfeld Follies." (She was deleted completely from the latter by the Memphis Censor.) In " Till The Clouds Roll By " she is co-starred with Judy Garland, Frank Sinatra and Robert Walker in a screen biography of the late Jerome Kern. This film marks her best billing to date, and it is possible that Lena Horne may yet make history and achieve something not known in Hollywood so far—stardom of a Negro in a film also featuring white players.

The rise to world fame and popularity of Lena Horne has been rapid and astonishing. She is a favourite with white audiences (and incidentally was a pin-up girl of thousands of white soldiers, as well as Negro G.I.s, during the war). Her beauty and personality have made her the most photographed Negro in the world, and her appearances in films have in themselves constituted great steps forward towards the general acceptance by American audiences of coloured people in leading film rôles. Perhaps it is too soon to assess the importance of Lena Horne's contribution to the cinema, for she has as yet appeared only in musical productions as a singer, as so many Negroes have done before her. In the two films in which she was given an opportunity to act,* namely " Cabin In The Sky " and " Stormy Weather," the entire cast was coloured—Jim Crow productions. Thus this actress has yet to make an appearance in a Hollywood film, playing an ordinary Negro girl in a story also featuring white actors. It will be seen, therefore, that Hollywood has again side-stepped the issue. Lena Horne is a star in Negro films and also of Negro *sections* in musical films, but she has not yet been given the chance to do what she most wants to—to play an ordinary girl of her race in a Hollywood film with an everyday American background.

Lena Horne feels very strongly about this. As she has declared : " I am not so much interested in playing parts of conventional glamour girls or even in being called the most glamorous Negro

*In " Leader Magazine," October 11th. 1947, James Mason included Lena among his list of the Six Best Actresses in Hollywood !

actress. I would rather establish myself as a prototype of the women of my race whose beauty both of body and character has never been properly presented to the public. As in any other group, they are the moving forces behind most of the accomplishments of the Negro race, and they deserve recognition. In this recognition I aim to play a leading part." Lena goes on to add : " It is a strange twist of fate that Hollywood publicity has labelled me ' tops,' ' unmatched,' and so on. As a matter of fact, this is quite untrue ; any Negro community can produce girls who measure favourably with Hollywood standards."

Lena, who is known for her downright and courageous attitude towards Hollywood attempts at discrimination, and for her refusal to play in stage or screen rôles which do not reflect credit on the Negro race as a whole, must rank as one of the most significant names in Negro theatrical history. (She entered the limelight in 1946 by refusing Broadway stardom in the play " St. Louis Woman," giving as her reason that the stereotyped Negro character she was asked to play did not realistically nor typically portray her people ; and this takes courage.) When she arrived in Hollywood she proved to be modest, sensible and likeable ; now that she has settled down to her screen career Lena is still modest, but she has become outspoken, condemning all forms of discrimination against her race in both the cinema and the theatre.

She is on the board of directors of the Hollywood Screen Actors' Guild, representing the Negro contingent in films, and it is under her leadership that Hollywood's coloured actors have become more militant, socially conscious and reluctant to accept stereotyped parts. Her immense popularity, like Paul Robeson's, is Lena's greatest weapon in her campaign for a fair deal for Negroes everywhere. Because of her screen prominence her influence is inestimable, and she is a valuable fighter, in the very front rank of the modern Negro struggle for progress.

Lena is today the most successful coloured actress in films, but as she says, " I am lucky. I am thankful for the chance I have been given to give my children an education and some sort of security. Indeed this may be the first generation in the history of our race where Negro families will have something to leave to their children. And that is something to think about."

Her ambition is to make a success as a straight actress. " I am gratified," she remarks, " that people accept my singing, but that's really a sort of frustration. I always wanted to be an actress ever since I travelled around with my mother in the Lafayette Stock Company. But it is easier for a coloured person to be a singer than an actress ; one's colour is a factor to be reckoned with in every field. A singer is accepted when an actress is not. Hollywood, however, has been very kind to me and has, I believe, presented me to the best of its ability."

Lena is a serious person, an omnivorous reader, intensely interested in world affairs, and particularly in race relations. She wants to be accepted by Hollywood and by filmgoers everywhere as a Negro girl, a symbol of her race, and says that her most exciting reading consists of books dealing with the distinguished coloured people of the past. One of her most satisfying experiences, she declares, was when she launched the Liberty Ship " George Washington Carver," named after the world famous Negro scientist, for whom she has long had an intense admiration.

In an interview with *P.M.*, July 8th, 1943, Lena stated : " All we ask is that the Negro be portrayed as a normal person. Let us see the Negro as a worker, at union meetings, as a voter at the polls, as a Civil Service worker or elected official. The Negro is human, too, you know."

As Charlotte Kay wrote in the magazine *Movieland*, August, 1945 : " Lena Horne is a forthright and intelligent champion of her people. She is proud of the strides they have made so far, and constantly stumps for greater educational opportunity for them. Only through education, she says, can their hopes for a better heritage for their children and their children's children be realised. That better heritage she defines as financial security, economic equality and a cultural background."

Clarence Muse

One of the outstanding character actors in Hollywood, a man who ranks with the Lionel Barrymores, Frank Morgans, Hume Cronyns, Beulah Bondis, Thomas Mitchells and the Spring Byingtons, is that fine and vastly experienced screen player Clarence Muse, who first entered films when he was called to Hollywood some eighteen years ago to play one of the leads in " Hearts In Dixie," the first all-coloured talking film. Muse was born in Baltimore, Maryland, and educated at Dickerson University, where he took a degree in law. As a child he showed great potentialities as a performer and while at the University decided to go on the stage, since he could see that there were few openings for Negro lawyers in the U.S.A. He possessed a very beautiful bass voice and indeed it was as a singer that he first became known on concert tours of the U.S.A. Afterwards he appeared in vaudeville, in a circus and on the radio, and ultimately was connected with every facet of American entertainment.

When the Lafayette Stock Company was founded in New York, Muse was among the founder members and in the seven years in which this famous Negro theatre group operated he was extremely prominent as one of the leading actors. Particularly outstanding were his performances as Svengali and as Dr. Jekyll and Mr. Hyde, in which he scored great successes both in New York and on the subsequent tours to such cities as Chicago, Washington and Baltimore. Clarence played character leads in nearly two hundred plays with the Lafayette Stock Company, and when this historic organisation was finally disbanded he formed his own companies, both straight and musical, to tour the Southern States. In the late 1920's the Clarence Muse Company was a popular and respected theatre group, and Muse himself had a reputation higher than that of any previous Negro actor, with the possible exception of Charles Gilpin.

In a letter to the author in 1946, Muse writes : " I was making my last stand against talking films in Columbus, Ohio, putting on shows at the Ogden Theatre, when a long distance call from Hollywood interrupted me one day at rehearsal. I was offered one of the leading rôles in ' Hearts In Dixie ' by producer William Fox but I was not very impressed. I had never made films before and my one and only love was the theatre ; so, not being interested in the offer, I asked for a sum as salary that was so high as to be ridiculous. To my surprise I received a telegram next day stating that Fox had agreed to my terms, and the part was waiting for me ! Thus in 1928 I went to Hollywood for twelve weeks, and I have stayed there since that time."

Muse has become one of the most well-known faces in Hollywood films. He invariably gives a perfect performance whether as a dignified old family retainer, as a servant with a sense of humour, or as a fiery young rebel of the kind he played in " So Red The Rose." Among the films in which he has been seen in good rôles are " Prestige," " Cabin In The Cotton," " Show Boat,"

" Way Down South," " Is My Face Red," " Tales of Manhattan," " Shadow Of A Doubt " and " In The Meantime Darling." In the latter he played the kind of part which has endeared him to thousands of filmgoers, a sort of sympathetic uncle to the hero of the film, a kindly, benevolent and altogether friendly person who helps to make the course of true love run smooth. This type of character, bringing out many of the good qualities of the Negro race, has become known in Hollywood as " a Clarence Muse part " and certainly nobody can play these rôles better than Muse himself. (It is sad to note, however, that an actor of his calibre is often forced to take " bit " parts of an infinitesimal size, examples being two lines in " Scarlet Street " for Universal and one line in " Night And Day " for Warners.)

He is a man of unusually varied talents ; he has written plays and songs (one of his most famous songs is " When It's Sleepy Time Down South "), and as well as appearing in scores of films he is well known as a stage producer in New York, and also as a screenwriter. He collaborated with Langston Hughes on the screenplays of such films as " Way Down South " and " Broken Strings " ; and in the latter, an interesting independent Negro production, he also starred. Muse was a star of " Hearts In Dixie," his first Hollywood film, and he has since managed to keep his name prominent in spite of the dearth of worth-while Negro parts in most films. Occasionally he has made a trip to New York, there to star in independent Negro films or to produce and appear in a stage play. For the Federal Theatre he produced Hall Johnson's play " Run Lil' Chillun," and for a long period he played the rôle of Porgy on the Pacific Coast. He is one of the most highly respected Hollywood actors, and also holds a position of prominence in the American theatre. Muse realises, however, that there is a dearth of plays or films giving adequate parts to coloured players. As he says : " There are few books and plays that can make good moving pictures in which the part of the Negro could be made dignified, and in which more of a comprehensive picture of the American Negro could be shown to the world. However, these books and plays do exist, and as I see it the only remedy is to keep them in print, create the demand, make them popular until finally will come the time when motion picture producers in America will feel that money can be made with this type of picture. And, when they feel this, the picture *will* be made and made well.

" The set-up in Hollywood is highly commercial," he goes on, " and I do not believe that the film city is in any sense truly creative. I think they reach out for successful books, plays, even people to build up their great industry, and in the material which they buy the Negro is invariably a stereotype. But in my opinion Hollywood would buy and make a best-selling book, a really sensational world-famous novel, even if it featured a Negro as the central character, if the book were successful enough. I don't think politics enters into the question at all. To sum up : Hollywood's treatment of coloured actors is determined only by the material which it buys and by the box office which it serves. As soon as better material, that is material which features the Negro in a more sympathetic light, becomes popular with the mass American public, then Hollywood will follow the trend. Already there have been improvements during the past few years. Let us hope for the time when *popular demand* will cause producers to make good Negro films and also to film good Negro plays and novels."

An intelligent and talented actor, Muse is in the vanguard of the Hollywood movement to improve the treatment of coloured players. He is highly respected and well-paid, and he will, as he once wrote, " keep on trying in my own quiet way to do the best I can with the rôles I am given, to clean them up and make them artistic and realistic. But the actor is essentially the highly finished tool of the author. What we need are more Negro authors and screenwriters. For when they furnish the material we actors can do the rest."

Muse once wrote a pamphlet, *The Dilemma Of The Negro Actor*, in which he showed the actor torn between two desires— the giving of his best talent in a serious way to Negro audiences, or the winning of financial success as a buffoon, clown and dancer before white audiences. His final chapter concluded with these words : " Some day someone is going to write fearlessly about the black man in America. And that will be great drama. The Negro has lived in a world of conflict and struggle for generations and of such influences are sublime works created."

Eddie " Rochester " Anderson'

A popular comedian, Eddie Anderson, has been appearing in films since 1935, and has given some extremely clever performances in a number of Hollywood productions, including his delightful portrayal of Noah in " The Green Pastures " and the faithful old friend of Bette Davis in " Jezebel." But although he has been in films for so long, it is only comparatively recently that Anderson has come into the limelight, and this is due mainly to his radio appearances, playing Jack Benny's amusing valet and confidante, " Rochester," in the popular series. In fact, so much have the public connected his name with this comic character that Anderson has in recent years dropped his real name in favour of his radio nomenclature.

He was born in Oakland, California, and entered show business when a youngster by joining the chorus of the revue " Struttin' Along," and afterwards singing with a vocal trio called " The Three Black Aces." He then went on tour with a band called The California Collegians (which, incidentally, featured a certain young Fred MacMurray on the saxophone). With a background of many years in variety and after undertaking countless vaudeville tours of the United States, Anderson eventually opened as a night-club entertainer at Sebastian's Cotton Club in Los Angeles, where his singing, dancing and remarkable personality made him a favourite for nearly three years. During his period here he made his first radio appearance, and shortly afterwards followed his meeting with comedian Jack Benny, which resulted in a new radio personality being born. Anderson first appeared in a brief sequence as a porter in a Benny programme, but within a few months his part had increased to such importance that he is now featured in the second largest rôle in the popular radio show.

It has been said that Eddie Anderson talks to more Americans every Sunday night than any other coloured man in history. He is one of the most popular of radio comedians and among the leading Hollywood screen personalities. His inimitable voice and expert sense of timing have rocketed him to fame in radio, while his success in Hollywood is due to his fine flair for musical comedy, a photographic personality and a considerable acting talent. Still under forty, "Rochester" is widely popular and has a fine reputation ; he is held in high esteem, not only by Negroes but by white audiences who find him amiable, attractive and talented. Principal Anderson film appearances are in " Gone With The Wind," " Kentucky," " Love Thy Neighbour," " The Music Goes Round," " Topper Returns " and " Kiss The Boys Goodbye," while with Jack Benny he has been seen in an amusing series of productions which include " Man About Town," " Buck Benny Rides Again," and " The Meanest Man In The World." More recently " Rochester " has become a featured player in his own right, and in films like " Cabin In The Sky," " Broadway Rhythm," and " Memory For Two " his rôles have increased in length and significance.

For example in Edward Small's production of " Brewster's Millions " " Rochester " was one of the star names ; likewise he co-starred with Phil Harris in Columbia's " Memory For Two," and was seen in important parts in M.-G.-M's. " The Sailor Takes A Wife " and others. He occupies a distinctive niche in Hollywood; his lovable personality has allowed him to give colour and character to many of his screen rôles.

" Cabin In The Sky " is in a slightly different category since it is an all-Negro film ; in this " Rochester " showed himself to be an excellent actor, running the gamut of emotion from the elation and good humour of the high-spirited dicing and gambling no-good to the genuine repentance of the penitent who sees the error of his ways in the latter part of the film. However, it is with his work in films featuring white actors that we are mostly concerned, for it is largely due to his appearances in these he has become one of the most famous Negro actors in the world today, and certainly one of the most beloved.

Does he follow in the tradition of Stepin Fetchit ? To an extent, yes. He tends to play good-natured, servile, comic, eye-rolling Negroes, but when given the opportunity, he can and does act with dignity and intelligence (an instance was his distinguished performance as Noah). One of the few Negroes occupying important positions in the entertainment world who refuses to commit himself on questions of racial relations, Anderson steers clear of all arguments about racial prejudice and as he puts it, " refuses to propagandise." " Rochester " asserts : " In my opinion a performer is a performer first and last. He has no business making propaganda. People want to be entertained not educated."

But as the magazine *Ebony* declared in the issue of November, 1945 : " Much as he likes to avoid controversy, ' Rochester ' was tossed right into the middle by the town of Memphis when the Censor Board banned his picture ' Brewster's Millions ' because the Negro acted too snappy and socialised too much with white actors in the film." Obviously Eddie " Rochester " Anderson could become a great power for good. His considerable popularity could surely be harnessed in the struggle of his people for social and artistic justice ; but it remains to be seen whether he will contrive to remain merely as a popular performer, or take his place with Robeson, Ingram, Lena Horne and the others who form the vanguard of the social-conscious and outspoken members of their race.

Ethel Waters

In 1924 Ethel Waters first introduced the song " Dinah " to New Yorkers, and since that time she has been a well-known name in the American musical and legitimate theatre. Her initial attempt at singing was at an amateur performance in Philadelphia, when she sang " St. Louis Blues." Ethel was a great success and decided to go on the stage professionally. During the next ten years she played in nearly every Negro theatre in the Southern States, as well as most of those in the larger Northern cities. In 1927 she made her first Broadway stage appearance in " Africana," since when she has been a tremendous and well-deserved success in such New York productions as " Blackbirds," " Rhapsody In Black," " As Thousands Cheer," " At Home Abroad " and " Mamba's Daughters." One of the most beloved of all Negro personalities, Ethel Waters ranks with Robeson among the best-known Negroes in the world of the theatre. In 1929 she made her first film appearance, singing in Warners' musical " On With the Show," and she afterwards starred in a short film called " The Cotton Club, New York." But Ethel preferred acting before flesh and blood audiences and, as film rôles for coloured actresses were limited, she returned to the stage. It was not until 1942, following her tremendous success in the Broadway play " Mamba's Daughters," that Ethel returned to Hollywood, appearing in an important rôle in M.-G.-M's. " Cairo," and following this by co-starring, with " Rochester " and Lena Horne, in " Cabin In The Sky."

Ethel was also seen as Paul Robeson's wife in the Negro sequence in " Tales Of Manhattan," and she confessed afterwards that she was not satisfied with her rôle in this film, which represented her as the typical spiritual-singing, religious, simple mammy of the South. However, in " Cabin In The Sky " she had much better opportunities and gave a performance full of richness and beauty. Long famous as a singer, she reached in this film full stature as an actress ; indeed some critics have claimed that her scenes at her feckless husband's death-bed are among the most moving in the annals of cinema acting. But as one reviewer remarked of her, " When Miss Waters finally decides to take that old coloured bandanna from her head, she will step into a place among the foremost Negro screen artists."

It is reported that the filming of " Cabin In The Sky " was held up at times because Miss Waters did not agree with the way in which her part was shaping. She possessed certain preconceived notions concerning the dignity and sincerity of her part of Petunia Jackson and she would not give way to the screenwriters who sought to invest it with the usual degree of out-dated, so-called Negroid humour. As she said, " The deeper religious emotions of Petunia could not be made light of, or in any way taken as a joke. I hope to establish this character as symbolic of one of the moral values for which men go to war, as symbolic of all that is best among Negro women." These are encouraging words from an actress who has been a stage star for more than twenty-five years, and has proved to have the potentialities which would ensure her becoming a really great screen personality.

Butterfly McQueen

Gauche, likeable, eccentric Butterfly McQueen has risen to screen fame by having a squeaky voice. She is, however, a talented actress, with a long stage background, and only recently have film critics come to realise that, almost imperceptibly, she has joined the ranks of the Hollywood " reliables " who never give a bad performance. Butterfly is one of those fortunate actresses, a " critics' darling " ; she has never received a bad notice for her acting on stage or screen. It was in the play " Brown Sugar," produced on Broadway by George Abbott, that she first came to the attention of dramatic critics in New York. The play ran for only three days, but Butterfly was given a special critics' award for her work, and as a result of this George Abbott signed her as a member of his celebrated stock company.

In such productions as " What A Life " and " Brother Rat," both enjoying long runs in New York, the diminutive coloured actress scored further successes, but her biggest triumph came when she played Puck in the Benny Goodman-Louis Armstrong musical " Swingin' The Dream " (based loosely, it is said, on Shakespeare's " A Midsummer Night's Dream "). It was as a result of this that Butterfly was given her first film opportunity in 1939 in David Selznick's " Gone With The Wind," following which she appeared for M.-G.-M. in " The Women " and " Cabin In The Sky," among others. Since then she has been seen in a number of comic maid characters, in fact in so many of them that she often declared herself to be heartily tired of being cast in the same perpetual groove.

And at last, in 1946, Butterfly issued a statement saying that following her appearances in Warners' " Mildred Pierce " and Selznick's " Duel In The Sun," she would no longer accept the sort of parts which she had previously been forced to play. Undoubtedly she has since found herself in the cleft stick which awaits all independent Negro film players—to act stereotypes or starve. Nevertheless it is to be hoped that her courageous stand will have some effect on Hollywood opinion, and in encouraging other Negro rebels. And in any case, one must applaud her strength of character in taking such a decision for her principles at a time when her acting in Warners' " Mildred Pierce " has served to indicate her talent for comedy and her perfect film timing (and, incidentally, resulted in her being offered several comic maid rôles—which she refused).

Well-known on the radio in ordinary American parts, not necessarily servile or Negroid (she once walked out of a radio rôle in a Jack Benny programme, protesting over the part of a stupid maid), Butterfly McQueen is on the fringe of a promising film career. Hollywood producers have said that although she is such a notable comedienne she has the capabilities of playing strong dramatic rôles, but as to that events will give a further indication. At any rate this actress has a flair for cinema and a love of acting.

Right: *Huckleberry Finn* directed by Richard Thorpe. Left: *The Song Of The South* produced by Walt Disney.

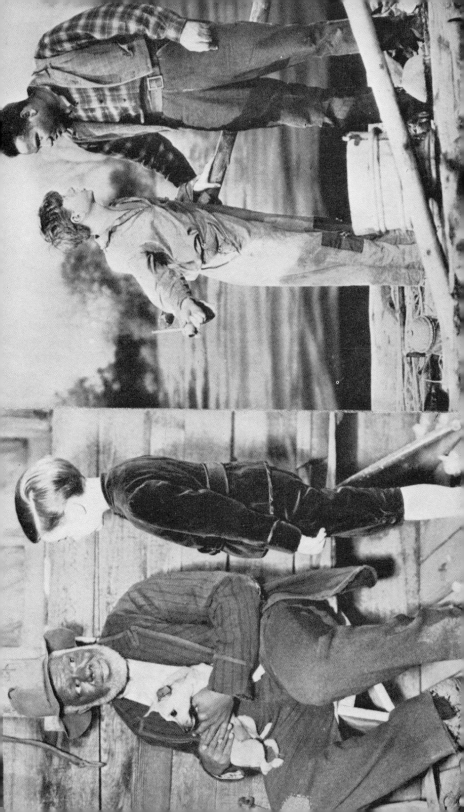

It would be heartening to be able to record incidents of other Negro players making protests against Hollywood's ever-prevalent colour prejudice, but unfortunately this has not happened often. For more than a year Butterfly was boycotted by film agents because of her refusal to accept what are described as " dumb coloured-maid parts," but she made a brave attempt to establish the right of her people to a just representation in the cinema.

Kenneth Spencer

In 1939 a young Negro giant understudied Paul Robeson in the Broadway musical " John Henry." His name was Kenneth Spencer, an actor who has recently invited comparison with Robeson due to his magnificent presence, physique and beautiful deep voice. He studied music at the Eastman School in Rochester, New York, and followed this with a brief Canadian concert tour. With the St. Louis Opera Company he appeared in " Show Boat," and afterwards scored a great success at the Hollywood Bowl in the opera " Gettysburg," which brought him to the notice of the studios. He received some film offers as a result of the opera, but decided in favour of continuing his concert career. In 1941 he made his New York concert début and following this he was heard extensively on his own radio programme and in many concerts in all parts of the U.S.A. At last he accepted a film offer and in 1943 he went to Hollywood to play a leading part in the M.-G.-M. production of " Cabin In The Sky," directed by Vincente Minnelli. Following this he appeared in " Bataan," in which he enjoyed a personal success.

In this film Spencer played the part of a young Negro G.I., Private Wesley Eeps, and so sincere and likeable was his personality and so powerful his acting that one soon forgot the colour of his skin, as one watched him sharing the same trials and sacrifices as his fellow soldiers, a small contingent left to defend the post as the Japs attacked unceasingly night and day. " Bataan," something of a revolution in its treatment of the coloured soldier in the U.S. Army, was a praiseworthy film and did much to further race relations; not the least of its achievements

Above left : PAUL ROBESON. Above right : REX INGRAM. Below left : EDDIE " ROCHESTER " ANDERSON. Below right : ORLANDO MARTINS.

was that it brought Kenneth to the notice of filmgoers in a fine and well written part.

Spencer's excellent baritone voice had made a deep impression at concerts and on the many radio programmes in which he has featured, and it is likely that his future will be divided between the concert stage and Hollywood. Since he is good-looking, dignified and an extremely talented actor and singer, it is to be hoped that he will remain in movies, for there are very few young Negroes of his type in the film city.

He likes film acting, and as he says : " Of the pictures I have made, I think I enjoyed ' Bataan ' most. This film was so real that it excited me. Every character was a true replica of those Americans who gave their lives at Bataan in the early days of the war. In addition I felt great sympathy in the drawing of the Negro soldier, and I feel that director Tay Garnett understood that my part, to an extent, represented the whole of the four million Negroes in the fighting services. I hope to do more films and to play further parts like the one in ' Bataan.' "

But Kenneth Spencer shares the same dilemma confronting Todd Duncan, Gordon Heath and other good-looking coloured actors in Hollywood, since there are so few films made which require a handsome, personable Negro in a sympathetic part. Either Spencer must conform to pattern, and take the meagre film rôles offered him, or else he can make a stand as Duncan did a few years ago. It is likely that Spencer's high reputation on the concert platform will guarantee his income for some time to come, which means that he can possibly be independent of Hollywood. Thus he should be in a position to accept only those screen rôles which are equivalent in significance and importance to those he played in " Cabin In The Sky " and " Bataan " and, as he has declared himself to be highly sensitive on racial questions and screen characterisation, we hope we shall see him soon in rôles worthy of his ability and which reflect no discredit upon his race.

Louise Beavers and Hattie McDaniel

" The Eternal Mammy Of Hollywood " is a title which may be shared by two actresses, Hattie McDaniel and Louise Beavers. Miss Beavers made a corner in the 1930's in the part of the good-hearted menial who always showed a keen interest in the personal affairs of her beloved master or mistress, and one encountered her ample figure and wide grin on the screen in dozens of movies. Lately she has been superseded to some extent by Miss McDaniel, who achieved the height of film acclaim in 1940 by winning an Academy Award for her acting in " Gone With The Wind." Both actresses are similar in style and appearance ; and both must share a responsibility in helping to perpetuate the " mammy " stereotype.

Louise Beavers was born in Cincinnati, Ohio, and soon afterwards went with her parents to live in Pasadena, California, being educated at Pasadena High School. She entered show business as a singer and had some experience of the legitimate stage before making her first film in 1924. Her many motion pictures include " Glad Rag Doll," " Barnum Was Right," " Coquette," " Reckless Living," " Ladies Of The Big House," " Girl Missing," " Blonde Bombshell," and literally dozens of others. Her appearance as the gentle, meek mammy in " Imitation Of Life " in 1934 aroused a storm of protest, but no one could deny that she acted with skill and tenderness. This is often the way with coloured players, genuine ability being wasted on mediocre material.

Other pictures in which she has appeared in recent years are " Virginia," " West Of The Pecos," " Farewell To Romance," " Reap The Wild Wind," " Holiday Inn," " The Big Street," " Seven Sweethearts," " Top Man," " Follow The Boys " and " Barbary Coast Gent." In " Jack London " she was able to give some sort of characterisation to a stereotyped rôle, and her scenes with the fiery, progressive London, played by Michael O'Shea, indicated that, given an opportunity, Louise could be an interesting dramatic actress. She had, in fact, demonstrated this in " Imitation Of Life " twelve years before, but Hollywood did not proceed to do anything much about it then, and her parts have rarely varied during her lengthy film career. Louise Beavers has been performing in the same groove since 1924, and possibly could not get out of it now, even if she wanted to. Her film career is a striking example of wasted talent.

The same may be said of clever Hattie McDaniel, who since entering films in 1933 has never managed to avoid playing humorous coloured servants except in one or two instances. Born in Wichita, Kansas, Hattie won a medal in dramatic art given by the White Women's Christian Temperance Association in 1916, and thenceforth made the stage her career. She worked mainly in Denver, the city where she was educated and brought up, and it was here that she achieved the distinction of being the first coloured girl ever to sing on the American radio. As a member of Professor George Morrison's coloured orchestra, the girl toured all over the U.S.A. during 1924 and 1925, finally forming her own act in Kansas City. Later on, it was in " Show Boat " that she became well-known on the stage, playing in the Edna Ferber-Jerome Kern operetta in every important city in the United States, before making her motion picture début in 1933 in Paramount's " The Story Of Temple Drake."

Since then Hattie has gained an enviable reputation and has worked more consistently in Hollywood than any other coloured actress. She has been seen in such films as " Blonde Venus," " I'm No Angel," " Judge Priest," " The Little Colonel," " Saratoga," and " Nothing Sacred " ; and also " Gone With The Wind," for which she received high praise from the critics. In the past few years Hattie has repeated her successful " Gone With The Wind " performance in similar rôles, good-natured mammys, in " Maryland," " Affectionately Yours," " The Great Lie," " The Male Animal," and " George Washington Slept Here."

In John Huston's " In This Our Life " she had a somewhat different part as the kindly mother of the Negro boy who wants to get on in the world and spends his spare time studying law. She cannot understand his desire to be anything other than a servant and believes that no good will come of his " unnatural ambition." And when, later, he is falsely accused of reckless driving and killing two people, the Negro woman breaks down and cries : " Ah knew this would happen if he tried to better himself. His place is with us, with the servants ; he shouldn't try to make himself better than he is ! " Hattie gave a beautifully restrained performance, which proved that she could act when given worth-while parts ; but she soon returned to the cap and apron. Hollywood had labelled her " Mammy," and " Mammy " she had to remain.

In this familiar characterisation Hattie has brightened a score of motion pictures since " Gone With The Wind." I can recall " Johnny Vagabond," " Janie," " Since You Went Away " and " Three's A Family." In the Selznick film Hattie offended the South by behaving too familiarly with the lady of the house and her gentleman friend, played by Claudette Colbert and Joseph

Cotten, while it is interesting to note that for her performance as the feckless maid with a *penchant* for gin in " Three's A Family " the portly actress was the object of severe criticism from members of her own race ! Negro opinion considered that the depicting of a Negro maid as an unreliable drunk was false and malicious, and that Hattie should have refused to play the part or else try to " clean it up." This actress has been the recipient of much of this type of criticism for some time, and is apparently little concerned with it.

During the past few years there has been only one other occasion when she did not play her usual rôle. This was in Warners' " Thank Your Lucky Stars," in which she featured in a particularly tasteless Jim Crow sequence with Willie Best. It seems a real pity that such an accomplished actress as Hattie McDaniel cannot use her popularity with screen audiences as a lever to ensure better and more dignified rôles from Hollywood producers.

Robert Adams

Robert Adams is now the leading Negro film actor in Europe. Just over ten years ago he arrived in England from the West Indies with exactly sixpence-halfpenny in his pocket ; since then he has been labourer, wrestler, private tutor, singer and actor. He bears many resemblances to Paul Robeson, with whom he has often acted on the stage and in films—he is over six feet tall, is an athlete, a singer and a lawyer. Like Robeson, he came into the theatre because it was one of the few professions in which a Negro could reach the top. For Adams, however, it has been a long, hard and difficult journey ; but today he is a star in British films and stands at the top of his profession, a position he deserves after ten years of stuggle.

Born of humble parents in Georgetown, British Guiana, forty years ago, Bob showed a remarkable aptitude for learning, and obtained scholarships quickly to high school and college, finally becoming a teacher at a Georgetown school. In between teaching he organised school shows, producing and acting in amateur plays, and also giving a number of concerts, for he possessed a fine tenor voice and a good stage presence. He had long wanted to act professionally but realised that there was very little opportunity to do so in the West Indies, where few theatrical activities flourished. For most West Indians Britain is the Mother-country, and eventually Bob's eyes turned eastwards towards London. He made up his mind to visit Europe, and finally, in 1934, he decided to try his luck in England, spending all his savings to book his passage to Plymouth.

Adams arrived here one night, a young giant of a man, full of ambition, eager to get to London and to work in the theatre. He had to borrow his fare from Southampton to Waterloo, but when he got to the capital he found that things were more difficult than he had imagined. The stage was not open to inexperienced Colonials, and parts for coloured people in the London theatre were few and far between. Months flew past, months of odd jobs as a labourer, and finally the Negro was persuaded by a sports promoter to become a professional wrestler. His splendid physique and background of athletics served him well and for more than a year Robert Adams was a well-known name in European wrestling circles. When he had become Heavyweight Champion of the British Empire, however, Bob decided that it was time to try to establish himself on the stage. He had achieved some sort of independence through wrestling, and could afford to spend a little time in trying to crash the film world. At last he started as a small-part player, his first film job being a very minor rôle in the Alexander Korda production " Sanders Of The River," Then Bob managed to get other and better parts, principally in such films as " Midshipman Easy," and " Song Of Freedom " and " King Solomon's Mines " (in both of which he acted with Paul Robeson). In " Song Of Freedom " he had a comic rôle as Zinga's friend Monty and was extremely amusing, the part contrasting vividly with that of the villainous Negro chieftain which he played in the Rider Haggard film.

He made his London stage début in André van Gyseghem's production of " Stevedore," by George Sklar and Paul Peters at the Embassy Theatre. Since then he has been seen on the stage in such plays as " You Can't Take It With You," " Toussaint L'Ouverture," " Chastity My Brother," " Colony " (in which he played the leading rôle, a West Indian strike-leader), " The House Of Jeffreys," " The Little Foxes," " The Judgment Of Dr. Johnson," " Cellar," " Caviar To The General," and others. More recently Adams formed the London Negro Repertory Theatre, a group of actors organised to perform plays giving

Negroes worth-while rôles and presenting racial problems on the stage. At London's leading political playhouse, Unity Theatre, Adams was seen in 1946 as the tragic Jim in Eugene O'Neill's " All God's Chillun Got Wings " with members of his group. Later he plans to extend the work of his Negro Theatre and may soon take it on a tour of the U.S.A. and the British Empire under the auspices of the British Council.

In the English cinema Robert Adams has become prominent very recently. He has been featured in Gainsborough's " Old Bones Of The River," the M.O.I. feature " An African In London," and also in " It Happened One Sunday," " Dreaming," and " Caesar and Cleopatra." But it is in the Two Cities film " Men Of Two Worlds," directed by Thorold Dickinson, that Adams receives his most important screen part to date. He is featured in the film with Eric Portman and Phyllis Calvert, and is equal to them both in billing and story importance. For this Adams had to act the part of an African composer and pianist ; in six months he learned to play the piano sufficiently well for the rôle (and is now a more than adequate pianist). This is just another indication of Bob's exceptional thirst for knowledge and experience and his capacity for hard work. In between studying his stage and screen parts, he writes plays, articles, prepares lectures and studies law and music ; he recently passed his first law examination. His book on the West Indies, " Caribbean Hurricane," will be published shortly, he has written several plays, and his screen story about Haiti may be made into a British film some time next year.

For his performance as Kisenga in " Men Of Two Worlds " Adams received much favourable comment from the British critics. A. E. Wilson in the *Star* said : " Robert Adams, with his stalwart figure, his pleasant personality and his resonant voice, is particularly striking as Kisenga." Dilys Powell in the *Sunday Times* wrote : " There is a moving piece of acting by Robert Adams," while Joan Lester in *Reynolds News* remarked on " the fine voice and dignity which he brought to the screen."

Adams is an unusually intelligent and sensitive person, who feels very strongly on questions relating to the colour problem both on the stage and the screen. He hopes to present his viewpoint on the stage with his Negro Theatre, and considers that only through obtaining important parts can coloured actors influence the trend in films and theatre. " If," he says, " all my screen parts were, for example, as dignified, human and moving as the one in ' Men Of Two Worlds,' then one might soon be able to influence cinemagoers in the right direction. And if they see Negroes playing cultured, intelligent people often enough, they will begin to realise that the coloured man is not necessarily a superstitious, hymn-singing buffoon."

Adams stated recently, in a conversation with the author : " The most powerful of all vehicles of education has been and still is the screen. Much has been written of this by way of criticism and I will not add a great deal except to remark upon some of the ways in which we have made progress. The white man shows his ghettoes and his Cockneys and his slums on the screen, but he counter-balances this with a positive and constructive picture of his people, so that white audiences can rejoice at the progress at the same time as they contemplate the shortcomings. But the portrayal of the Negro has always concentrated on the latter— the shoe-shine boy, Pullman porter, semi-idiot *a la* Stepin Fetchit, hallelujah-shouters as in ' The Green Pastures,' the rolling-eyed, funny man like ' Rochester,' the black mammy with the cap and apron and the fat smile, the half-naked savage as in ' Sanders Of The River ' and many others of that *genre*.

" Hollywood has much to answer for, but British studios have had the courage to make a step forward. In ' Midshipman Easy,' ' Song Of Freedom,' ' The Proud Valley ' and a few others, Negroes were not exactly jungle types. And now further progress has been made in ' Men Of Two Worlds,' the first picture in the history of the screen where a Negro has a real starring opportunity in company with white actors. Some light is indeed breaking into what was formerly unrelieved darkness, and the courage that urged the making of ' Men Of Two Worlds ' is the courage that is breaking down the barriers of misunderstanding and misrepresentation of my people. Out of the suffering of the last war people have learned to have a measure of understanding ; and we wish earnestly that this spirit of co-operation and helpfulness will persist. The result will be a real cementing of the bonds of empire and a confirmation of the Christian message—love one another."

Orlando Martins

In 1946, for his magnificent work as the witch doctor, Magole, in Thorold Dickinson's " Men Of Two Worlds," Orlando Martins received great praise from the Press. He has thus come into prominence after twenty years of professional acting, for he has had a long and interesting career, beginning with an appearance with the Diaghileff Ballet in London early in the 1920's. His part in " Men Of Two Worlds " is his most important to date, and is the culmination of many years of hard and constant work. Born in Lagos, West Africa, in 1900, Orlando took his school certificate and went to work as a clerk for a French firm. He has very vivid recollections of the First World War : his grandmother became a prisoner of war when the Germans held the Cameroons, and it was her suffering at German hands that caused Martins to give up his job in Africa and come to London, with the object of joining up in the British Navy. He was too young, however, to get into the Navy, and managed to join the Merchant Marine, serving until the end of the war.

In the post-war years Orlando did many things ; he was successively a wrestler, a " super " with the ballet, a snake-charmer with Lord John Sanger's Circus and an extra in silent films. His first British movie part was in " If Youth But Knew," which starred Godfrey Tearle, and since that time he has appeared in numerous films, including " Black Libel," " Tiger Bay," " Sanders Of The River," " Song Of Freedom," " Jericho," and " Murder In Soho." He made his début as an actor on the legitimate stage at the Criterion Theatre in 1930 in the play " When Blue Hills Laughed," and afterwards was seen as Bobo Valentine in André van Gyseghem's production of " Stevedore," in which Paul Robeson played Lonnie. In 1938 Orlando played the rôle of Boukman in " Toussaint L'Ouverture " at the Westminster, but did not really come into theatrical prominence until he played the leading Scottsboro' boy, Heywood Patterson, in André van Gyseghem's production of John Wexley's fine play " They Shall Not Die," a dramatisation of one of the great injustices of American legal history. Afterwards Herbert Marshall chose him to play the lead in Geoffrey Trease's new play " Colony " at Unity Theatre, in which Martins alternated the part with Robert Adams.

During the war Orlando was for four years engaged in important war work, and was consequently unable to continue his professional career. In 1945, however, he returned to the London stage, playing Blossom in John Patrick's " The Hasty Heart," produced by Murray Macdonald at the Aldwych Theatre, a performance for which he received a great deal of appreciation, one critic declaring that " he almost stole the show without uttering a single word."

He has also recently appeared in three films, " Good-Time Girl," " The Man From Morocco " and " Men Of Two Worlds." In " The Man From Morocco " he gave a fine performance as Jerimiah, the Negro International Brigadier, and it was following his good work in this production that director Thorold Dickinson cast him for his most important part to date. Magole was a real triumph for Orlando, the culmination of many years of hard work in the theatre and in films. And Martins is deeply grateful to Dickinson for not seeking Negro talent in the U.S.A., preferring to give British coloured actors an opportunity to prove that we have the talent here in this country, if only it is given the chance. As he said : " I am proud and happy to have been connected with the production of a truly magnificent film, which I am sure will do a great deal to sweep away colour prejudice."

Orlando is married and has a son of eighteen, a musician. The African actor has no particular preference for either stage or screen, but likes to play rôles which have some character in them, no matter whether they are heroic or villainous. " Rather," he remarks, " have a Negro villain than yet another stupid Negro servant." Martins believes further that talent in any field will break down discrimination by itself. " If you are good enough as an actor," he declares, " you will be given good parts and receive fair treatment." And that is exactly what Orlando Martins has succeeded in doing during his professional career. His motto would seem to be " Merit destroys discrimination " (which, however, may hold true in Europe but, unfortunately, not so true in the United States).

Martins is a tall, powerful figure of a man with a deep bass voice, friendly, hospitable, and with a grand sense of humour. He is keenly interested in the foundation of a Negro Theatre in London. As he points out : " If this ever comes into being it will mean not only that Negro talent in every theatre art can be shown to the world, but a continuity of employment for this talent which is now going sadly to waste." Like Robert Adams and the other coloured actors in " Men Of Two Worlds," Orlando is happy to have been given an opportunity in this film, and hopes to do others like it. " It is a courageous venture," he adds, " and I hope that it will go a long way towards showing Africa and her people as they really are to the millions of ignorant unthinking people who regard the African as just a savage. The film shows African and European working side by side in amity and understanding, and that is how it should be."

Some Other Players

In addition to the aforementioned stars and featured players in Hollywood there are quite a number of well-known coloured character actors who have given consistently good performances over a long period. One of the earliest-known Negro film actors was Noble Johnson, born in Colorado Springs more than fifty years ago. He has been in pictures for some thirty years, and was one of the best-known character actors on the silent screen. He entered films in " Topsy And Eva," followed by " The Ten Commandments," " Gateway Of The Moon " and many others. (He played Friday in " Robinson Crusoe," in 1922, one of the few Negroid parts in which he has acted.) His first sound film was " Black Waters " in 1929, since when he has been seen in dozens of productions, including " Moby Dick," " She," " Lives Of A Bengal Lancer," " Lost Horizon " and " The Ghost Breakers," (in which he gave a terrifying performance as a zombie). More recently Johnson has appeared in fairly prominent rôles in " The Cowboy And The Lady," " Jungle Book," and " The Desert Song." This actor has achieved a great distinction ; he is probably the only Negro actor who has acted in non-Negroid parts, for he has been seen as a Mexican, Chinese, Spaniard, Cuban, Tibetan, South American—and even as an Eskimo. (He was a Tartar in " Hounds Of Zaroff ".) It is, indeed, rare that one finds him playing American Negro rôles, since he is light-skinned and quite European in appearance.

Another old-timer is George Reed, who was seen as long ago as 1915 in " The Birth Of A Nation " and other silent films. He was born in Georgia in 1867, and began his movie career in a screen version of " Uncle Tom's Cabin," afterwards acting in others for the old Selig Studio. His career has been long and distinguished, and his fine voice and presence have added character to many coloured retainer rôles. I remember him particularly in the Griffith film, and also in more recent productions such as " River Of Romance," " The Witching Hour," " The Green Pastures," " So Red The Rose," " In Old Kentucky," " The Cowboy And The Lady," " Swanee River," " Dr. Gillespie's New Assistant," " Tales Of Manhattan," and " Home In Indiana." Reed is a white-haired lovable actor whom most filmgoers know by sight, even if they are not aware of his name. He has natural dignity, tries bravely to bring this quality to some of his more thankless rôles, and has been responsible for a great deal of good film acting during his thirty-five years in Hollywood.

Stepin Fetchit, so prominent in the early 1930's, appears to have disappeared from films latterly ; his last productions being " It's Spring Again " and " His Exciting Night," both made in 1939. He has had a remarkable career. Born in 1902 in Key West, Florida, his real name is Lincoln Theodore Perry. After making his stage début in musical comedy he took the name he later made famous and appeared in his first film, " Show Boat," for Universal. Following " Big Time," and " Movietone Follies Of 1929," Fetchit was awarded with a long-term contract by Fox, and within the next few years he is reported to have earned fabulous sums. This was the period of the development of the sound film, the crazy days of the early talkies, and Fetchit rocketed to fame with his wide-grinned inanity, shuffling and dawdling, bringing to the screens of the world the eternal American conception of the " darky."

In quick succession he appeared in " Hearts In Dixie," " Salute," " The Ghost Talks," " Stand Up And Cheer," " Carolina," " Judge Priest," " David Harum," " The Country Chairman," " Steamboat Round The Bend," and " Virginia Judge." But gradually his popularity lessened, as audiences grew tired of the same performance in film after film, and he has not made an appearance in a major film for six or seven years. Stepin Fetchit typified all that is worst in the Negro character ; he debased his race in film after film, year after year. And he had many imitators, some of whom are still playing the perpetual type of " nigger " rôle in Hollywood today.

The most prominent of these are Willie Best and Mantan Moreland. Best was for some years known as Sleep 'n' Eat, but was eventually persuaded to use his real name for screen purposes.

Born in Mississippi, he worked with a travelling show and toured in California, finally reaching Hollywood, where under the name Sleep 'n' Eat he appeared in a series of short comedies. These were made in the tradition of " Rastus," " Sambo " and Octavius Roy Cohen, with the tall, thin Negro going through all the hackneyed rigmarole of the vaudeville black-face comedian. Eventually he graduated to feature films by playing stooge to comedians Wheeler and Woolsey in such productions as "Kentucky Kernels " and " The Nitwits," after which he reverted to his own name and was put under contract by R.K.O. Radio.

His films for R.K.O. and other companies include " West Of The Pecos," " Murder On A Honeymoon," " The Arizonan," " The Littlest Rebel," " Nancy Drew, Detective," "Blondie," " Spring Madness," " I Take This Woman," and " The Ghost Breakers." For Paramount he has made a number of recent appearances, invariably as a gangling, dim-witted man-servant in true Fetchit tradition (an example being " The Bride Wore Boots ") even to the lazy walk, the rolling eyes, the trembling lower lip and the continual air of a frightened rabbit at the approach of danger in any form.

His constant appearances as the amiable stereotype are duplicated by Mantan Moreland, an actor who has come into prominence only comparatively recently. A graduate from the New York vaudeville stage, he commenced his film career in 1938 in " Frontier Scout," followed by " Irish Luck," " Riders Of The Frontier," " Millionaire Playboy " and other Hollywood films. In 1940 he returned to New York to star in an independent Negro production, " Mr. Washington Goes To Town " ; and the standard of his work in this film may be gauged by one of the now-notorious line of dialogue he used in it : " Pork chops is the fondest thing I is of ! "

In the past few years Moreland has made dozens of Hollywood appearances, and was prominently featured with white actor Frankie Darro in a series for Monogram. Some of his pictures are " King Of The Zombies," " The Gang's All Here," " Law Of The Jungle," " Footlight Serenade," " Girl Trouble," " Eyes In The Night," " Melody Parade," and about a dozen in the " Charlie Chan " series made for Monogram. In the latter he plays the coloured chauffeur to Sydney Toler's Charlie Chan, a stooge in true tradition. No Negro actor has ever rolled his eyes with such abandon as Moreland, no coloured actor has ever tried so hard to revert

181

to the Stepin Fetchit sub-human characterisation. He is the accepted U.S.A. idea of the Negro clown supreme, and performs before the cameras like a well-trained monkey. This is a pity, for Moreland is a fine actor with a delightful sense of humour. He was excellent as one of the Devil's myrmidons in " Cabin In The Sky," and even better as a vaudeville comedian, in partnership with Ben Carter, in "Bowery To Broadway," but Hollywood will obviously keep him playing " nigger " parts for as long as they want him to. Recently he was seen in " Charlie Chan In Black Magic," " The Red Dragon," " Shanghai Cobra," " Dark Alibi," " The Scarlet Clue," " The Jade Mask," and others in the Monogram series, but it is significant that as he was unable to appear in some of the latest Charlie Chan productions, being busy at another studio, his place was taken by Willie Best, who stepped easily into the stereotype. In a review of one of these films, " The Red Dragon," the critic in *Kinematograph Weekly*, September, 1946, ended his notice with these words : " Willie Best makes the most of the conventional coloured comedy relief." Need more be said ?

An actress for whom I have long had a great admiration is Theresa Harris, a beautiful Negro girl with a striking screen presence who has too rarely been given an opportunity to reveal her ability. She has been appearing in Hollywood films for some ten years, and one remembers her particularly in " Baby Face," " Blood Money," " The Toy Wife " and " Jezebel." In the latter, she played the part of Bette Davis's maid, and indeed her career has of necessity been restricted to parts of this kind. But she revealed flashes of real intelligence in this rôle, and even the most meagre of parts, as in a notable film, " Tell No Tales," directed by Leslie Fenton in 1939. Into an ordinary murder melodrama was inserted a powerful section dealing with a Negro wake, and Theresa Harris had a number of well-directed scenes with the private detective, played by Melvyn Douglas, in which she was outstanding. Unless her rôle demands the kind of " niggerisms " that Hollywood is so fond of inserting into dialogue for coloured players, she usually speaks in perfect English, without any trace of the dialect so often used by Negro characters.

More recently she has been seen as " Rochester's " girl friend in " Buck Benny Rides Again " and " Love Thy Neighbour," and in 1943 she again distinguished herself with her work in that

curiously compelling motion picture " I Walked With A Zombie."
Like Fredi Washington, Theresa finds difficulty in getting straightforward American rôles, and has had to accept numerous parts as
maid-servants and comic relief. But even in these stereotyped
characterisations, as in " Three Little Girls In Blue," she is still
able to command attention, and has proved herself to be deserving
of recognition.

Well-known on the New York stage for his performances in
" Native Son," " The Tempest " and " The Duchess Of Malfi "
is Canada Lee, who has made only infrequent screen appearances.
His best part was in Hitchcock's " Lifeboat," in which he played
a serious, intelligent and admirable character, a steward on board
a liner who is one of the survivors in a lifeboat adrift in the Pacific.
Lee gave a fine performance, and was promptly offered other
coloured parts by Hollywood producers. However, the Negro
actor preferred to return to New York where he has been given
rôles more suitable to his talents. He has a considerable reputation
on Broadway, and in 1946 made an outstanding success in Webster's
" The Duchess Of Malfi," produced by George Rylands, with
Elisabeth Bergner as the Duchess. As the London *Daily Telegraph,*
October 16th, 1946, remarks : " Perhaps the most interesting
feature of the whole production is the appearance of a well-known
Negro actor, Canada Lee, as Daniel de Bosola, the part played
in London, in the John Gielgud season, by Cecil Trouncer. It is
the first time any Negro actor has appeared in New York in a
white rôle. The choice was made simply on Canada Lee's outstanding histrionic ability."

Lee will probably not make any further films until he is given
parts which compare with this stage rôles. (In 1947 he signed a
contract with Enterprise ; only a handful of coloured players
are under contract to studios, among these being Lena Horne,
Eddie " Rochester " Anderson, Mantan Moreland and Willie
Best.) Like Paul Robeson, Todd Duncan and others he will
not accept film rôles which do not show the Negro to be an
ordinary human being. Duncan, for example, born in Kentucky forty-one years ago, is another actor who shares the
same dilemma. He is one of the finest baritones on the American
concert stage. After teaching music and English at Howard
University, he made his operatic début in a Negro version of
" Cavalleria Rusticana," and came into prominence in the

part of Porgy in the operetta " Porgy And Bess," with music
by George Gershwin.   He played this more than one thousand
two hundred times, and repeated his success in London in
1939, when he came over to play a leading rôle in " The Sun
Never Sets," produced by Basil Dean at the Drury Lane Theatre.
Following his appearance in New York a few years ago in " Cabin
In The Sky," Duncan received a Hollywood offer to appear in
Dieterle's " Syncopation."   He was given a fine part, in which
he shared equal importance with Bonita Granville and Adolphe
Menjou, but producers did not follow up this film with other
interesting parts.   Of his offers since " Syncopation " was made,
Duncan himself has said : " Hollywood is obviously not looking
for my type. Dis, dat, dese ! I can learn to talk that way but not
very well."   It is a great pity that there are few opportunities in
films for such actors as Duncan, Lee, Robeson and Rex Ingram,
but screenwriters apparently do not write parts for personable
young coloured men.   Until they do, these actors will remain in
New York, or make films in Europe.

Leigh Whipper went to Hollywood from the New York stage
and has made some interesting appearances in such films as " Of
Mice And Men," " The Hidden Eye," " Vanishing Virginian " and
" Undercurrent."   He also starred in " The Negro Soldier,"
made by the U.S. Government, and has found his niche in Hollywood
in the kind of part played by Clarence Muse and George Reed.
Often he has to play the usual type of Uncle Tom character,
but his work in Milestone's " Of Mice And Men " and Wellman's
" Strange Incident," indicate that he may yet make a corner
in dignified, kindly coloured characters of the kind which did not
exist in Hollywood films of a decade ago, but which occasionally
have found their way into the productions of the war and post-war
period.

A talented young coloured actress, Louise Franklin, has made a number of notable appearances in recent years. Her pictures include
" Carolina Blues," " Hollywood Canteen," " Crazy House,"
"Atlantic City," "Ghost Of The Vampire" and "Ziegfeld Follies."
She has come to the fore in
the past year, playing "Roches-   **Above :** *Gone With The Wind*
ter's "screen sweetheart in such   **directed by Victor Fleming. Below :**
films as " Brewster's Millions "   *King Solomon's Mines* **directed by**
and " Memory For Two."   **Robert Stevenson.**

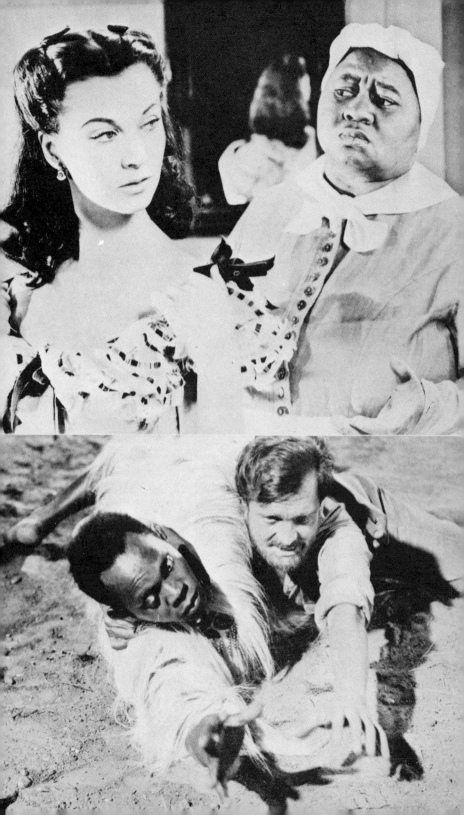

In 1935 a young actress, Fredi Washington, was acclaimed by the critics for her sensitive study of a light-skinned Negro girl in " Imitation Of Life " ; in fact many critics pointed out that her work was so outstanding that it gave undue prominence to the sub-plot of the film in which she featured as the central character. Miss Washington has never had such an interesting part as Peola, and makes rare appearances in Hollywood only when the rôle interests her. Too light-skinned and personable to play coloured maids and comic relief, she has received better treatment on the New York stage. Born in Georgia in 1903, she sang with Duke Ellington's Orchestra for a time, afterwards appearing on the stage in " Shuffle Along," " Singin' The Blues," " Black Boy " and " Porgy." She made her screen début in " The Emperor Jones," and afterwards went to the West Indies to star in " Ouanga " for Paramount, in which she played a half-caste girl who comes between a white planter and his wife. " Imitation Of Life " followed, after which she returned to New York, only going back to Hollywood in 1938 to play the sympathetic rôle of a Negro girl who brings up a little white boy as her own child in " One Mile From Heaven." Since then she has concentrated on stage appearances—which is a great pity for, like Lena Horne, she is both beautiful and talented and would be an excellent screen advertisement for the Negro people.

Nina Mae McKinney still makes occasional film appearances. She was brought to Hollywood in 1929 from New York's Cotton Club to play the leading rôle in King Vidor's " Hallelujah," and later acted smaller parts in such films as " The Lost Lady," directed by William Wellman. Though extremely lovely, this young dancer found that Hollywood had no real place for her, and she was forced to return to the New York stage. In 1935, however, she came to England to play opposite Paul Robeson in Alexander Korda's " Sanders Of The River," afterwards returning to the American stage. In recent years her film appearances have been infrequent, but in 1945 she made her Hollywood comeback in " Without Love," followed by " Night Train To Memphis " and " Dark Waters," in which she played opposite Rex Ingram.

The late Ben Carter was also a well-known theatrical agent.

Right: FLORA ROBSON as a Negro in *Saratoga Trunk* directed by Sam Wood. Left : *A Thousand And One Nights* directed by Alfred E. Green.

187

He was born in Fairfield, Iowa, in 1911, and first came into prominence in the " Happy-Go-Lucky " radio programmes. He first went to Hollywood as an agent for coloured actors ; in 1939 he was persuaded by David Selznick to play his first screen part in " Gone With The Wind." Since then he has been seen in " Little Old New York," " Maryland," " Tin Pan Alley," " Chad Hanna," " Dressed To Kill," " Reap The Wild Wind," " Happy-Go-Lucky," " Her Cardboard Lover," " The Harvey Girls " and a number of others. (He died in 1947.)

Most of his screen rôles have been in the accepted tradition, but in two recent films he was given much more significant parts. In " Bowery To Broadway," in which he was seen, with Mantan Moreland, as a dancing team, much of the dialogue he was given was adult and out-of-the-rut. He was allowed to act like a human being, and was treated by the others in the film—Jack Oakie, Donald O'Connor and Peggy Ryan—as equal in importance in the vaudeville world. Carter had an even better part in " Crash Dive," in which he played a soldier said to be modelled on Dorie Miller, a coloured mess-servant in the U.S. Army who manned a machine-gun during a Japanese raid in the Pacific, bringing down four enemy planes.

Other Negro players who have been prominent in Hollywood in the past few years are Etta McDaniel, Sam McDaniel, Lew Payton, Dorothy Dandridge, Harold Nicholas, Oscar Polk, Lilian Randolph, Lillian Yarbo, Libby Taylor, Marguerite Whitten, Nicodemus Stewart, Ruby Dandridge and Clinton Rosemond. The latter first came into prominence with his striking performance as the coloured janitor in Mervyn Le Roy's " They Won't Forget," in 1937, since which time he has played in " The Green Pastures," " Stand Up And Fight," " Young Dr. Kildare," " Golden Boy " and a number of other Hollywood productions. He is an actor with considerable charm, and can carry the weight of a whole film, as he did when he played the title rôle in M.-G.-M's. " Life Of George Washington Carver." Unfortunately since his great success in " They Won't Forget," Rosemond has found difficulty in obtaining parts of real significance, as, indeed, have all Negro players in the film city.

In 1932 two actors scored successes in the New York production of the play " Bloodstream "—Ernest Whitman and Frank Wilson. The former went to Hollywood a year or two later, appearing in

" The Prisoner Of Shark Island," " White Hunter," " The Green
Pastures," " Daughter of Shanghai," " Jesse James," " Congo
Maisie," " Maryland," " Drums Of The Congo " and a number
of others. In 1943 he appeared in " Cabin In The Sky " in which
he gave a first-rate performance. A well-known face to filmgoers,
Whitman specialises in playing the type of big, good-natured, bluff
Negro ; his work in " The Prisoner Of Shark Island " and " The
Green Pastures," among others, reveals his dramatic powers.

Frank Wilson has had a long and distinguished career. Born
in Harlem in 1891, he studied for the stage at the American
Academy of Dramatic Arts, and made his theatrical début in
1924 playing Jim in " All God's Chillun Got Wings," at the
Provincetown Theatre. He then acted in " The Emperor Jones,"
" The Dreamy Kid," " In Abraham's Bosom " and " Porgy."
In the title rôle of the latter play he made his first appearance in
London in 1929, and has played the part in England and America
more than eight hundred and fifty times. He has also appeared in
such New York plays as " Sweet Chariot," " Singin' The Blues,"
" They Shall Not Die," " The Green Pastures " and " Kiss The
Boys Goodbye," while he was prominently associated with the
Federal Negro Theatre, as actor, playwright and producer, during
the four years in which the Federal Theatre Project functioned.

Well-known as a playwright, Wilson has also been responsible
for a number of screenplays and has had several plays produced in
New York, including " Brother Mose " and " Walk Together
Chillun." While he was appearing on the Broadway stage in
1933 he was persuaded to make his first film appearance, with
Paul Robeson in " The Emperor Jones " produced in New York,
and three years later he went to Hollywood to play his original
part in the screen version of " The Green Pastures." His other
Hollywood films include " The Devil Is Driving," " All-American
Sweetheart " and " Watch On The Rhine." During the last
few years, however, Wilson has been working in New York, both
as actor and filmwriter. He wrote the screenplays of " Murder
On Lenox Avenue " and " Sunday Sinners," both produced by
Jack and Dave Goldberg ; and for the Goldbergs he also starred
in a series of films, which included " Paradise In Harlem," in
which he played a great Negro comedian who finally realised his
ambition to act the part of Othello. Wilson is a versatile actor
and a talented playwright who has refused several offers to return

189

to Hollywood, giving as his reason that the parts allocated to him were the usual kind of menial stereotypes, and not worth the trip to California.

Another Wilson, Dooley, has found a niche in Hollywood, and will be best remembered for his charming study of Humphrey Bogart's friend, Sam, in Warners' " Casablanca." Born in Texas in 1894, Dooley toured Europe with his own band from 1919 to 1930, making his stage début as a straight actor in the productions of Orson Welles and John Houseman for the Federal Theatre in 1934. He then played Crooks in the play of " Of Mice And Men," and was afterwards featured prominently in the New York production of " Cabin In The Sky." During the run of this play he was offered a film part in " Cairo," followed by " Casablanca." Since then he has been seen in " Two Tickets To London," " Stormy Weather," " Seven Days Ashore " and " Higher and Higher." In 1945 he returned to New York to take a prominent rôle in the musical play " Bloomer Girl," and will probably return to Hollywood if, and when, the parts offered him are tempting (and sympathetic) enough.

CHAPTER NINE

WARTIME DEVELOPMENTS IN HOLLYWOOD

" Hollywood until recent years has never accepted as its responsibility the function of helping to destroy race prejudice. In the years 1942 to 1945, however the Hollywood film industry demonstrated a conscious effort to bring about a better understanding among most races and groups in this country and, in a broader field among the nationalities and races allied with us in the Second World War. This came about through the acceptance of specific responsibilities by the industry and a general consent to fulfil the function of using the entertainment film medium to present and expand the principal issues of the war. Thus the exploitation of prejudice by the enemy evoked a response through films which was especially noteworthy in respect to anti-Semitic, anti-British, and anti-Soviet thinking and, to a considerably lesser degree, in helping to challenge anti-Negro and anti-Labor prejudice."

JOHN McMANUS and LOUIS KRONENBERGER,
" *Hollywood's New Deal for Negroes,*" *Negro Digest, June, 1946.*

During the Second World War it was inevitable that a number of great social changes occurred, not only in Europe but also in America. The re-orientation of the British film industry, the new and vital realism of feature films, the increased production of movies containing important sociological themes—these were some instances of a considerable alteration in cinematic (as well as in human) values. A new liberalism in the anti-Fascist democracies made itself apparent. The war against Fascism which had been brewing for twenty years took concrete shape, with a consequence that the democratic nations fighting the war inevitably adopted some measure of anti-Fascist psychology in their Press, radio and screen. Britain, which was nearer the heart of the struggle for a longer period than the United States, soon reflected in her rapidly improving film industry this vigorous new spirit ; it took Hollywood much longer to demonstrate a similar liberalising fervour. In fact, it has been often remarked that to some extent the U.S.A. stood still during the war while the British film industry forged ahead on its new and enlightened policy of realism and vitality in its documentary and semi-documentary output. Hollywood, nevertheless, did succeed in giving some illustrations of this spirit ; this may be noticed in its attitude latterly of increased tolerance towards racial minorities, and especially to the American Negroes.

Cynical critics have affirmed that as it naturally became Hollywood's policy to line itself up behind the war effort of its Government, it also suited its book to portray on the screen with some fairness those fourteen million American citizens, who although their skins were not white were nevertheless valuable units in the war effort, and in the Services and factories. This is, of course, quite true, but perhaps this new liberalism will be continued in the post-war years ? Dr. Alain Locke wrote as follows in *New Masses*, January, 1944 : " As to Hollywood, under the spur of wartime pressure for more democratic morale, even that recalcitrant colossus, whose stubborn and undemocratic stereotyping has hitherto raised such a formidable barrier to a full and proper knowledge and appreciation of the Negro by the great American public, has been moved to make a few concessions. Technically in such full-length Negro films as ' Stormy Weather,' and ' Cabin In The Sky,' then in the approximate parity for Negro talent in the many war cavalcades of stars—' Stage Door Canteen,' ' Thank Your Lucky Stars,' ' Thousands Cheer,' ' By Hook Or By Crook,' which brought Lena Horne, Ethel Waters, Hazel Scott and others to stellar position, and substantively in such subject-matter integrations as the roles of Kenneth Spencer in ' Bataan ' and Canada Lee in ' Lifeboat,' the great American movie, if it does not retreat, has set out some distance on the road to Negro cultural freedom."

Hollywood producers did, in fact, make some movies containing sequences in which Negroes were shown in a sympathetic light. Some of these were excellent ; during the war period perhaps a dozen important films have succeeded in escaping from the usual racial groove. It is an interesting fact that of all the stories centred around the American Civil War period and dealing with the South generally, remarkably few have attempted to view the subject through the eyes of an impartial observer. The majority have been distinctly pro-South, sentimentally remarking on the glories long departed, of " the great white house above the plantation," of the kindly old Southern colonel, of the mint juleps in the cool of the evening, and the fascinating singing of the faithful plantation blacks after a hard day's work in the fields. These then are the aspects of the Southern States which have featured largely in modern movies, Mervyn Le Roy's " They Won't Forget " in 1937 being one notable exception.

From the early days of D. W. Griffith's " The Battle," " A Child's Stratagem," " American Aristocracy " and others, through the period of Buster Keaton's " The General," J. Walter Ruben's " Secret Service," Henry King's " The House of Connelly," King Vidor's " So Red The Rose," David Butler's " The Littlest Rebel " and Victor Fleming's " Gone With The Wind," and up to the more modern era of Leslie Fenton's " Arouse And Beware," Raoul Walsh's " The Dark Command," Michael Curtiz's " Santa Fé Trail " and Frank Borzage's " The Vanishing Virginian " American film-makers have concentrated on whitewashing the South and dealing with those phases of American history which give sympathy to the Confederate Army and the Southern cause generally, while portraying the Northern " nigger lovers " as " the villainous destroyers of the Old South and its glorious traditions." It is not suggested that this is done with any consciously sinister motive, although the facts support this contention.

Even in the war period, 1940-45, the period of a new vigour and of an increasedly liberal conception of human relationships, Hollywood continued to turn out a regular quota of anti-Negro subjects. Typical of these was " Santa Fé Trail," in which the great abolitionist John Brown, admirably played by Raymond Massey, was depicted inevitably as a crazed fanatic. The implication of this film was the one used variously in American films in the past thirty years ; that the abolitionists were crazy eccentrics, and that their revered leader and hero, central figure of the famous song " John Brown's Body," was a creature of inhuman fanaticism. All those who advocated the abolition of slavery are placed in an unfavourable light, and time and time again the moviegoer is led to believe that the United States would today be a better place to live in if those muddle-headed anti-slave traders had not succeeded eighty years ago and if the black man had been kept in his rightful place in U.S. society.

The treatment of the Negro mob rivals even the treatment of the individual. American Negroes *en masse* are depicted with regularity as blood-thirsty, eye-rolling, demented creatures with thick, blubbering lips, almost demented with hate and yelling for white blood. This distorted picture has been presented not only in such famous films as " The Birth Of A Nation," and " Gone With The Wind," but also in productions such as " The Prisoner Of Shark Island," " The Texan," " So Red The Rose," and dozens of minor pictures. African Negroes, in various Hollywood jungle films, have fared no better, always being represented as hate-filled barbarians, savages, head-hunters or cannibals, only one degree removed from the wild animals of the jungle.

In the past few years, however, it is agreeable to note that the number of films glorifying the Old South appears to have been on the decrease. And it is even more pleasing that one can draw attention to some recent and important Hollywood efforts in which the coloured man has appeared as a dignified American citizen. For instance there is Lewis Milestone's outstanding film made from John Steinbeck's novel, " Of Mice And Men," in which a Negro, beautifully played by Leigh Whipper, appears as Crooks, one of a group of ranch workers in the West. Crooks is a kindly, sympathetic character who befriends the two heroes of the film, George and Lenny (played by Burgess Meredith and Lon Chaney) and gives them much useful advice and the benefit of his sagacity and philosophy. Never obtruding into the central situation of the film, yet always quietly in the background, ready with a kind word or a generous action, this charming old Negro does much in his characterisation to atone for the immense harm done in previous Hollywood productions. Milestone, a noted humanitarian whose " All Quiet On The Western Front " is one of the great classics of the cinema, must take some credit for his unconventional treatment of the Negro in this film, while praise is also due to that fine actor Leigh Whipper, who never fails to give a good performance and whose quiet dignity has enriched a number of other Hollywood films.

Whipper was also seen a year or two ago in William Wellman's film " Strange Incident," from the novel *The Ox-Bow Incident* by Walter van Tilberg Clark, a passionate indictment of lynch law. Into a small Nevada town in the late 1800's ride two cowboys, and no sooner are they ensconced in the local saloon than they are involved in drama. A local ranchowner has been found dead on his ranch and it is rumoured that the rustlers responsible for the action are heading North. The sheriff calls for a posse and, under the leadership of an ex-colonel of the Confederate Army, the lynch-minded townsfolk excitedly ride after the rustlers.

The two cowboys follow, hoping to bring a measure of justice to the proceedings.

The same night they come across a party of three armed men encamped in the canyon. Assuming them to be the rustlers in question and in spite of their protests, the mob grab them, tie them up and declare their intention of lynching all three at dawn. The posse is divided into two sections : those who are in favour of the lynching, and a minority who ask that the three men be brought into the town and given a fair trial. The strongest group, the lynchers, are led by the fanatic renegade colonel, who had ridden at the head of the posse in full Confederate Army uniform, complete with spurs and sword. A typical example of the most terrifying type of narrow-minded bigoted Southerner, this character was obviously meant to point to the worst in Old Southern mentality. And, indeed, it is largely through the efforts of this man that the unhappy strangers are finally lynched.

The scenes leading up to the actual lynching are harrowing in the extreme ; and the audience is never allowed to know until the final few moments whether the three men are the rustlers in question. The two cowboys, the strangers who had joined the posse to see justice done, are strongly against the lynching and there are several stormy scenes before the eventual hangings. Among the anti-lynchers is a Negro preacher, a beautifully-drawn character, played exquisitely by Leigh Whipper. The preacher has dignity, courage, passion ; opposing the Southern colonel, quietly and unemotionally he declares himself on the side of those voting for a fair trial. As he declares, he comes from a race which has had to bear the brunt of lynch law, and lynching is no way to settle things for either black or white people. His speech is as effective as a douche of water, and many of the would-be slayers are affected by his words.

Unfortunately his pleadings and efforts, like those of the others, are however in vain. And although the Negro protests until the very last moment, the hate-blinded posse set about hanging their three doomed suspects, who still protest their innocence as the ropes are being put around their necks. At last the lynching is over. There is a strained feeling of anti-climax as the men mount their horses slowly and ride with set, grim faces back towards the town. As they reach the road back they are met by the sheriff himself who tells them that the man said to be found dead on his ranch was only wounded and that the two rustlers who had confessed to the deed had been arrested some miles south of the town. The men exchange startled glances ; their three victims were innocent ! Shamefaced, with hearts of lead, they struggle back to the town. And in the final poignant scene Henry Fonda, as one of the two strangers, reads them a letter left by the leader of the three men they have murdered by mistake. None of the lynchers will ever forget his part in the affair ; the grim lesson has been learned. As the film ends the two cowboys ride out of the town ; the strange and terrible incident is over. This is the outline of Wellman's powerful attack on a social evil. Not only is the film itself to be commended for its subject, but it will also be long remembered for its sincere handling of a Negro character.

A film such as " Strange Incident " can do a great deal to counterattack those many Hollywood productions showing the coloured man as a grinning idiot. William Wellman, the director, Twentieth Century-Fox, the producers, and actors Henry Fonda, Dana Andrews, Anthony Quinn, Frank Conroy, Henry Morgan, Marc Lawrence, Henry Davenport, William Eythe, Leigh Whipper, Paul Hurst and the others are all to be congratulated on this fine and moving effort. It is interesting to note that, for no apparent reason, this film did not receive a London West End showing, and was therefore not reviewed by the film critics of the daily Press. Instead, it was quietly given a modest release, and shown in some suburban cinemas a year or more after it had been seen in America. Nevertheless the critics who saw this film when it was given a revival run by the Academy Cinema in London in 1946, agreed unanimously that it was one of the most magnificent productions ever to come out of Hollywood. As a social document, "Strange Incident " ranks with Fritz Lang's " Fury " and John Ford's " Grapes Of Wrath."

Of the half a dozen films made during the war in which Negro themes were included with any degree of prominence, two were all-coloured musicals while the others treated the Negro character in a fairly sympathetic manner. Once again it was Warners' who were responsible for making another outstanding contribution to screen tolerance, " In This Our Life," directed by John Huston in 1942. The film featured Bette Davis, Olivia de Havilland, George Brent and Dennis Morgan and was a faithful filmic transcription of Ellen Glasgow's sincere novel. The central character, played by Bette Davis, is a headstrong, self-willed and extremely spoiled girl who in one mad moment of hysteria knocks down a woman and her child, killing the child and seriously injuring the mother. To save herself from imprisonment the girl swears that she had not used her car, and that in fact she had lent it for the evening to a coloured boy whose job it is to keep the car in good condition, and whose mother is employed by her family. The young man is arrested and in spite of his protests is confined to jail. Things look very bad for him since it is his word, the word of a Negro, against the word of his white mistress. It seems that he has very little hope.

Luckily the girl's sister (Olivia de Havilland), who is extremely fond of the Negro boy and his mother, suspects that her self-willed sister is lying and, with the help of a young lawyer, played by George Brent, she finally manages to extract a confession from the guilty woman, so that the Negro boy is eventually set free. The direction of the sub-theme in this excellently-acted film is a fine example of intelligent treatment of racial problems on the screen, and John Huston, talented director, screenwriter and playwright, has handled his subject in a straightforward, hard-hitting manner. The Negro boy, extremely well played by Ernest Anderson, is portrayed as a hard-working, ambitious youngster who works as a clerk during the day and studies to be a law student in his spare time. In his verbal clashes with the Southern girl in prison he is shown in almost an heroic light, while she is portrayed as the spoiled, neurotic type that she is. In the jail scene, when she threatens him and tries to bribe him to keep quiet and "take the rap " for her reckless driving, he refuses to do so and responds to her threats with courage and dignity. The boy realises that as a Negro he stands very little chance of justice in a Southern community, but in spite of this he is steadfast. Protesting his innocence, he will not let his own people down, he says.

Previously, in his scenes with the kindly sister, the boy talks intelligently in perfect English and behaves naturally and un-affectedly. When he is asked why he studies to be a lawyer, he replies, " It is the only profession in which an American citizen can be black and still do his work without interference or persecution; that is why I have chosen it. I am determined to play my part in the advancement of my people, for we need good lawyers *and better laws* " (author's italics). " In This Our Life " was a landmark in the history of American films dealing with race problems. It was awarded a place on the Honour Roll of Race Relations for 1942, and remains one of the finest examples of how a progressive Hollywood director is able to present a controversial theme without the marked colour prejudice which had been a striking feature of so many Hollywood films before the Second World War. Warners', incidentally, were also to be commended for the unconventional handling of Humphrey Bogart's Negro friend, played by Dooley Wilson, in that excellent film " Casablanca."

" Sahara," directed by Zoltan Korda for Columbia in 1943, owed much in its theme to the Soviet film " The Thirteen " (Michael Romm) and to the British film " Nine Men " (Harry Watt). Written by John Howard Lawson, it told the story of a group of Allied soldiers in the Sahara Desert during the North African campaign, and how their numbers gradually decreased as they were shot by Nazi snipers or died from thirst and general fatigue. The group narrows down to half a dozen men, including Humphrey Bogart as the American and Rex Ingram as the coloured French officer (it is well known that in France no colour bar exists and that there are many Negro officers in the French Services, and very fine soldiers, too). The character is sympathetically drawn, is handsome, brave and intelligent. He is perhaps the first Negro in screen history allowed to have a white man—in this case a captured Italian soldier—as his personal servant in a Hollywood film. Throughout " Sahara " he is shown as an integral part of a brave group, a comrade, a man on a level with his fellow-soldiers. In one scene he uses his hands as a cup for the dripping water which quenches the thirst of the other men. Each of the whites drinks out of the water in the hands of the Negro, and none of them appears to find this extraordinary ; a small point but none the less subtle, and certainly effective.

In one of the final sequences of the film the French officer, in spite of gun-fire from the enemy, runs after a fleeing Nazi soldier and, following a struggle, overcomes him. This was possibly the first time that a Hollywood producer has ever allowed the spectacle of a Negro vanquishing a white man in fair combat to appear in a film. Rex Ingram as Tambul adds more laurels to his brow with his excellent performance in " Sahara," a film which was yet another reflection of Hollywood's increased liberal outlook during the wartime period. One of the most significant features in " Sahara " is the friendship between Tambul and a white boy from Texas, played by Bruce Bennett. The Texas boy spends many hours confiding in Tambul. He has a wife and a home in Texas, and is looking forward to going home. So is the Negro ; he too has a wife waiting, he too is fighting to preserve the spark of civilisation and culture which he had begun among his people before the war started. The two young men find they had much in common, and become firm friends.

The spirit of this film can best be summed up by a comment made in an article on " Sahara " which appeared in an American film magazine : " Among the group of men whose destinies we watch in this film are a Free Frenchman, dreaming of a new France, an Italian who has quickly realised the perfidy of the Nazi regime, Americans, English, and a fine, dignified Negro. Differences of opinion or race do not matter any more. All religions, all people, are one ; fighting for their very existence. Only by working together can they survive, only by understanding one another's problems can they win the war and preserve an everlasting peace."

In the M.-G.-M. film " Bataan," directed by Tay Garnett from an original screenplay by Robert D. Andrews, there is also another Negro soldier, this time in the American Army. Similar in plot to " Sahara," this interesting motion picture shows a group of American soldiers besieged at Bataan by the Japanese Army. One of the most powerful war films ever made, "Bataan" was presented with a special award by the National Association for the Advancement of Coloured People, one of the very few Hollywood productions deserving of this recognition.

Kenneth Spencer, well known Broadway actor and singer, played the Negro G.I. and, as in "Sahara," he formed part of a small but gallant body of soldiers besieged by the enemy at Bataan. The group narrows down to eight or nine men. They fight, sleep, joke, laugh together, wait patiently for help, face death with courage. Not by one lapse does director Tay Garnett differentiate in his treatment of the white soldiers and the Negro boy. On the contrary, Spencer is made to appear just as courage-- ous as his comrades ; obviously he represents in this film those many thousands of coloured soldiers who fought in the United States Army on all fronts. M.-G.-M. probably had in mind that, in some way, this film might be a tribute to the great contribution of the Negro race to final victory. But whatever the reasons behind the making of this film, for the treatment of this particular character one must be grateful to the producers of " Bataan." The courage shown by the characters in the film was second only to that of the director who probably had to face a barrage of criticism from the South for his friendly handling of the Negro soldier.

" Cabin In The Sky," a successful New York musical play, was made into a film by M.-G.-M. in 1943. Directed by Broadway producer Vincente Minelli, now one of Hollywood's most successful directors of musical films, " Cabin In The Sky " marked some developments in the featuring of coloured actors in Hollywood. Admitted it was all-coloured, therefore still in the same Jim Crow groove ; and in addition it was a fantasia and therefore not to be judged by the yardstick of realist films. But it was an entertaining production which revealed the natural acting talents of a dozen good coloured players, actors who were often neglected in other Hollywood films.

The story, never very important in these " all-coloured epics," concerns Little Joe, a good-natured gambler who is continually the centre of a struggle for his soul. On one side is his devoted wife, Petunia, trying to keep him on the straight and narrow path, and on the other side is the beautiful night-club singer continually enticing him to leave his wife for a career of gambling and high life. Little Joe is finally shot in a night club fracas, and as he lies on his death bed the struggle still goes on, this time for his immortal soul. In a cleverly-conceived fantasia, one of the best dream sequences ever seen on the screen, we are shown (though perhaps a trifle unsubtly) the two factions opposed on the question of the destination of Little Joe's soul. Those from " above " are shown as serious, dignified individuals wearing white suits, while those " below " are depicted as grinning, malevolent, dice-playing, petty criminals, with tiny horns growing out of their foreheads and ill-concealed forked tails. After some interesting and amusing sequences Little Joe is finally saved from purgatory by the faith of his wife and, recovering from his wound, declares that in his delirium he has realised the error of his ways.

Eddie Anderson, already well-known as Jack Benny's celebrated stooge on his radio programmes, as well as in a number of films, proved in " Cabin In The Sky " that he was capable of making a fine showing as an actor rather than as a comic performer. In

previous films he had shown his powers as a straight actor, and
" Cabin In The Sky " proved that given adequate rôles Anderson
could easily forsake the " Rochester " stereotype occasionally and
play more worth-while parts. The acting triumph of the film,
however, belonged to Ethel Waters, the Broadway singer and
actress, who in one of her infrequent appearances in Hollywood
gave a performance which marked her out as one of the leading
emotional actresses of the screen. As one New York film magazine
pointed out, " *If it wasn't for her colour* (author's italics) Miss Ethel
Waters would undoubtedly become one of Hollywood's top names
in the dramatic field."

" Cabin In The Sky " was also the first film to draw attention
to Lena Horne, a striking new screen discovery, with great beauty,
personality and talent. In addition it was the first directorial
effort of Vincente Minelli, who has since directed such notable
musicals as " Meet Me In St. Louis," " Under The Clock " and
" Ziegfeld Follies." The film gave rôles of importance to such
fine actors as Rex Ingram, Kenneth Spencer, Nicodemus Stewart
and Ernest Whitman ; and, as this was a Negro musical, there
were naturally a number of lively coloured performers, dancers
and singers, including " Buck And Bubbles," Louis Armstrong,
Mantan Moreland and Duke Ellington and His Orchestra, all
of whom were seen to good advantage in the night club sequences.

" Cabin In The Sky " was excellent entertainment, and certainly
gave some parts of prominence to a number of Hollywood's coloured
actors. Nevertheless, like all exclusively Negro movies, it suffered
from the same defects : complete unreality and relentless continuance of the stereotypes, such as the dice-throwing, razor-carrying,
good-for-nothing, jazz-playing, gambling " darkies." It had a fair
success, though not, of course, in the Southern States, where all
films featuring coloured actors in any degree of prominence are
subject to a virtual boycott.

The other all-coloured musical of the war period was " Stormy
Weather," described by its makers, Twentieth Century-Fox, as
" something sensational in musicals." I quote from a publicity
sheet : " ' Stormy Weather ' is a tribute to the magnificent contribution of the coloured race to the entertainment of the world
during the past twenty-five years. It is gay, light-hearted musical
entertainment at its finest, for here is a picture which has assembled
the most striking personalities of screen, stage and radio and here

is sparkling entertainment that key-notes brilliant dancing ensembles, tuneful songs and melodies, eye-filling sets, gorgeous costumes and laughter-filled comedy. Lena Horne, Bill Robinson, Cab Calloway and His Band, Katherine Dunham and her famous dancing troupe, the Shadrack Boys, the Nicholas Brothers—these are a few of the lively and talented entertainers who parade across the screen in scenes of music, revelry and song. Every type of audience will be attracted to the manifold entertainment facets of this film. Millions will be electrified by the golden mellow voice and the striking personality of Lena Horne, one of today's most sensational coloured singers ; others will thrill to the skill and artistry of Bill Robinson's tap dancing and Katherine Dunham's brilliant ballet dancing ; and vast numbers will be captivated by the catchy song and dance rhythms dispensed by Cab Calloway and His Band, and Fats Waller. Add to these the incomparable Nicholas Brothers and you get an idea of the truly magnificent entertainment offered by ' Stormy Weather.' "

To what extent was this extravagant blurb justified ? It did, at least, seem that writers Jerry Horwin and Seymour Robinson had evolved a story which endeavoured to give prominence to the Negro's contribution to entertainment during the past decade, but the film was, on the whole, a disappointment. The central character, Corky, played by Bill Robinson, is a singer and dancer with Jim Europe's Jazz Band, that well-known coloured combination which played to the Allied troops in France during the First World War. On his return to the United States Corky meets Selina, a singer, played by Lena Horne, and they fall in love. The rest of the film follows a conventional pattern of boy meeting, losing and finally getting girl, but " Stormy Weather " concerns itself mainly with the spectacle of bands, dancers, vocalists, floor shows, all of which form the background to the slight love theme. Opportunities for acting were limited, although Bill Robinson, departing a little from his usual Uncle Tom characterisation, was pleasant enough and Lena Horne, Dooley Wilson, Ernest Whitman, Babe Wallace and Cab Calloway were each as good as their material allowed them to be.

As a revue, " Stormy Weather " was adequate screen entertainment with some good coloured performers. Right : *Stormy Weather*, directed by Andrew Stone. Left : KATHERINE DUNHAM.

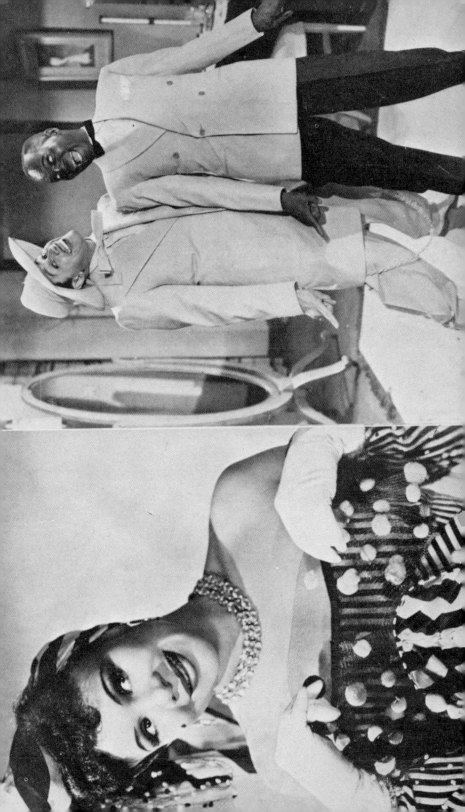

Certain film critics were, however, condemnatory. Denis Preston, well-known British radio writer and producer, devoted a long review in the magazine *Jazz Music*, October, 1943, to an attack on the film. He writes: "The Uncle Tom attitude still reigns supreme in Hollywood, and this latest monstrosity is well and truly in the tradition. It is a revolting hotch-potch of comico-pathetic 'nigger characterisation.' As the bathetic cant of ' The Green Pastures ' served to prostitute the Negro's histrionic ability, so ' Stormy Weather ' presents his vital functional art in its most debased form. . . . The emaciated plot is loosely held together by the twenty-two year long romance of Bill Robinson and Lena Horne, a romance which becomes sickening, it's so *doggy* ! Big black faithful spaniel snuffling in the tracks of dainty yellow bitch. None of the Fred Astaire-Ginger Rogers delightful intimacies here, or the inner yearnings of a Gable or Turner, the enchanting propriety of Judy Garland's adolescent hitherness and thitherness, upon which Hollywood lavishes its celluloid, its dollars and almost its entire æsthetic resource. But then who has ever heard of a ' nigger ' with ordinary human emotions ? Certainly *not* Hollywood." Mr. Preston adds as a footnote : " As a sop, presumably, for race rape theorists, Hollywood conscripted a regiment of the yellowest high yellows, female, which helped to set off the blackness of the chosen male characters more than somewhat. Subtly psychological this ! "

Both " Cabin In The Sky " and " Stormy Weather " throw into prominence the basic inadequacies of all-Negro films. Among many Negro actors themselves there is a great deal of dissatisfaction felt about these Jim Crow films, and it may be that they will soon be discontinued since Hollywood has recently discovered that they are not particularly profitable. It is in fact doubtful if any major company will undertake the production of an exclusively Negro film again, for not only do they tend to alienate intelligent Negro opinion, but they also are " box office poison " in the South. Some indication that the Southern States do wield a vast amount of power in influencing Hollywood opinions may be gauged from the following extract from the American newspaper *P.M.*, July 31st,

ROBERT ADAMS, above : with ERIC PORTMAN in *Men Of Two Worlds* and below : with author PETER NOBLE.

1945: " The Memphis, Tennessee, Board of Film Censors this year banned ' The Southerner ' which it was claimed does not represent the South in a good light, cut Lena Horne out of ' Ziegfeld Follies,' and also banned ' Brewster's Millions,' because of its friendly treatment of a Negro character, who played a sort of major-domo in charge of office staff, acted amusingly by Eddie ' Rochester ' Anderson." In addition, " The Sailor Takes A Wife " was censored in Memphis because in it Robert Walker tips his hat to a Negro !

These were by no means isolated cases ; it is possible to quote dozens of instances where various Southern States have banned films because the coloured actors who appeared in them were *not* always depicted as lazy, ignorant, good-for-nothing inferiors. A writer in *Negro Digest* pointed out recently : " Southern film audiences total about one-eighth of the total American film audience, which is an indication of the way in which minority prejudice and pressure may control the policy of an international industry. Because of the prejudices of this one-eighth and its effectiveness in preventing wholesome treatment of the American Negro in films, the rest of the world, which depends entirely on Hollywood for its views on America, has seldom seen the American Negro in his true position, however second-class it may still be, in American society."

And as Carleton Moss, producer of " The Negro Soldier," stated in *Our World*, May, 1946 : " There is a lot of money in making motion pictures. The industry stands tenth in American business. Profit is the primary motive of the men who control the making of motion pictures. A large percentage of the annual net profit of the industry comes from the six thousand three hundred and fifty cinemas which are situated in the deep South and border States (thirty-one per cent. of the total cinemas in the U.S.A.). Especially does the South influence the use of Negroes in the industry. A story analyst in one of Hollywood's major studios reports that stories dealing realistically with Negro life are never given any consideration. Producers have made it a policy to consider only Negro stories that can be made into all-Negro musicals. Here again is the influence of the South. Since the days of the big house, when the master would allow his most talented slaves to entertain his guests, the South has approved of Negro entertainment. Stories of the gay days of the old South with its magnolias and happy house servants cannot be told often enough for the ' good families of the South.' As long as the

Negro portrays these ' acceptable characters ' there will be no objection from the owners of the six thousand three hundred and fifty cinemas in the South.

" There is a growing number of progressive-minded people in Hollywood. Many directors, writers and actors give their time to lecturing and teaching at schools open to all races. Some determined writers and directors have, during the war period, broken through the rigid studio censorship and created Negro characters other than the stereotypes, e.g. : ' Sahara,' ' Strange Incident,' ' In This Our Life,' ' Under The Clock,' ' Crash Dive ' and ' Miss Susie Slagle's.' But the strength of the democratic people in Hollywood is not yet strong enough to break through the Southern pattern that dominates the studios." Nevertheless certain actors were able to gain sympathy by virtue of their talent ; one such was Canada Lee.

This actor gave a magnificent performance in Alfred Hitchcock's " Lifeboat," made for Twentieth Century-Fox in 1944. The film tells the story of a group of assorted characters cast adrift in a lifeboat following a shipwreck. The Negro steward, played by Lee, saves a white woman from drowning and is throughout the film shown as an heroic American. He receives his only hint of discriminatory treatment from a Nazi U-boat captain, also picked up by the lifeboat, and one of the messages of the picture appears to be that it is only Nazi bestiality which views the Negro as an animal but that good American citizens regard him on a level with themselves ! Perhaps the fact that the film was directed by Englishman Hitchcock was responsible for this highly erroneous suggestion, since it is well-known that racial discrimination does indeed exist strongly in everyday life in the U.S.A. Nevertheless the quietly intelligent work of Lee, with its exquisite underplaying, and the considerable charm exercised by his study of a gentlemanly coloured seaman surely contributed largely towards the general betterment of race relations in the war years. " Lifeboat " must, on the whole, be considered one of the major contributions to increased racial harmony made by Hollywood in the period 1940-46.

In " Follow The Boys," produced by Universal in 1944, an interesting sequence occurred when an entertainer (George Raft), on a tour of Army Camps to entertain American Forces, came on a Negro battalion stationed behind the battle-zone. He danced and entertained them and afterwards shook hands warmly with the coloured officer in charge, who thanked him for helping to keep up the morale of his men. That excellent young Negro actor Nicodemus Stewart played the part of the officer.

As I have noted previously, most films dealing with the Civil War have a strongly partisan attitude. Invariably it is the South who are portrayed with sympathy, while Northerners are shown as egotistical fanatics with an idealistic but unpractical approach to Southern politics. "The Man On America's Conscience," directed for M.-G.-M. by William Dieterle in 1944, was an example of a modern film which, while quite good of its kind, yet trod the same prejudiced rut. When it was first made in Hollywood it was called "Tennessee Johnson," under which name it was released in America. The title referred to Johnson, one-time president of the U.S.A. (Apparently the U.S.A. thought that European filmgoers would find the title obscure and forthwith gave it a new one which was more obscure than ever). The film deals with the exciting period of the Reconstruction after the Civil War, and shows Andrew Johnson (excellently played by Van Heflin) as Abraham Lincoln's vice-president, and a man who faithfully follows in Lincoln's footsteps. After Lincoln is assassinated Johnson succeeds him as President and following a stormy period in his career he is finally impeached by Congress. His life thus ends in ignominy, making him "the man on America's conscience"; and for a hundred years historians and Southern writers have sought to whitewash Johnson's political misdemeanours.

Dieterle's film shows Johnson as the staunch upholder of the Southern bourgeoisie against the North, and the main part of the action is concerned with his clash with Thaddeus Stevens (played by Lionel Barrymore), a Northern politician who believes in giving the ex-slaves equal rights with the white Southerners. The sympathy of the entire film is, however, with Johnson, who stubbornly affirms that although the Civil War is over and although the slaves are admittedly now free, the South should be allowed to continue in the same tradition as before. The political implications of the whole film are obscure (especially to European filmgoers), but it is obvious that Stevens who stands up for Negroes is the villain of the piece, while Johnson who maintains that the coloured man should be kept in his proper place in American life is, in fact, the hero. That Johnson is finally discredited does not alter the main implication, since we are left at the end of the film with the feeling that he has been scurrilously treated and that his name will live in American history as an example of a politician who " let patriotism come first."

The film may therefore be bracketed with " The Birth Of A Nation " ; both deal with the same period and contain the same villain (Stevens in Dieterle's film and Stoneman in Griffith's). Griffith depicts him as an insincere careerist while Dieterle shows him as a scheming egotist. " The Man On America's Conscience " is from an original story by Milton Ginsberg and Alvin Mayers. Presumably they have both been influenced by Thomas Dixon's " The Clansman " ; certainly their combined sympathies are entirely with the South here, and the whole film is a reflection of this.

The Negro Press in the U.S.A. attacked the film, and it caused some controversy when it was first shown in America. As the *Negro Handbook*, 1944, records : " Negroes protested about ' The Man On America's Conscience,' because Andrew Johnson, who was well-known for his low opinion of Negroes, was portrayed as a hero. The protests reached the Office of War Information in Washington and resulted in the Government's request for the producers to change certain parts of the film. Several scenes were re-taken to represent the question of slavery in a more sympathetic manner. But the film, as it was completed, was still not satisfactory to Negroes."

Not until two years later was it exhibited in England, with the political content considerably watered down. Most English critics failed to note the implications of the film, but an exception was Lionel Collier, in *Picturegoer*, July 6th, 1946, who shrewdly remarked in his review, " Andrew Johnson's opponent, Thaddeus Stevens, who stood for Negro rights, is depicted in a very bad light." In the U.S.A. most liberal film critics were indignant that in the middle of a war such a film could still be made by a Hollywood studio, and several reviewers of the daily newspapers deplored the fact that whenever the Civil War was featured in a motion picture the North was shown as the villain, principally because of its advocation of the abolition of slavery. That a film company in 1944 could still make a motion picture depicting a sincere abolitionist like Stevens as a kind of monster is indeed a censure on Hollywood, and represents a considerable backward step.

Lawrence Reddick asserts that the film was definitely reactionary and notes that it was fought by the National Negro Congress and a number of Left groups and trade unions as being anti-Negro and anti-democracy in the sense that it glorified President Andrew Johnson and his co-operation with the " Southern bourbon aristocracy." The film underwent certain modifications at the suggestion of the N.A.A.C.P., but a large body of public opinion was ranged against the eventual showing of a production, which in any case did not prove to be a box office success.

" Tales Of Manhattan," directed by Julien Duvivier in 1942, was the last film in which Paul Robeson appeared. It was a mammoth affair, comprising several distinct sections, related to each other by a dress suit worn by various of the characters in the separate incidents. One of these scenes caused a number of objections among Negroes. It was a Jim Crow scene amid half a dozen ordinary American episodes, and showed the Negro as a superstitious, hymn-singing, gullible, good-natured dolt. In fact the central idea of the scene in which the coloured characters appeared was quite preposterous in that it showed a group of Southern Negroes who, picking up a dress suit which had been thrown from an aeroplane with the pockets stuffed with money, believed that this was really a gift from Heaven in answer to their prayers for a new church ! A tasteless and naïve sequence saw such eminent artists as Paul Robeson, Ethel Waters, George Reed and Eddie Anderson demeaning themselves by impersonating superstitious " niggers," thanking the Lord for his goodness in sending them the money from the skies, praying, kneeling, sobbing, and behaving generally in the same old credulous, sub-human manner.

Paul Robeson responded to public criticism of his part in this film by stating that he did not realise what he was doing until he had got too far into his lines and contract to stop. He was, however, so incensed by it when it was finally shown that he volunteered to join a picket line around any cinema showing the film. Indeed so disappointed was Robeson by " Tales Of Manhattan " that he left Hollywood for good, resolving never to return until he could supervise the choice of vehicle. Some critics admitted that his rôle in this film might have been worse, and it was pointed out that he did get a chance in the final scene to speak some brave words about democracy. But, all things considered, " Tales Of

Manhattan " rates inclusion among the anti-Negro films of the past few years.

Nevertheless this Duvivier production was something of an exception. Generally speaking, Hollywood's treatment of coloured actors during the war years did show an improvement. Certainly such productions as " Bataan," " Sahara," " In This Our Life " and " Strange Incident " could never have been made fifteen years ago. Referring to this, some cynics assert that in the post-war period Hollywood will probably revert to its former attitude, since it will then be no longer necessary to appeal to Negro audiences in the same way that they had to during the war, at a time when coloured citizens and soldiers were of far greater importance than ever they had been during times of peace. There may be some truth in this. But it is also true that so increasedly strong has American public opinion become on this question latterly that it is quite possible that Hollywood may decide to take heed of those many American organisations which have been continually striving towards a fair treatment of minorities on the screen.

Let us, here and now, try to get one point straight. Film production is a business, out of which occasionally emerges *some* art. Such are the complications and ramifications of the production and distribution field that film-makers are forced into the position of being guided by certain prejudices which still exist in the movie markets.

The *Afro-American*, of May 17th, 1930, quoted an important executive of the Hollywood industry as saying the following : " We are in the game to make money, not to make friends or enemies. We produce whatever it pays to produce, regardless of the colour or creed of the subjects. In order to realise adequate profits on a production, distribution must be nation-wide. Thus it does not suffice that the East, West and North accept Negro pictures, while the South refuse to accept pictures in which Negroes are starred or featured." This is Hollywood's viewpoint, then and now.

We have already seen that film companies have to be careful concerning the type of movie shown in the South, and also that a producer will eliminate the entire Negro section of his film, or cut out the coloured characters completely, if he considers their presence would upset the notoriously sensitive Southern audiences.

It can also work the other way, of course, for Hollywood has made intelligent, sympathetic and progressive films in order to appeal to the admittedly-growing audience for a better class type of motion picture. One cannot help being reminded of recent American films like " Strange Incident " and " In This Our Life " (or, for that matter, " Scarlet Street," " The Lost Week-End," " The Searching Wind," and " The Southerner "), all of which deal intelligently with a problem, and which are without any question aimed at an audience of more than average intelligence. And they have often been successful. This is a good sign, for although we know it will be many years before Hollywood stops making mass entertainment musicals and frivolities and other films of the type which appeals to the lowest common denominator in cinema audiences, the fact remains that in the fifty years of its existence the film itself has grown up, to a considerable, if not remarkable, extent. Although it must be admitted that Hollywood's product has certainly been influenced during the war by the fact that alienation of Negro cinemagoers would be detrimental to the common cause, one must also take heart by remembering the general improvement in the standard of American motion pictures today, and the work of a handful of fine and intelligent directors, among whom Edward Dmytryk, Richard Whorf, Tay Garnett, Archie Mayo, William Dieterle, Jacques Tourneur, William Wellman, Lewis Milestone, Frank Capra, Garson Kanin, William Wyler, John Ford, John Huston, Irving Rapper, Robert Siodmak and Vincent Sherman may be noted.

We have already remarked that Eddie " Rochester " Anderson has virtually been co-starred in " Memory For Two," " Brewster's Millions," " The Sailor Takes A Wife " and others. Monogram, an independent studio in Hollywood, has during the past few years made a constant practice of co-starring Mantan Moreland and Frankie Darro in a series of films in which the white boy and his coloured friend and helper solve mysteries, bring crooks to justice and generally play a sympathetic part on the right side of the law. The first of these, " Chasing Trouble," was directed by Howard Bretherton from a screenplay by Mary McCarthy, but the rest in the series were written by Edmond Kelso, who was also responsible for other screenplays in which the coloured characters were un-usually prominent. Of the Darro-Moreland series a few titles are worthy of mention—" Farewell To Fame " and " In The Night," both directed by Jean Yarborough, and " Up In The Air " and " You're Out Of Luck," both directed by Howard Bretherton. By 1943 Moreland was co-starred also with Dick Purcell, e.g., " The Phantom Killer," directed by William Beaudine. But when Monogram began to make the popular Charlie Chan series they cast Moreland as Sidney Toler's stooge, and the Negro actor's rôles became more and more stereotyped. Occasionally he was able to get better parts at other studios, e.g., "Bowery To Broadway " at Universal, but generally his career has followed the conventional pattern in the past few years. As the film critic of the Negro magazine *Ebony*, May, 1946, remarked bitterly : " In ' Dark Alibi ' Mantan Moreland, playing Charlie Chan's chauffeur Birmingham again, runs through his usual pop-eyed antics. Moreland, whose forte is sweating through cliché rôles with watermelon, dice and rabbit's foot, has an encounter with a skeleton in this opus, with the inevitable results."

The growing Hollywood trend towards liberalism may also be seen in two further films made in 1946—Archie Mayo's " Angel On My Shoulder " and Edward Dmytryk's " Till The End Of Time." In the former there is a sequence showing a group of speakers on a political platform. Among the whites are two coloured priests, who intermingle with the other speakers, joke with them, join in the discussion and are generally part of the political group supporting the liberal judge, played by Paul Muni. In another part of the film, where the judge is greeted by a delegation of school-children, it is noticeable that included in the group of white youngsters are one or two nicely-dressed and well-spoken Negro children, the implication being that they too are part of the youth of the city, and are treated just as the white boys and girls —a small but significant point.

In the latter, which deals with the trials and tribulations of returning Servicemen in the U.S.A., a part of the film is concerned with a sub-plot about a semi-Fascist body, calling itself the American Patriots' Association, which is endeavouring to band all war veterans together in one big group to demand fair play from the Government. We see some representatives of the American Patriots, in a saloon, trying to interest two young ex-Marines, played by Guy Madison and Robert Mitchum, in joining the organisation. (Previously we had noticed that they were playing pin-ball with a coloured soldier, a sympathetic and pleasant character.) When the American Patriots come up to the two white boys and ask them to join their organisation, one of them (Robert Mitchum) asks : " What kind of people do you have in your organisation ? " To which the spokesman replies, " We take all Americans, that is everybody except Negroes, Catholics and Jews."

At this remark the coloured soldier with a hurt expression on his face begins to disappear into the background but the ex-Marine motions him back, grabs the spokesman by the collar and hisses, " My best friend, a Jew, is lying back in a foxhole at Guadalcanal. I am going to spit in your eye for him, because we don't want to have people like you in the U.S.A. There is no place for racial discrimination here now ! " He has the support of all the ex-Servicemen in the saloon, and there, follows a fracas in which the American Patriots are ejected and arrested.

The above are interesting examples of the manner in which Hollywood occasionally endeavours not to be left behind in the general development of liberal thought in the post-war world. It is certain that a sequence in a big popular film like " Till The End Of Time," directed specifically against racial discrimination, is a valuable antidote to the prejudice existing in American social life, and our thanks must go to that excellent young director Edward Dmytryk, and to the studio, R.K.O.-Radio.

Two other recent films produced in Hollywood give hope that film-makers are beginning to face up to modern developments, and to realise that motion pictures presenting actual problems of every-day life can no longer be rated as " box office poison." Edward Dmytryk directed a revolutionary American film in 1947. Titled " Cross-fire," it dealt with the hitherto " banned " subject of anti-Semitism. At first, other Hollywood producers and the film trade Press in the U.S.A. were aghast at the fact that R.K.O.-Radio had allowed the production of a film on that most controversial of all topics, racial discrimination.

Dmytryk, long noted for his vigorous pronouncements and his progressive tendencies, has said that " Cross-fire " is only the first in a series of films which he intends to direct dealing with subjects of controversy and dispute. Among them, he asserts, will be a picture facing up to the position of the Negro in post-war American life.

Another indication of Hollywood's new approach to modern problems was " The Burning Cross," directed by Walter Colmes for Somerset Pictures, a new producing group. The film, described as " a daring exposure of the Ku Klux Klan " was refused finance by every national bank in the U.S.A. and was eventually screened despite the advice of " everybody in the picture business." The film describes the K.K.K's. efforts to keep Negroes from voting, and includes one scene in which the Negro hero, an ex-sailor, is being persuaded by the K.K.K. not to enter his vote. He replies, " Ask me for one of my eyes—for all my money—I'll give you that but I cannot, and will not, give you my birthright."

Director Walter Colmes and producer S. Levinson admit that they were told, " we were fools to make this film after the banks called it ' too hot to handle '." The leading rôle in " The Burning Cross " is played by Joel Fluellyn, formerly seen in " The Negro Sailor." His part, that of a Negro ex-Serviceman killed by the Ku Klux Klan, was originally written in dialect, but was rewritten in straight English at the suggestion of the Eric Johnston Office. Henry Cass, former Special Prosecutor in Atlanta, Georgia, acted as Technical Adviser, and the production was based on careful research into Ku Klux Klan methods over the past thirty years.

In a moving scene, Charlie, the Negro veteran, paraphrases the message of " The Burning Cross " when he says, " There is something I will always remember. I learned it in school. President Lincoln said, ' Government of the people, by the people, for the people.' I was born in America. My father was born in America, and his father before him. So I figure that what Mr. Lincoln said includes me too."

Many of us would be interested to know if Hollywood's " new liberalism " will continue in the post-war years. Leon H. Hardwick, noted Negro writer, does not think so. He points out, in *Hollywood Quarterly*, January, 1946 : " From 1941 to 1944 there was a decided improvement in Hollywood's treatment of the American of colour. The emphasis on morale-building entertainment as part of the war effort resulted in an increased employment of Negro players. They took part in entertaining members of the armed forces at various camps and recreational centres and in bond-selling drives and other war-related activities. During the same period the Negro public displayed a growing interest in coloured players and in the types of rôles assigned to them. Most of the studios answered affirmatively the demand for better and more dignified rôles for coloured artists, but in the past year or so, since the end of hostilities, there has been a decided drop in the employment of Negro actors and actresses. It is said that orders have been given to ' write out ' Negro characterisations in story scripts for fear of giving offence." (Nevertheless it is reported that full-length feature films are being planned at the time of writing, based on the lives of Negro scientist Dr. George Washington Carver, and Captain Hugh Mulzac, the first Negro master of a white crew in the modern American Merchant Marine. As to this, we shall see.)

Red Kann, Hollywood commentator, writing in the trade journal *Motion Picture Herald*, February 22nd, 1947, points out : " It is interesting to note that the Motion Picture Export Association is stepping up a self-regulation of product designed for the thirteen countries in which M.P.E.A. operates for most producing and distributing organisations. As Eric Johnston explained in Washington, the idea is to seek to eliminate those films which fail to reflect America as she is, not as some insular producer in Hollywood imagines her to be.

" Involved here, it ought to be understood, is no question of the right of the American industry to export what it wants within the formula applying to the nations serviced by the Export Association. But motion pictures are so much an influence and our national reputation so incalculably vital to the national scene that inevitably there enter considerations reaching beyond the normal channels of commerce.

" Once more this serves to stress the undeniable truth that, while films have entertainment as their primary function, at the same time they cannot escape being a method of communication as well. What is communicated, here and everywhere around the world, therefore must be given the most serious consideration— politically, economically and morally within the entertainment package."

Let us hope that many producers will take heed of the words of David O. Selznick, who in spite of having been the man responsible for the film of " Gone With The Wind," apparently experienced a change of mind and declared in December, 1945 : " Hollywood studios stand ready to make pictures emphasising racial unity." Also allying himself with the New Deal for Negroes is Eric Johnston, President of the Motion Picture Association of America, who is reported, in the *Motion Picture Herald*, December, 1945, as saying : " If our American ideal does not prevail, some other, embodying the ideology of some slave state will prevail. We can no longer afford to avoid this challenge in our Press, on the radio, in our airways. Everyone of us who has a rôle, however small, in the making of opinion and the fashioning of institutions has a duty to perform. And that we must fight divisive ideas, that we must smash myths of previous races and groups, goes without saying."

CHAPTER TEN

WHAT OF THE FUTURE?

" Even today the motion picture has not quite outgrown its immaturity. It still uses talented Negro players to fit into the old sterotypes of the loving Mammy and the comic servant that have both almost disappeared from the theatre."

EDITH J. R. ISAACS *in " Theatre Arts," August, 1942.*

" The coloured American recognises that he has a tremendous stake in the current struggle to highlight the importance of the social responsibility of motion pictures in the custom of new patterns of universal understanding and inter-racial adjustment,"

LEON HARDWICK, secretary, *International Film and Radio Guild.*

In the past ten years forceful protests against Hollywood type casting have come from various American organisations, including the Writers War Board, the Hollywood Writers Mobilization, various sections of the Negro Press and of the Liberal and Left white Press, including such papers as *P.M., The Nation* and the *New York Daily Worker.*

The two principal groups in the U.S.A. to have made the most concentrated efforts in this campaign in recent years have been the National Association for the Advancement of Coloured People (N.A.A.C.P.), and the International Film and Radio Guild (I.F.R.G.). Both organisations have been in the forefront of the move towards a just depiction of the Negro in American films, and both have done a great deal to improve the situation, especially during the war years. For example in 1946 they both led the campaign against the contemplated screening of " Uncle Tom's Cabin " by Metro-Goldwyn-Mayer, resulting in that studio's decision to abandon the project. They persuaded Twentieth Century-Fox to alter the title of René Clair's film " Ten Little Niggers " to " Ten Little Indians," and to delete the word " nigger " from the film's dialogue, in order not to give offence to coloured Americans. They also staged protests against the filming of " Song Of The South," the Walt Disney film which presents once more that beloved menial figure of early American fiction, Uncle Remus, " the superstitious, dialect-speaking lovable nigger of the South," and a character, to quote from *Time*, November 22nd, 1946, " bound to enrage all educated Negroes." In the latter case they were not so successful, for the film was screened in 1947.

(Frederic Mullally brings up an interesting sidelight on the above in *Tribune*, November 22nd, 1946. He writes : " I put a question to Mr. Walt Disney at a Press conference held this week. I thought it was a fair enough question from a film critic to a film producer. It was about Mr. Disney's latest film, ' Song Of The South,' an adaptation of Joel Chandler Harris's classic tales about the philosophical old Negro Uncle Remus, Brer Rabbit, Brer Fox and the other well-loved Harris creations. I asked Mr. Disney if it is true that educated Negroes in America are protesting about the treatment of Uncle Remus in his film, regarding it as a not very subtle attempt to confirm the white American's argument that the Negro was a much more likeable fellow when, like Uncle Remus, he ' knew his place ' and had no impertinent political or social aspirations.

" If Mr. Disney had replied, in effect, that he was conscious of this criticism, was sorry that some Negroes took it that way, but had decided that Uncle Remus ought to be above the hurly-burly of contemporary minority struggles, I would have been glad to leave it at that. Instead he denied that there would be any real antagonism towards the film, went on to assert that the criticism came from the radicals, 'who just love stirring up trouble whenever they can,' and, in reply to a supplementary from myself, declared that the time had not yet come when Negro susceptibilities could be treated with as much delicacy as Hollywood reserves for, say, the American Catholics ! ")

In 1945 the N.A.A.C.P. set up an organisation in Hollywood to advise producers and to analyse screenplays containing Negro characterisations, but, surprisingly, it was fought by Negro artists in Hollywood, who, later on, formed the Institute of Progressive Artists of America. This group was composed of coloured film players, and declared itself to be an organisation " to protect and safeguard the interests and employment possibilities of Negro film artists." Apparently some Negro actors are not so much concerned with the type of rôles that they play as with the *number* of rôles. Although one can easily appreciate their point of view since acting is in any case a precarious means of livelihood, it is to be hoped that the Institute of Progressive Artists of America will work in close collaboration with the N.A.A.C.P. and the I.F.R.G., so that, in general, the treatment of Negroes on the screen will become more realistic at the same time as their employment possibilities become of a less casual nature.

For it would seem that if Negro parts become more important in themselves, then Negro actors would share in increased benefits in every direction, both æsthetically and financially. Indeed it has been noted that one of the results of the rising protests by Negro groups has been that some studios have, in fact, improved Negro characterisations. (In some cases, however, as Leon Hardwick has noted, they have responded to objections by completely writing out the part. This might have been due to a fear of giving offence to Negro opinion, or maybe it was merely to safeguard their own interests by appeasing the South.) It must be agreed, in any case, that some of the improvements in the general situation apparent during the past five or six years are due in no small measure to the increased militance of various Negro organisations, and often to the courageous and defiant attitude of some important Negro players. Paul Robeson, for example, has rejected a number of screen rôles in the past few years, and it is to be hoped that other prominent Negro actors will emulate his example, and that of Charles Gilpin, for instance, who left the cast of at least two films, " Uncle Tom's Cabin " and " Hearts In Dixie," because he felt that the parts as written were an insult to his race. Gilpin had great courage, for it is not an easy task to reject a film rôle and retard one's progress in one's chosen profession simply because of a question of principles ; his name will always be revered for his bravery, dignity and pioneer work in protesting so practically against the stereotype.

The N.A.A.C.P. has, of course, been doing much valuable work in improving Negro conditions and social relations for a number of years. It is the most famous American organisation of its kind, and Walter White, the National Secretary, is a nation-wide figure of great repute. As long ago as 1928 White was conducting courageous attacks on producers. He expressed the hope in *Close Up*, August, 1929 : " Perhaps in time we may evolve to the point where film-makers may have intelligence and courage enough to utilise the excellent material contained in some of the more notable novels written about the Negro by Negro and white

writers during the last few years." White has always been in
the forefront of all movements to improve race relations, both
on the stage and screen and in social life in the U.S.A.

In 1944 the International Film and Radio Guild was formed,
as an educational organisation dedicated to a programme of
fostering and developing inter-racial understanding, protecting
the interests of minority groups as represented through the media
of motion pictures, radio, television and other fields of entertainment, and to the protection of national unity through the process
of audience education. The I.F.R.G. is composed of those who
believe in the idea that, for the film (and radio) industries to
assume their rightful rôle of leadership in the new world, each
must base entertainment values on fact not fiction, on realism not
fallacies. The organisation is directed at screen and radio writers,
directors, producers, actors, actresses and others, as well as to the
mass of laymen who support these industries.

The basic aims of the I.F.R.G. are as follows :—

(a) To create an awareness of misrepresentations of minorities
among theatre, film and radio audiences and to organise these
audiences into I.F.R.G. and keep them informed concerning
conditions in the entertainment world regarding the presentation of minorities.

(b) To influence producers, directors, writers and performers
towards creating truthful, realistic and democratic presentations
of minorities.

(c) To watch carefully portrayals and presentations of minorities
and to scrutinise and analyse thoroughly motion pictures and
radio programmes, thus acting as a guard against distortion of
characters which would cast in any way a derogatory light on
any minority group because of race, creed, colour or religion.

I.F.R.G., with headquarters in Los Angeles and maintaining
close contact with Hollywood through its National Secretary,
Leon H. Hardwick, well-known publicist, screenwriter and lecturer,
seeks more equitable employment of coloured people in all branches
of motion pictures and radio industries. It also aims at the
complete abolition of group stereotyping on a colour, cultural,
racial or religious basis in Hollywood motion pictures, demanding
a fuller integration of minority characterisations into films dealing
with the typical life of any community, state or nation. The
organisation has attempted also to obtain Negro and minority

representation from various motion picture boards of review in communities throughout the United States.

In addition to sponsoring mass meetings, panel discussions, forums and other types of affairs designed to keep the American people informed as to the contributions of the film and radio industries to public welfare, I.F.R.G., through survey and study, examines the policies of film and radio corporations, and through detailed analyses of motion pictures it seeks to acquaint the general public with the significance of these productions as well as with their entertainment value.

The organisation compiles a regular list of approved films produced by each studio, submitting this list to its members and to newspapers, civic groups and persons and units in sympathy with the aims and objects of the Guild. It has commenced publication of a national monthly magazine, featuring articles, comments, and statistical data on the motion picture and radio industries of the United States and other countries. To sum up : with every means at its disposal the International Film and Radio Guild actively opposes all motion picture and radio presentations which conflict with its campaign against undignified and un-American portrayals of minorities. On the other hand the organisation makes it quite clear that it will encourage actively the production of films and radio programmes which tend to promote greater unity and understanding among the peoples of the world through balanced and realistic characterisation. Among the leading American actors and actresses associated with the I.F.R.G. in the work it is doing are John Garfield (vice-president), Lena Horne, Joseph Calleia, Rita Hayworth, Rex Ingram, Paul Robeson, and Clarence Muse.

A group which has recently done some good work in the field of race relations is the Independent Citizens' Committee of the Arts, Sciences and Professions. Inspired by Franklin D. Roosevelt, the Committee came into being in 1944 and most of the politically-conscious workers in the field of literature, art, theatre and cinema belong to the organisation. Among the members of the I.C.C.A.S.P. are Walter Huston, Fredric March, Charles Boyer, Humphrey Bogart, Edward G. Robinson, Charles Laughton, Robert Young, Lena Horne, Hazel Scott, Bette Davis, Jo Davidson and Frank Sinatra. (Frank Sinatra, long known for his interest in racial questions, and who has been speaking at various meetings all over the U.S.A. for the past few years against all forms of racial and religious persecution, is a member of the committee of the I.C.C.A.S.P. and other similar organisations. In 1945 he received a special Academy Award for his work in sponsoring and acting in a splendid short film, " The House I Live In," a powerful plea for racial tolerance.) In its issue of September 9th, 1946, *Time* stated, " I.C.C.A.S.P. is a unique leverage on thousands of U.S. voters."

It was founded in 1944 by half a dozen notabilities, including Ethel Barrymore, Van Wyck Brooks, Quentin Reynolds and sculptor Jo Davidson. " We were mostly virgin voices in things politically," states Davidson now. " Most of us had been liberals, which meant that we did a lot of yapping and intellectualising about things, but few of us had actually participated. And until you participate it doesn't count." Today I.C.C.A.S.P. is growing rapidly, and under the leadership of Harold Ickes it has become, as *Time* says : " A political phenomenon unique in U.S. history." It has made a strong stand against Jim Crow and the existence of all forms of discrimination. In the U.S.A. where film-stars and big names in literature and the theatre have a great sway with the public, it is quite likely that the I.C.C.A.S.P. will be able to exert something of a major influence over Americans in the next few years. At any rate it has made a very good start.

The Negro Actors' Guild of America, under the guidance of Mabel Roane, exerts a considerable influence in the theatre world and has made a number of important moves towards the bettering of rôles for coloured actors and the elimination of sequences in plays and shows which are considered racially out of date. Among the actors on the executive board and committee of the N.A.G.A. are Todd Duncan, Katherine Dunham, Paul Robeson, Bill Robinson, Leigh Whipper, Ethel Waters, Dooley Wilson, Fredi Washington, J. Rosamond Johnson, Bing Crosby, Louis Armstrong, Mary McLeod Bethune and Marian Anderson.

There is also the Common Council For American Unity, in New York, which was formed for the following purposes :—

1. To help create among the American people the unity and mutual understanding resulting from a common citizenship, a common belief in democracy and the ideals of liberty, the placing of the common good before the interests of any group, and the

acceptance, in fact as well as in law, of all citizens, whatever their national or racial origin, as equal partners in American life.

2. To further an appreciation of what each group has contributed to America, to uphold the freedom to be different, and to encourage the growth of an American culture which will be truly representative of all the elements which make up the American people.

3. To overcome intolerance and discrimination because of national origin, race or creed.

4. To help the foreign-born and their children to solve their special problems of adjustment, know and value their particular cultural heritage, and share fully and constructively in American life.

The C.C.A.U. publishes its own magazine, *Common Ground*, and among the distinguished names connected with this organisation and its work are Van Wyck Brooks, Pearl Buck, Mary Ellen Chase and Langston Hughes. In *Common Ground* a number of articles have appeared on the subject of the Negro's position in Hollywood, and racial interpretation on the screen is one of the topics most often discussed by the group.

In Great Britain there are two main bodies with a common aim, the abolition of discrimination : The League of Coloured Peoples and the Racial Relations Group. The League, founded by Dr. Harold Moody, who is also the president at the present time, has a long and distinguished record. Among its objects are those of improving relationships between the races, and co-operation with all other peoples. " For co-operation there must be understanding and this can only come if the better qualities of both sides can be seen," Dr. Moody declares, and goes on : " Evidence seems to point to the emphasising of the worst features of the Negro to the exclusion of his better qualities and recognition of his steady contribution to world improvement. The screen is one of the most powerful organs of education and the League deplores what appears to have been a constant tendency to stereotype the Negro as shoe-shine boy, Pullman porter and generally what is known as the ' Yes Boss Nigger ' in America."

The League has always protested at this stubbornly-held attitude, but has realised that apart from the merely commercial aspect an extensive process of education was necessary. It noted that British studios have been the first to take any steps in the required direction, though in some respects they have, in the past, been as guilty as Hollywood. For example, Dr. Moody refers to the film " Sanders Of The River," in which a white man asks a Negro, " Whose dog are you ? " ; and a great Negro artist playing the native rôle has to affirm his servility. " We consequently welcome," says Dr. Moody, " the forward trend, particularly as shown in the recent film ' Men Of Two Worlds,' in which Robert Adams plays a leading part. Here for the first time in the history of the screen a Negro is portrayed as an artist, a human individual with the normal passions and reactions of a man, and an associate and an equal with the white man. England has made the first move, a momentous one, in race relationships. May we hope that America will soon follow, and that this will be the dawn of a new understanding between the races."

The League has done much good work in the past years, helping, advising, sending lecturers to all parts of the country and intervening in disputes between film studios and coloured players. In fact, in many ways the League is the guardian angel of coloured peoples in the British Isles, and has worked hard to further the betterment of race relations in Europe generally. It has been helped considerably in this work by the formation of an independent body, known as the Racial Relations Group, an organisation associated with the Institute of Sociology. The Group has as its aim to explore available sources of information relative to the problems of race and inter-racial contacts, with the ultimate purpose of improving racial and natural relations. It was formed in 1938 and exists to spread a knowledge of the findings of science and the teachings of ethics and religion on the unity of mankind. Its aim is to remove racial and natural prejudices and to spread a spirit of mutual esteem, co-operation and friendship between all members of the human family. It looks forward to the achievement of harmony among all peoples, the free exchange of material products and cultural values and the final ending of war.

The Group recognises that its aim cannot be attained by denying or ignoring differences in the institutions and culture of races and nations. Many distinguished writers, however, agree in the conviction that such differences are not fundamental nor irreconcilable, and that they can be harmonised and turned to account, by education in mutual understanding and goodwill. The Group carries on several activities. Regular meetings are held at which members and visitors give addresses on racial problems, which are followed by discussions. It has also published a successful series of booklets entitled *Studies In Conflict And Co-operation*. There exists a panel of lecturers and distinguished men of letters whose services are available to societies and schools. Descriptive notes on current literature on racial questions are circulated to members, and newspaper cuttings and other materials on these problems are collected to form a permanent library on racial relations. It is intended to collect facts and opinions on all aspects of race relations with the object of the annual publication of a year-book. Furthermore, the use of such materials for study and research will be placed at the disposal of any organisation to whom an information service is avai.able. The Group offers its co-operation to institutions and movements interested in similar aims, e.g., universities, scientific societies, missions and organisations for educational and social work.

Apart from the work of these two bodies in Great Britain, the Communist Party and its newspaper the *Daily Worker* is extremely active in all matters dealing with the treatment of coloured citizens and the improvement of race relations generally. Also there are several newspapers, such as the *News-Chronicle*, *Sunday Pictorial* and *Reynolds News* which give wide publicity to racial injustice, and in fact it has often been the case that outspoken articles in such British publications as *News-Chronicle*, *Tribune* and *New Statesman* have often seriously embarrassed American opinion, noticeably sensitive on the question of its treatment of its Negro minority.

In addition, the Socialist Book Centre has a wide distribution organisation which handles such Negro magazines as *Ebony*, *Negro Digest* and *Our World* in Europe. The author himself, who is the European representative of the International Film and Radio Guild of America, is also active in work towards the betterment of race relations and since 1944 has headed a rapidly growing group, the Society for the Prevention of Racial Discrimination. This body, with Robert Adams as president, carries on much the same kind of work as the Racial Relations Group, but with a certain concentration on aspects relating particularly to stage and screen characterisation.

Each of these various bodies has its own conception of the best method to end discrimination on the screen ; the main work of the N.A.A.C.P. and the I.F.R.G. in the U.S.A., and the L.C.P. and the R.R.G. in Britain is to co-ordinate and co-relate the activities of those scattered organisations and individuals who are working with a common aim. There are a number of such individuals in the U.S.A. and Europe. For example, Phil Carter, well-known Hollywood writer, outlines, in an article in *The Crisis*, what he describes as " his seven point plan for action," as follows :—

1. Negro spokesmen should talk to Hollywood, not in moral terms, but in realistic terms of the box office. The figures are there, and all they need is dramatic and purposeful interpretation.

2. Negroes should give more of their patronage to the smaller cinemas where audience reaction is of vital importance to the producers, and also since it is here that most of the box office receipts in the U.S.A. are taken.

3. More Negro capital should be invested in cinema ownership and management.

4. Independent producers should be persuaded to show their films in Negro theatres at the same time as they are shown in white cinemas.

5. All Government moves towards regulation of the film industry should be noted by Negro commentators, for this is Hollywood's Achilles' heel.

6. Greater concern with the entry of the sixteen millimetre film into the commercial field should be shown. These films require less money to produce, and the fact that they can be accepted in places other than the usual commercial theatres may create a new conception of values. Furthermore, since the major Hollywood producers are concerned about the new sixteen millimetre industry, Negroes might try to establish themselves in this field as quickly as possible.

7. Finally, the Negro Press should assign competent and uncorrupted writers to deal regularly with criticism of all new films.

Carter's programme has received wide publicity and much support in the U.S.A. Thus the move against discrimination grows daily, not only by the N.A.A.C.P. and the I.F.R.G., but by private individuals, writers, artists, social workers and others in Hollywood, Europe and elsewhere, who are striving in their various ways towards a common aim. What can each of us do personally, those of us who believe that conditions can and will be improved if a large enough number of filmgoers desire it ? The situation involves tremendous difficulties. It is not enough to say we will *not* patronise films which we know depict Negroes in a bad light, although that is a considerable step. We must also write letters to film companies and to the newspapers, letters of protest, letters of constructive suggestions as to what we wish to see in our motion picture entertainment. Here, for example, is the kind of letter I mean ; it appeared in the *New York Times*, September 9th, 1945.

" To the Editor,

I wish to call your attention to an important small detail in an important long picture. The picture is ' Wilson.' The detail is the short scene in which a non-white has a speaking part. The massive, smiling Negro servant tells Mrs. Wilson that he ' 'members her from Alabama 'cause his mammy used to wash for her mother.' Mrs. Wilson responds graciously, and the man rejoices that he now has someone who's ' gwine to speak my language.' The importance of this detail is that it is the only contact between races that this two and a half hour long picture of a great democrat and an American era depicts. The democrat, Mr. Wilson, gives verbal service to racial equality freely. But the action illustrates Hollywood's conception of racial equality with this little 'ole massa ' scene.

Now you may flick over your memory of ' Wilson ' and decide that it must be a pedant indeed who would hold such a casual little incident against a picture filled with such noble ideals. But you saw the picture in New York. I saw it in North Carolina. Here, the audience broke into spontaneous applause for this servant-master vignette. (The only other applause of the evening heralded the first appearance of the North Carolinan, Josephus Daniels.)

Well, you may reason, perhaps the good Southerners were just pleased that the servant-master relationships can be so happy— maybe they were showing their love for the little black brother. In that case the applause would be from one side only. For theatres in our little town don't bother with segregation, they just exclude all Negroes.

Seriously, I believe that the movies have an unmatchable opportunity to improve race relations. What many people need to see is simply that individuals can work together and play together without regard to colour lines. Just to have a camera pick up faces in a crowd without emphasis or discrimination is something.

The film on the Liberation of Paris, shown by the Free French, did this. Why should a picture such as ' Wilson ' botch such a chance ?

> Yours sincerely,
> (Signed) MARY RENTZ,
> Chapel Hill,
> North Carolina."

If letters like the above were sent to national newspapers often enough, and printed often enough ; if people who cared about these things did everything in their power to make their protests felt, then Hollywood would eventually have to take heed of this current of opinion. Here in England many of us feel deeply about the anomaly of the position of the Negro minority in the U.S.A. For instance, political journalist S. L. Solon, writing in the *News-Chronicle*, May 8th, 1944, states : " American Negroes figure with distinction in sciences, literature, art and the entertainment world. The stereotyped Hollywood characterisation of the Negro as a humorous, spiritual-singing, habitual servitor is a serious distortion of the contribution which the Negro has made to American life." And this is the general belief of all clear-thinking people, both in Europe and the U.S.A. But whether Hollywood takes any account of clear-thinking people when it is planning, producing and casting its films is another matter entirely.

There are fourteen million Negroes in America, a considerable audience body which should be encouraged to make its demands heard. But as William Grant Still, the Negro composer, pointed out in an article in *Opportunity*, Spring, 1945, we must first of all clarify the issue in our own mind, which is that film producing is a business, first and last. Therefore if Negroes want Hollywood to do anything for them they must make it unprofitable for them *not* to do it, and therefore profitable for them to do it.

There are eight major companies in Hollywood, each of which obtains money to finance its productions either from its own resources, or from banks, which have direct financial interest in the studio. In addition to these major companies, there are also a number of independent producers working in Hollywood. Briefly, the procedure when an independent producer wishes to make a film is as follows. He must first sell his idea for a film to his backer, or to the bank which finances him. Obviously the bank which puts up the money will demand to study the outline of the film in question, taking into consideration the treatment, the central idea, the stars who will appear in it, its appeal to a wide audience, and so on. Thus the bank has a great deal to say about the kind of films being made by many Hollywood producers ; and if a bank considers that a film dealing with a controversial theme will fail to make a considerable return for their outlay, then they will refuse to finance the film. So Hollywood, on the whole, plays safe.

It follows therefore that all æsthetic, social, and other considerations aside, we must concentrate on Hollywood as a business centre, and attempt to convince producers that there is good business in making good Negro films, i.e., films in which Negroes appear in sympathetic rôles. This is obviously a long job, but no one will deny that the racial situation has eased considerably during the past ten years, and continued agitation by interested bodies will eventually, I am sure, make some indent on Hollywood's apparently implacable surface.

And there are a growing number of social-conscious directors that we can look to for help in this matter. As Elmer Anderson Carter, editor of *Opportunity*, once remarked : " Only a motion picture impresario endowed with exceptional courage will attempt to film a great epic of the Negro in America, or will dare to fight in the heroic struggle of this unfortunate people for the universal human attributes of mankind. And unless he fights these things, easy for the unprejudiced eye to see, he will never attain that height of artistry, the basis of which has been and must always be the truth." Some Hollywood directors are even now managing to get sequences into their films which would have been left on the cutting room floor ten years ago. It is to these enlightened men that we must look for aid against cinematic discrimination.

Lawrence Reddick has written, in his pamphlet on race relations : " The treatment of the Negro by the movie is inaccurate and unfair. Directly and indirectly it establishes associations and drives deeper into the public mind the stereotype conception of the Negro. By building up this unfavourable conception, the movies operate to thwart the advancement of the Negro, to humiliate him, to weaken his drive for equality and to spread indifference, contempt and hatred for him and his cause. This great agency for the communication of ideas and information, therefore, functions as a powerful instrument for maintaining the racial subordination of the Negro people."

" If all this is true," Reddick continues, " it goes without saying that any real programme of correcting the mistreatment of the Negro by the movie industry must include basic changes in the social order of which the movies are a part. But more immediately and directly such a programme would surely need to consider the following :—

(*a*) The use of non-commercial movies which treat the Negro favourably. There are any number of worth-while films which have been produced or distributed by Government agencies, labour unions, film libraries or other educational institutions. The entertainment quality of this type of film is being constantly improved. Churches, schools, libraries, clubs, Y.M.C.A.'s and other organised groups could make wide use of these inexpensive shows ; and

(*b*) The production of more and better films by Negroes themselves. So far most of the movies made by Negro producers have been of poor quality. Yet the success of Oscar Micheaux with his melodramas suggest what could be done if those who know better would help.

Dr. Reddick goes on to make the following suggestions for exerting some pressure on Hollywood :—

1. There should be local committees for cultural democracy as part of the race relations betterment organisations. These should be affiliated to a national committee of this sort.

2. Such committees should undertake sufficient research to document, chapter and verse, the generalisation that the Negro is inaccurately and unfairly presented on the screen.

3. The widest dissemination ought to be given to this information so that the movie-going public, movie critics, actors, screenwriters and producers will be aware of these facts.

4. Direct contact should be established and maintained with all of the elements which enter into the production and distribution of films. This means that such conferences as those of Walter White and the late Wendell Wilkie with Hollywood executives should be repeated and that the organisations of the screenwriters, actors, distributors, film reviewers and so forth should be worked with and induced to impose upon themselves a code such as has been worked out by the Emergency Committee of the Entertain-

ment Industry.   Negro actors in particular must be supported when they refuse to accept Uncle Tom and Aunt Jemima rôles.

5. All of the devices of leaflet, news story, picket line and so forth should be used to " educate " theatregoers to the end of organising boycotts of anti-Negro films.   A good start may be made with the five hundred odd theatres in Negro neighbourhoods.   But the fight must extend far beyond these limits.   A special effort should be made to gain the support of progressive, liberal, religious and labour-union-conscious groups.

6. Present censorship councils and boards of review should be worked with to include treatment of the Negro in films as part of their codes.   These bodies include not only the movie industry's self-imposed Eric Johnston Office, but The National Legion of Decency, National Board of Review and various religious, civic and state councils.

7. Though the Office of War Information has declined to advise Hollywood on the question of the treatment of the Negro, it and other Governmental agencies may be persuaded to throw their great influence in the right direction, as is now done with reference to rôles or scenes which may be offensive to Latin America, China and other parts of the world.   As a beginning the Government might ban the use of such terms as " nigger," " darky," " piccaninny," " Smoke," " Sambo," " coon " and " WACoon."

In an article which asks " How Do We Stand In Hollywood? " appearing in *Opportunity*, William Grant Still sums up the message of this chapter as follows :   " Hollywood has shown, with rare exceptions, only one side of Negro life to such an extent that one Negro writer, in desperation, begged for a coloured villain, just to break the stereotype !   The Negro is willing to be portrayed on the screen in any truthful way, as long as aspiring Negro people are filmed along with the servants and the theatrical figures.   He does not want to be stuffy.   He wants to laugh too, but until a few more decent portrayals come along, he has to remain a crusader.

" There may come a day when the Negro will have seen so many other sides of Negro life on the screen that he can afford to condone quaint Negro characters and folky acting.   At present he cannot do so for the simple reason that many white people are coming to regard those simple characters as typical of an entire race, and that will not aid good race relations in America, nor will it please people in foreign countries whose skins are not white.

" For the present, we would like to see ridiculous, criminal, superstitious and immoral characterisations eliminated ; Negroes cast in other than servant rôles ; Negroes' contribution to the war and to American life pictured truthfully ; Negroes included as extras in background groups ; Negroes employed in studios in other positions than those of actor and menial ; Negroes employed as authorities on the Negro. We would like to see all-Negro films abolished for, no matter how expensive and glamorous they are, they still glorify segregation. In short, we would like to see the Negro presented to the world and to America as a normal American. If this were done, the film could make a real contribution to inter-racial understanding and to a better world."

APPENDIX A

A BRIEF NOTE BY THE AUTHOR ON THE HISTORICAL BACKGROUND OF THE AMERICAN NEGRO

" From the time the first slave ship anchored off the coast of Virginia in 1619 until the present time, the Aframerican, as he has been felicitously designated, has been the most persistent insoluble in the chemistry of Americanization. As a result, around him have whirled the mightiest forces of American life. He has been the cause of bitter strife, the genesis of devastating conflicts, and the source of endless speculation and perplexity."

ELMER ANDERSON CARTER, *Editor, Opportunity.*

The first Negroes to enter America landed at Jamestown, Virginia, in 1619, when a Dutch trading vessel exchanged fourteen black men from Africa for fresh food and supplies. By 1662 there were some two thousand Negro slaves in Jamestown. The slave trade had become extremely profitable, and gained momentum in the Southern States of America to such an extent that by the end of the 17th Century the Negro slave had become an accepted part of the American scene. The misery of the bewildered black men, torn from their own homes and brought in chains to this cruel New World, was indescribable. A new era of horror commenced. But not only in the South.

In 1626 eleven Negro slaves were imported from Africa to a Dutch outpost in North America called New Amsterdam. Some forty years afterwards the British took over this outpost, and the province became known as New York. It is interesting to note that thenceforward the by then enlarged colony of slaves was treated with increased cruelty : they were forbidden by law to own property, were not permitted to gather in groups of more than three, and were not allowed on the streets at night without carrying a lantern. Apart from that, the personal cruelties and indignities inflicted on them were varied and extensive. The cruel system of segregation commenced, the same segregation which resulted from fear and which has been responsible for the continuance of racial conflict these past three hundred years. The slave trade increased in scope (more than two million slaves were imported to the British colonies between 1680 and 1780), while the treatment of the slaves seemed to become more inhuman in proportion.

More than a hundred years passed, years of cruelty by the whites and revolt by the blacks. Various Negro rebellions against slavery were crushed, their leaders were put to death, and the business in human flesh continued unabated, with occasional bouts of protests from liberal-minded whites, protests which had very little effect. In 1808 a bill became law, prohibiting slave trading, but all the slave-owners resisted any move to free the slaves they already possessed.

But following the war of 1812 a movement became apparent among the slaves themselves, a movement which grew steadily as their conditions worsened. The Negroes demanded freedom to meet socially, more education and better conditions of work. In 1812 the African Society for Mutual Relief was formed and did much good work of a reformist kind. Other similar Negro groups also sprang up. The slaves were beginning to realise that they were human beings too, though as yet they had not come to demand complete freedom from their serfdom. The desire for self expression also became apparent. In 1821 a body of professional-class Negroes—butlers, better-class servants, valets and so on—managed to form their own theatrical group and even took a New York theatre, known as the African Grove, to present a season of legitimate drama. The programmes were received with great interest by mixed audiences, but the group was later suppressed.

And generally the conditions of the Northern slaves began to improve as their masters realised that the blacks were men just as they themselves were. Many gave their slaves their freedom, and over a period of years slavery virtually disappeared from the North. But down in the South rumblings of discontent were heard. Here the slave trade had become even more considerable ; indeed in some districts the blacks out-numbered their white masters. In the Southern States the whites had exceeded in cruelty and barbarism even the earlier vicious measures of the North. Runaway slaves were the order of the day, and among progressive white people grew a movement which steadily gathered voice and momentum, the movement for the abolition of slavery. Many Negro leaders, former slaves who had escaped from the South, found their way to the Northern cities where slavery had been allowed to disappear, and where they could get work as free men. Gradually an invisible line of demarcation could be seen dividing the South from the more liberal North. In 1832 the first Negro newspaper was founded and called *Freedom's Journal* ; the black man was beginning to find himself, and the conscience of America showed signs of stirring. By 1840 such organisations as " The Friends of Immediate Abolition " and " The New York Anti-Slavery Society " were rousing opinion in the whole of the United States, and the movement to free the slaves grew more rapidly, especially in the North. A convention was held in Philadelphia, at which a national body was formed called " The American Anti-Slavery Society " ; at this meeting a resolution demanding " immediate and unconditional abolishment of slavery " was adopted. New York was selected as headquarters and such was the vigour of the movement that by 1845 this Society had over 2,000 branches throughout the United States.

The passion aroused by the strong division of opinion on the question of slavery was indicated by the storm which greeted the publication in 1852 of Harriet Beecher Stowe's famous anti-slavery novel *Uncle Tom's Cabin*. This memorable book had a profound effect on the South, and was immediately followed by a score of pro-slavery novels and books by Southern writers. But by this time the tide had turned ; the great mass of liberal opinion was in favour of the complete abolition of slavery. It was a nation-wide issue ; as Frederick Douglass, great Negro-leader and friend of Lincoln, declared, " After the execution of the famous abolitionist, John Brown, together with his Negro and white comrades, the whole line rocked with this great controversy."

Then came the war, the Civil War, which arose out of Lincoln's declared object to save the Union. Nevertheless it was regarded by abolitionists everywhere as a move towards complete Negro emancipation, and eventually there came a great step forward. Black men were allowed to enter the Union Army, and in 1862 the Emancipation Proclamation decreed that all persons held as slaves in the Southern States were to be set free, and could, if they liked, be received into the Armed Services of the United States ! In other words, Lincoln by this diplomatic measure invited all slaves in the rebel states to come over to the side of the Union. And they did ; they rallied to the Union flag, and as Abraham Lincoln himself wrote, " Many of the most important battles would have been lost if the Negro soldiers had not flocked into the Northern Army."

The war of 1860-64 ended in a decisive victory for the North, and soon followed the Thirteenth, Fourteenth and Fifteenth Amendments, ending slavery, giving the rights of citizenship to Negroes, and giving Negroes the vote. The latter was passed in 1871, but oddly enough in the next half-century the Negro's status as a citizen gradually began to decline, for a variety of reasons.

Following the wave of liberalism and the widespread demands for the abolition of slavery which had swept the country over a long period, the inevitable reaction set in, and to an extent the sweet taste of victory of the Negroes in their fight for emancipation seemed to turn to ashes in their mouths. Now that slavery was abolished the mass of Americans seemed to care very little what happened to the liberated black men among them, and in fact a number of former abolitionists, in an endeavour to pin the cause of the Civil War on to a scapegoat, fastened the blame on the Negroes, with some results in affecting public opinion. Such was post-war psychology, the search for a scapegoat, a not unusual feature of all the great wars in history. The first victorious flush of the abolition movement gradually faded away, and in the South there came a sharp reaction against the former slaves, now working as labourers and share-croppers, and, indeed, in all the various menial tasks in which they had previously been engaged. For a long time freedom meant very little, in actual fact, to millions of coloured people. The dreaded Ku Klux Klan made its emergence in the South, ostensibly to protect the whites from the increasing menace of the emancipated blacks. And in the next few years the Klan and similar organisations committed countless outrages against human decency : lynching, whipping and beating Negroes for various " crimes," ranging from impudence to their white " superiors " to alleged mass rape of white women. Many freed slaves were turned adri without a job and thousands of Southern Negroes left their homes and decided to go North to New York and Chicago, there to make an attempt to escape the rising tide of Southern anti-Negroism which had developed so strongly in the middle 1800's.

All movements towards the furthering of human progress seem to exist in waves and cycles, and it was the same with the Negro struggle. After almost a quarter of a century of comparative quietude, suddenly, about ten years before the end of the Nineteenth Century, what had been up till then a steady ripple became a great wave of indignation, the indignation of the Negroes themselves. For some thirty years they had endured "freedom," but although the end of the Civil War had brought with it this great and wonderful concession they soon discovered that it was "freedom" either to starve or to slave for the white man. The contempt which white masters had felt for their slaves during the previous two hundred years had now turned into bitter, searing hatred. The basis of this hatred was fear of Negro equality—or worse, dominance, the fear which caused the formation of the Ku Klux Klan and similar fascist groups, the fear which caused the white men to pass vicious laws of segregation. It was this fear which caused miserable, foul Negro ghettoes to spring up in the big cities, where unofficial curfews prevailed and where any blacks found wandering in or near the white district at night were certain to be beaten, or worse.

As *Picture Post* aptly phrased it, in a special issue dealing with the United States : " The Civil War of 1860-64 was ostensibly fought by the North to bring an end to slavery in America. Actually it was nothing more than a successful attempt by the North to gain political dominance over an agricultural South, and the slavery issue merely provided the North with a moral justification for war. Neither the war nor the so-called Emancipation which followed in 1865 onwards materially altered the status of the Negroes. Technically they were free to earn a living, but they were everywhere denied equal competition with the white man."

And by 1890 this situation had brought about a new revolt, mostly among the better-educated Negroes. A class of literate black men had steadily grown up through the years, since the end of the Civil War, a class which included Negro revolutionaries, intellectuals, school-teachers, preachers, politicians and journalists. Heading this movement was the famous Booker T. Washington, who travelled about the country on lecture tours, demanding more education for his people, seeking funds for his school, and writing speeches and books, the most well-known of which was *Up From Slavery*, published in 1900. It has often been said that while *Uncle Tom's Cabin* was acknowledged to be the first book to cry out against slavery, Washington's famous and widely-read book was the first justification and fulfilment of Negro freedom. Known as " the father of his people," he passionately advocated further opportunity and education for Negroes and as Jonathan Daniel says, in the preface to *Up From Slavery* : " A whole race and a whole people can remember and respect such a fine American as Booker T. Washington." Hailed also as the

" economic emancipator of the Negro," this former slave succeeded over a long period in winning the support of many influential white people in both the North and in the Southern States, and coincident with his teachings and his great influence came a mass migration of Negroes to the North. Every month hundreds of coloured men and women poured into the Northern cities, particularly into Chicago and New York. All those who could manage to, left the South and the vicious discrimination which prevailed.

In 1900 New York's coloured population was in the region of sixty thousand, living mostly in the " Black Belt," called Harlem. Formerly a pleasant residential centre, Harlem gradually became the abode of Negro families after Bert Williams, the famous actor, and Harry Burleigh the Negro composer, both went to live in this district. Over a period of years the little colony of Negroes quickly expanded across Lenox Avenue and into St. Nicholas Park. Negro schools, clubs and churches sprang into existence rapidly, and soon a white face in the Harlem district became a rarity. Today more than 300,000 Negroes live in this district.

As Roi Ottley remarks in his book *New World A-Coming* (published in England under the title *Inside Black America*) " Harlem is now the nerve centre of Black America." It is indeed a complete country within a country. Here, as he says, as well as in Chicago and Washington, Negro newspapers, educators, politicians, lecturers, writers, artists, journalists, teachers, preachers all continue in their daily efforts to bring tolerance to the everyday scene. But it is hard work ; for as *Picture Post* stated a few years ago : " The economic and social discrimination in the region of the Black Belt in the Southern States, and the Negro districts of Harlem, Chicago and Washington, represents the most complete denial of democracy in the Western Hemisphere."

The treatment of coloured American citizens varies considerably from area to area. A third of the Negro population lives in the Northern States. Here they have, theoretically at least, the same political and social rights as the white population. They attend the same schools, are able to visit the same public places, use the same hospitals, transport facilities, restaurants and so on. Any discrimination by proprietors of restaurants against Negroes is an offence. During the war the position of all American Negroes showed much improvement economically. Some of America's biggest trades unions began to accept coloured members on the same basis as whites, and in thousands of factories and war plants Negro and white workers were employed side by side, sharing the same difficulties, and working under the same conditions. In the South, also, the Negro has made considerable progress in the past fifty years. Many more schools have been opened for coloured pupils and in industry the Negro's position has steadily increased in importance.

There are more than a hundred universities and colleges in the United States devoted to Negro education. There are fifty-six thousand Negro teachers, many of them teaching in mixed classes of both white and coloured students. It has been estimated that more than ninety per cent. of all American Negroes are now literate. And when one remembers that it is only eighty years ago that the practice of slavery still existed in the Southern States, this must be considered a considerable advancement.

It is provided in the American Constitution that colour should not be a bar to the political rights of an American citizen. And in spite of the fact that, in practice, many Southern States make it difficult for the Negro to use his vote by the use of poll tax and other means, slowly some of the local restrictions are disappearing. Today more than three hundred Negro newspapers and periodicals play their part in drawing attention to inequalities and injustices, and the Negro Press has a most important rôle in the modern scene.

In the past fifty years the conditions of U.S. Negroes have undergone certain improvements. It is still, however, a struggle for most black Americans to break down the mental attitude of the white population, which in the South assumes almost pathological proportions. It remains to be seen whether the Second World War has brought with it a drastic change in the social position of the black citizen. During the war he was employed side by side with white workers, fought side by side with white Americans in the U.S. Army, and in every way made the same sacrifices for final victory. It is possible that these contributions and sacrifices will be recognised and that the Negro will be able to take his place alongside his fellow citizens in the building of a post-war world and a permanent peace for all peoples. But it is certain that unless the American nation decides to do something about its Negro problem there can never be any hope for the world at large.

By 1946 there were more than fourteen million Negroes living in the United States of America. Their part in the re-making of the post-war world is becoming of ever-increasing significance. An American commentator writing in *Courier*, June, 1946, makes the following statement, which most of us would like to believe : " It is good to see that there is far less wild emotion on the one side, or wild romanticism on the other surrounding the Negro problem than there was even ten years ago. The curve of lynchings has fallen steadily over the years, almost to extinction-point. The new forces in American life—the young labour leaders of the Congress of Industrial Organisations, for example, or the young writers and politicians of the South—seem bent on working out solutions which will be to the benefit of white men as well as coloured men. They realise that they are all Americans in the same boat together and the boat doesn't look quite so large and commodious as it did some twenty-five years ago. They see that the America of the future must either be an amalgam or an anarchy. The metals in the melting pot are not yet fully fused. The Negro question in 1946 is still a challenge to American unity ; it is my faith now that Americans have a strong instinct in favour of unity. They can't make slaves of fourteen million Negroes—for there is no going back along the road—so it must make free men and women of them, not for their own sakes so much as for the sake of the community at large."

This may be true, but there is the more sinister aspect too. I quote from a leader article headed *Lynch Law*, which appeared in the London

Star, July 27th, 1946 : "There has been an explosion in Dixieland as sinister as those at Bikini. Two Negroes and their wives have been lynched by a gang of whites. A week ago Georgia's Eugene Talmadge was voted back as State Governor on the ticket, ' Show the nigger who is boss ! ' Evidently the black man is being shown. The U.S. Attorney-General has launched an investigation into this recrudescence of racial bestiality. It might be well if the Administration remembered that though Huey Long is dead his evil spirit goes marching on in the Deep South."

And this cynical paragraph appeared in *Newsweek*, August 27th, 1946 : " A tricky scheme to ban Negroes from Democratic primaries in the South and thus to evade the Supreme Court's 1944 ruling got its first test last week in South Carolina. It worked. Unlike other Southern states, which have permitted some Negroes to vote in Democratic primaries this year, South Carolina didn't let its 800,000 Negroes vote on August 13th.

" The plan had been patiently devised by ' white-supremacy ' advocates in the party : First, the party organisation converted itself into a club— ' a private voluntary association of individuals, mutually acceptable to each other,' in which Negroes obviously would not be acceptable. Next, the state legislature whipped through 141 new laws, repealing all primary statutes from the state's books and making party business strictly a club affair—theoretically exempt from Federal laws and court rulings. Finally, the club decided that all members must be ' able to read or write, and interpret the state constitution,' in order to make doubly sure to ' keep out of our party at least 90 per cent. of the people we don't want.'

" Even if the Democratic party was a private club as claimed, its primary last week was still tantamount to election. The result : Governor Ransome J. Williams, seeking renomination, ran a poor third in an eleven-man free-for-all. The two leading candidates were J. Strom Thurmond, former lieutenant colonel and circuit court judge, and James A. McLeod, surgeon and political novice who heads the State Medical Association. The one candidate who favoured letting Negroes into the party, A. L. Wood, polled only 2,500 of the 250,000 votes cast, running a poor tenth."

So there it is : discrimination and lynching. And this in 1946 !

Dr. Gunnar Myrdal has called his book on this problem *An American Dilemma*, and it is just that. More important than at any other time in history will be the inter-racial developments of the next few years. Assuredly the Negro problem, as a moral, social and economic issue, will become the personal concern of every American citizen. And in the struggle for complete equality, justice and recognition of the Negro's essential rights as a free citizen, the Press, radio, and more specifically the cinema, will continue to play their all-important rôles.

APPENDIX B

BIBLIOGRAPHY

BOOKS ON GENERAL ASPECTS OF RACE RELATIONS IN THE U.S.A.

(Note : Books specially recommended for study are marked with an *asterisk*).

ADAMS, JAMES TRUSLOW, *America's Tragedy*. New York : Charles Scribner's Sons, 1934.

*ALLEN, JAMES S., *The Negro Question in the United States*. New York : International Publishers, 1936.

AMES, JESSIE DANIEL, *The Changing Character of Lynching*. Atlanta : The Commission on Inter-racial Co-operation, Inc., July, 1942.

*BENEDICT, RUTH, *Race, Science and Politics*. New York : Modern Age Books, 1940. (Revised in 1943.)

BOND, HORACE MANN, *The Education of the Negro in the American Social Order*. New York : Prentice-Hall, Inc., 1934.

*BROWN, STERLING A., *The Negro in American Fiction*. Washington, D.C. : The Associates in Negro Folk Education, 1937 (Bronze Booklet No. 6).

*BROWN, STERLING A., *The Negro in Poetry and Drama*. (Bronze Booklet, 1938).

*BROWN, STERLING A., ARTHUR DAVIS and ULYSSES LEE, *Negro Caravan*. New York : Dryden Press, 1943.

BUCK, PAUL H., *The Road to Reunion*, 1865-1900. Boston : Little, Brown and Company, 1937.

*BUCKMASTER, HENRIETTA, *Let My People Go*. New York : Harper and Brothers, 1941.

BURNS, ROBERT E., *I am a Fugitive from a Georgia Chain Gang*. New York : The Vanguard Press, 1932.

CABLE, GEORGE W., *The Negro Question*. New York : American Missionary Association, 1888.

CAMPBELL, SIR GEORGE, *White and Black in the United States*. London : Chatto and Windus, 1879.

CARPENTER, MARIE E., *The Treatment of the Negro in American History School Textbooks ;* a comparison of changing textbook content, 1826 to 1939, with developing scholarship in the history of the Negro in the United States. Menasha, Wisconsin : George Banta Publishing Company, 1941.

241

*CARTER, HODDING, *The Winds of Fear*. London : Victor Gollancz, 1945.

CASH, WILBUR J., *The Mind of the South*. New York : Alfred A. Knopf, 1941.

*The Chicago Commission on Race Relations, *The Negro in Chicago*. Chicago : The University of Chicago Press, 1922.

COLLINS, HENRY HILL, JR., *America's Own Refugees*. Princeton : Princeton University Press, 1941.

COLLINS, WINFIELD H., *The Truth about Lynching and the Negro in the South*. New York : The Neale Publishing Company, 1918.

The Commission on Inter-racial Co-operation, *The Inter-racial Commission Comes of Age*. Atlanta : The Commission on Inter-racial Co-operation, Inc., February, 1942.

*The Commission on Inter-racial Co-operation, *The Mob Still Rides*, a review of the lynching record, 1931-35. Atlanta, Georgia : 1936.

The Commission on Inter-racial Co-operation, *A Practical Approach to the Race Problem*. Atlanta : The Commission on Inter-racial Co-operation, Inc., October, 1939.

COOLEY, CHARLES HORTON, *Social Process*. New York : Charles Scribner's Sons, 1918.

*DAVIS, ALLISON, and JOHN DOLLARD, *Children of Bondage* ; the personality development of Negro youth in the urban South. Washington, D.C. : American Council on Education, 1940. (Prepared for the American Youth Commission).

*DAVIS, ALLISON, BURLEIGH B. GARDNER and MARY R. GARDNER, *Deep South ;* a social anthropological study of caste and class. Chicago : The University of Chicago Press, 1941.

DAY, CAROLINE BOND, *A Study of Some Negro-White Families in the United States*. Cambridge : Peabody Museum of Harvard University, 1932.

Detroit Bureau of Governmental Research, *The Negro in Detroit*. Detroit : Detroit Bureau of Governmental Research, Inc., 1926.

*DETWEILER, FREDERICK G., *The Negro Press in the United States*. Chicago : The University of Chicago Press, 1922.

DEWEY, JOHN, *Freedom and Culture*. New York : G. P. Putnam's Sons, 1939.

*DINGWALL, E. J., *Racial Pride and Prejudice*. London : C. A. Watts, 1946.

DODD, WILLIAM E., *The Cotton Kingdom*, a chronicle of the Old South. New Haven : Yale University Press, 1919.

DOUGLASS, FREDERICK, *Life and Times of Frederick Douglass*. Boston : De Wolfe, Fiske and Company, 1895.

DOYLE, BERTRAM WILBUR, *The Etiquette of Race Relations in the South.* Chicago : The University of Chicago Press, 1937.

*DU BOIS, W. E. BURGHARDT, *Black Folk, Then and Now ;* an essay on the history and sociology of the Negro race. New York : Henry Holt and Company, 1939.

*DU BOIS, W. E. BURGHARDT, *Black Reconstruction;* an essay toward a history of the part which black folk played in the attempt to reconstruct democracy in America, 1860-80. New York : Harcourt, Brace and Company, 1935.

DU BOIS, W. E. BURGHARDT, *Dusk of Dawn ;* an essay toward an autobiography of a race concept. New York : Harcourt, Brace and Company, 1940.

DU BOIS, W. E. BURGHARDT, *The Negro.* New York : Henry Holt and Company, 1915. (Home University Library of Modern Knowledge, No. 91).

DU BOIS, W. E. BURGHARDT, *The Philadelphia Negro ;* a social study. Together with a special report on domestic service, by I. Eaton. Philadelphia : The University of Pennsylvania Press, 1899. (Publications of The University of Pennsylvania series in Political Economy and Public Law, No. 14).

DU BOIS, W. E. BURGHARDT, *The Souls of Black Folk.* Chicago : A. C. McClurg and Company, 1903.

*EMBREE, EDWIN R., *Brown America ;* the story of a new race. New York : The Viking Press, 1931.

EMBREE, EDWIN R., *American Negroes.* New York : John Day, 1942.

EMBREE, EDWIN R., *Brown Americans.* New York : Viking Press, 1943.

EPPSE, MERL R., *The Negro, Too, in American History.* Chicago : National Educational Publication Company, Inc., 1939.

*FORD, NICK AARON, *The Contemporary Negro Novel ;* a study in race relations. Boston : Meador Publishing Company, 1936.

FRAZIER, E. FRANKLIN, *The Negro Family in the United States.* Chicago : The University of Chicago Press, 1939.

FRAZIER, E. FRANKLIN, *Negro Youth at the Crossways ;* their personality development in the Middle States. Washington, D.C. : American Council on Education, 1940. (Prepared for the American Youth Commission).

GALLAGHER, BUELL G., *American Caste and the Negro College.* New York : Columbia University Press, 1938.

*GARTH, THOMAS R., *Race Psychology ;* a study of racial mental differences. New York : McGraw-Hill Book Company, Inc., 1931.

GIDDINGS, FRANKLIN H., *Studies in the Theory of Human Society.* New York : The Macmillan Company, 1922.

GOSNELL, HAROLD F., *Negro Politicians ;* the rise of Negro politics in Chicago. Chicago : The University of Chicago Press, 1935.

GRADY, HENRY W., *The New South.* New York : Robert Bonner's Sons, 1890.

*GRAHAM, SHIRLEY, *Paul Robeson.* New York : Julian Messner, 1946.

GREENE, LORENZO J. and CARTER G. WOODSON, *The Negro Wage Earner,* Washington, D.C. : The Association for the Study of Negro Life and History, Inc., 1930.

HARRIS, ABRAM L., *The Negro as Capitalist ;* a study of banking and business among American Negroes. Philadelphia : The American Academy of Political and Social Science, 1936.

*HERSKOVITS, MELVILLE J., *The American Negro ;* a study in racial crossing. New York : Alfred A. Knopf, 1928.

HOFFMAN, FREDERICK L., *Race Traits and Tendencies of the American Negro.* New York : The Macmillan Company, 1896.

*HOLMES, SAMUEL JACKSON, *The Negro's Struggle for Survival ;* a study in human ecology. Berkeley, California : University of California Press, 1937.

HOSHOR, JOHN, *God in a Rolls Royce ;* the rise of Father Divine, madman, menace, or messiah. New York : Hillman-Curl, Inc., 1936.

*HUGHES, LANGSTON, *The Big Sea,* an autobiography. New York : Alfred A. Knopf, 1940 ; London : Hutchinson, 1943.

HUGHES, LANGSTON, *Not Without Laughter,* a novel. New York : Alfred A. Knopf, 1930.

HURSTON, ZORA NEALE, *Mules and Men.* Philadelphia : J. B. Lippincott Company, 1935.

*ISAACS, EDITH J. R. *The Negro On The American Stage.* New York : Theatre Arts, 1947.

*JAMES, C. L. R., *History of Negro Revolt.* London : Fact Books, 1938.

*JAMES, C. L. R., *The Black Jacobins.* London : Secker and Warburg, 1938.

JENKINS, WILLIAM SUMNER, *Pro-Slavery Thoughts in the Old South.* Chapel Hill : The University of North Carolina Press, 1935.

JOHNSON, CHARLES S., *The Negro in American Civilisation ;* a study of Negro life and race relations in the light of social research. New York : Henry Holt and Company, 1930.

JOHNSON, CHARLES S., *Shadow of the Plantation.* Chicago : The University of Chicago Press, 1934.

*JOHNSON, JAMES WELDON, *Along This Way ;* the autobiography of James Weldon Johnson. New York : The Viking Press, 1933.

*JOHNSON, JAMES WELDON, *The Autobiography of an Ex-Coloured Man*. Boston : Sherman, French and Company, 1912.

JOHNSON, JAMES WELDON, *Black Manhattan*. New York : Alfred A. Knopf, 1930.

*JOHNSON, JAMES WELDON, *Negro Americans, What Now?* New York : The Viking Press, 1934.

JOHNSTON, SIR HARRY H., *The Negro in the New World*. London : Methuen and Company Ltd., 1910.

KEY, V. O., JR., *Politics, Parties and Pressure Groups*. New York : Thomas Y. Crowell Company, 1942.

KIPLINGER, WILLARD M., *Washington is Like That*. New York : Harper and Brothers, 1942.

KLINEBERG, OTTO, *Race Differences*. New York : Harper and Brothers, 1935.

*LAWSON, ELIZABETH, *Thaddeus Stevens : Fighter for Negro Rights*. New York : International Publishers, 1942.

*LEWINSON, PAUL, *Race, Class, and Party ;* a history of Negro suffrage and white politics in the South. London : The Oxford University Press, 1932.

LEYBURN, JAMES G., *The Haitian People*. New Haven : Yale University Press, 1941.

*LOCKE, ALAIN, *Negro Art : Past and Present*. Washington, D.C. : The Associates in Negro Folk Education, 1936.

*LOCKE, ALAIN, *The Negro and His Music*. Washington, D.C. : The Associates in Negro Folk Education, 1936.

*LOCKE, ALAIN, *The New Negro ;* an interpretation. New York : Albert and Charles Boni, 1925.

*LOCKE, ALAIN, *The Negro in Art*. Washington : Associates in Negro Folk Education, 1940.

*McKAY, CLAUDE, *Harlem : Negro Metropolis*. New York : E. P. Dutton and Company, Inc., 1940.

*McKAY, CLAUDE, *A Long Way From Home*. New York : L. Furman, Inc., 1937.

MECKLIN, JOHN M., *Democracy and Race Friction ;* a study of social ethics. New York : The Macmillan Company, 1914.

MILLER, KELLY, *Race Adjustment ;* essays on the Negro in America. New York : The Neale Publishing Company, 1908.

MONTAGUE, LUDWELL LEE, *Haiti and the United States, 1714-1938*. Durham : Duke University Press, 1940.

MOTON, ROBERT RUSSA, *What the Negro Thinks*. Garden City, New York : Doubleday, Doran and Company, Inc., 1929.

*MURRAY, FLORENCE (editor), *The Negro Handbook*. New York : Wendell Malliet and Company, 1942, 1943, 1944, 1945 and 1946.

*MYRDAL, GUNNAR, *An American Dilemma*. Parts 1 and 2. New York : Harpers, 1944.

ODUM, HOWARD W., and HARRY E. MOORE, *American Regionalism ;* a cultural-historical approach to national integration. New York : Henry Holt and Company, 1938.

*OTTLEY, ROI, *New World A' Comin'*. New York : Houghton Miflin Company, 1943 (published in England in 1947, by Eyre and Spottiswoode, under the title *Inside Black America*).

*PEEPLES, EDWIN A., *Swing Low*. London : Sampson Low, Marston and Company, 1946.

PHILLIPS, ULRICH B., *American Negro Slavery ;* a survey of the supply, employment and control of Negro Labour as determined by the plantation regime. New York : D. Appleton and Company, 1918.

*POWDERMAKER, HORTENSE, *After Freedom ;* a cultural study in the Deep South. New York : The Viking Press, 1939.

*POWELL, ADAM CLAYTON, Jr., *Marching Blacks*. New York : Dial, 1945.

PUCKETT, NEWBELL N., *Folk Beliefs of the Southern Negro*. Chapel Hill : The University of North Carolina Press, 1926.

*QUILLIN, FRANK, *The Color Line in Ohio ;* a history of race prejudice in a typical Northern State. Ann Arbor : George Wahr, 1913. (University of Michigan Historical Series).

*RAPER, ARTHUR F., *The Tragedy of Lynching*. Chapel Hill : The University of North Carolina Press, 1933.

REID, IRA, *In A Minor Key ;* Negro Youth in Story and Fact. Washington, D.C. : American Council on Education, 1940. (Prepared for the American Youth Commission).

REID, IRA, *Social Conditions of the Negro in the Hill District of Pittsburg*. Pittsburg : General Committee on the Hill Survey, 1930.

REUTER, E. B., *The American Race Problem ;* a study of the Negro. New York : Thomas Y. Crowell Company, 1927.

*REUTER, E. B., *The Mulatto in the United States ;* including a study of the rôle of the mixed-blood races throughout the world. Boston : R. G. Badger, 1918.

REUTER, E. B. (editor), *Race and Culture Contacts*. New York : McGraw-Hill Book Company Inc., 1934.

REUTER, E. B., *Race Mixture ;* studies in inter-marriage and miscegenation. New York : Whittlesey House, McGraw-Hill Book Company, Inc., 1931.

ROBERTSON, WILLIAM J., *The Changing South*. New York : Boni and Liveright, 1927.

*ROBESON, ESLANDA GOODE, *Paul Robeson, Negro*. London : Gollancz, 1930.

ROMAN, CHARLES V., *American Civilization and the Negro ;* the Afro-American in relation to national progress. Philadelphia : F. A. Davis Company, 1916.

ROYCE, JOSIAH, *Race Questions, Provincialism and Other American Problems*. New York : The Macmillan Company, 1908.

*RUSSELL, WILLIAM, *Robert Cain*. London : Nicholson and Watson, 1944.

*RUSSELL, WILLIAM, *A Wind Is Rising*. London : Nicholson and Watson, 1945.

SCHRIEKE, B., *Alien Americans*. New York : Viking Press, 1936.

*SHAY, FRANK, *Judge Lynch ;* his first hundred years. New York : Ives Washburn, Inc., 1938.

SHUFELDT, ROBERT W., *America's Greatest Problem : The Negro*. Philadelphia : F. A. Davis Company, 1915.

*SMITH, LILLIAN, *Strange Fruit*. London : Cresset Press, 1945.

SMITH, SAMUEL DENNY, *The Negro in Congress, 1870-1901*. Chapel Hill : The University of North Carolina Press, 1940.

SMITH, THOMAS LYNN, *The Sociology of Rural Life*. New York : Harper and Brothers, 1940.

STEPHENSON, GILBERT T., *Race Distinctions in American Law*. New York : D. Appleton and Company, 1910.

STODDARD, LOTHROP, *The Rising Ride of Color Against White World Supremacy*. New York : Charles Scribner's Sons, 1920.

STONE, ALFRED HOLT, *Studies in the American Race Problem*. Garden City, New York : Doubleday, Page and Company, 1908.

STOREY, MOORFIELD, *Problems of To-day*. Boston : Houghton Mifflin Company, 1920.

*SUTHERLAND, ROBERT L., *Color, Class and Personality*. Washington, D.C. : American Council on Education, 1942. (Prepared for the American Youth Commission).

THOMAS, WILLIAM H., *The American Negro, A Critical and Practical Discussion*. New York : The Macmillan Company, 1901.

Twelve Southerners, *I'll Take My Stand ;* the South and the agrarian tradition. New York : Harper and Brothers, 1930.

*VAN DEUSEN, JOHN G., *The Black Man in White America*. Washington, D.C. : Associated Publishers, Inc., 1938.

WARNER, ROBERT AUSTIN, *New Haven Negroes ;* a social history. New Haven : Yale University Press, 1940.

WASHINGTON, BOOKER T., *The Future of the American Negro*. Boston : Small, Maynard and Company, 1899.

WASHINGTON, BOOKER T., *The Story of the Negro ;* the rise of the race from slavery, vols. 1 and 2. Garden City, New York : Doubleday, Page and Company, 1909.

*WASHINGTON, BOOKER T., *Up From Slavery ;* an autobiography. Garden City, New York : Doubleday, Page and Company, 1900.

WERTENBAKER, THOMAS J., *The Old South ;* the founding of American civilisation. New York : Charles Scribner's Sons, 1942.

*WHITE, WALTER, *Rope and Faggot ;* a biography of Judge Lynch. New York : Alfred A. Knopf, 1929.

WOODSON, CARTER G., *A Century of Negro Migration.* Washington, D.C. : The Association for the Study of Negro Life and History, Inc., 1918.

WOODSON, CARTER G., *The History of the Negro Church.* Washington, D.C. : The Associated Publishers, Inc., 1921.

*WOODSON, CARTER G., *The Mis-Education of the Negro.* Washington, D.C. : The Associated Publishers, Inc., 1933.

WOOFTER, THOMAS J., JR., *Races and Ethnic Groups in American Life.* New York : McGraw-Hill Book Company, Inc., 1933.

WOOFTER, THOMAS J., JR., and Associates, *Negro Problems in Cities.* Garden City, New York : Doubleday, Doran and Company, Inc., 1928.

*WORK, MONROE N. (editor), *Negro Year Book ;* an annual encyclopædia of the Negro. Tuskegee Institute, Alabama : Negro Year Book Publishing Company, 1931 and 1932.

*WRIGHT, RICHARD, *Native Son.* New York : Harper and Brothers, 1940.

*WRIGHT, RICHARD, *Black Boy.* London : Gollancz, 1946.

*WRIGHT, RICHARD, *Twelve Million Black Voices ;* a folk-history of the Negro in the United States. New York : The Viking Press, 1941.

*WRIGHT, RICHARD, *Uncle Tom's Children ;* four novellas. New York : Harper and Brothers, 1938.

ADDITIONAL BIBLIOGRAPHY

(Articles, books, magazines, and sections in books relating to the appearances of Negroes in films, or to films containing racial themes.)

BLAKESTON, OSWELL : *Black Fanfare.* " Close Up " (London), August, 1929.
　　Acclaims the æsthetic potentialities of the Negro as screen material, condemning the producers for their exploitation of artificial trappings in preference to the realities of life. Also discusses Jacques Feyder's *Thérèse Raquin* (1928, Germany) as an example of social satire and analyses the absence of time values in *The Stationmaster* (1925, Russia) and Frank Borzage's *Seventh Heaven* (1927).

BROWN, STERLING : *The Negro in the Movies* In his " Negro Poetry and Drama " (Washington, D.C.) Associates in Negro Folk Education, 1937.

Gives a brief general note on Hollywood's inability to treat its Negro actors with truth or justice. Deplores the lack of Negro writers for films.

CARTER, ELMER ANDERSON : *Of Negro Motion Pictures.* " Close Up " (London), August, 1929.

A survey, by the editor of " Opportunity," of the Negro on the stage and in the cinema. Attributes the failure of both mediums in projecting the beauty and pathos of Negro life in America to racial antagonism. Condemns *Hearts In Dixie* (1929), but anticipates King Vidor's *Hallelujah* (1929) and the development of comedy shorts exploiting the Negro's singing and dancing talents.

CHOWL, HAY : *London and the Negro Film.* " Close Up " (London), August, 1929.

Hails the film programmes of the London Polytechnic cinema house as an enterprising contribution to English knowledge of Negro art. Discusses the merits of films there exhibited including *South* (1928) a travel picture, *Nionga* (1925, Great Britain), *Chang* (1927, United States), as evidence of general interest in films about Negro life. Deplores the falsification of native folklore and customs in *Under The Southern Cross* (1929, New Zealand), a film based on a Maori legend.

" CLOSE UP " : (London), August, 1929.

An issue devoted to *The Negro in the Film.*

Contents : As Is, by Kenneth Macpherson ; The Negro Actor and the American Movies, by Geraldyn Dismond ; Black Shadows, by Robert Herring ; Letter from Walter White ; Letter from Paul Green ; The Aframerican Cinema, by Harry Alan Potamkin ; Of Negro Motion Pictures, by Elmer Carter ; Black Fanfare, by Oswell Blakeston ; London and the Negro Film, by Hay Chowl ; Robert Herring makes some points about *Hearts In Dixie* (1929) ; and Henry Dobb gives some critical variations on the same theme.

DICKINSON, THOROLD : *Making A Filmn in Tanganyika,* In " The British Film Yearbook 1947-48, edited by Peter Noble (London).

Discusses very fully the making of " Men Of Two Worlds," with Robert Adams as Kisenga, the Negro composer.

DISMOND, GERALDYN : *The Negro Actor and the American Movies.* " Close Up " (London), August, 1929.

Surveys the evolution of Negro characterisations on the screen from the production of *The Birth Of A Nation* (1915) to King Vidor's *Hallelujah* (1929). Notes the establishment of three Negro producing companies, listing five of their pictures. Also discusses the Our Gang comedies, *West Of Zanzibar* (1929), *Hearts In Dixie* (1929), *Melancholy Dame* (1929), *Show Boat* (1929) and other current American films with Negro themes or Negro players.

DRAPER, ARTHUR : *Uncle Tom Will You Never Die?* " New Theatre " (New York), January, 1936.
Attacks Hollywood for its continuance of the stereotype, examining " So Red The Rose " and other anti-Negro films in some detail. Suggests measures for combating Hollywood prejudice.

FISHER, ETHEL : (1) *Behind the Camera with Men Of Two Worlds.* " Film Quarterly " (London), Autumn, 1946.
Claims that Thorold Dickinson's film makes history in that it virtually co-stars two white players and a Negro actor, Robert Adams. Quotes the latter's views on racial discrimination in films. (2) *Men Of Two Worlds*, novelisation of the screenplay by Ethel Fisher, from the original by Thorold Dickinson, Herbert Victor and Joyce Cary (World Film Publications, London, 1946). The story of a great Negro film.

GEBHART, MYRTLE : *The Chocolate Comedy.* " Extension Magazine " (Chicago), November, 1929.
Anecdotes concerning Negro players : Stepin Fetchit, " Farina," Nina Mae McKinney and George Reed. Also notes the series of Negro comedies being made from some of the Octavius Roy Cohen stories.

GLOVER, HUGH : *Renaissance Of The Negro.* A sketch of his accomplishments in the drama and the cinema. " St. Louis Chronicle," April, 1930.
On the emergence of the Negro as a serious cultural force in America. Includes references to the development of Negro characterisations in the film, from *The Birth Of A Nation* (1915) to *Hallelujah* (1929) and *Hearts In Dixie* (1929).

GOLDEN, HERB : *The Negro and Yiddish Film Boom.* " Variety " (U.S.A.), January 3, 1940.

GREEN, PAUL : *A Letter From Paul Green.* " Close Up " (London), August, 1929.
A short letter from the author of *In Abraham's Bosom*, applauding the efforts of the editors of " Close Up " to promote Negro art in the cinema.

HARDWICK, LEON : *The Negro Looks At Hollywood.* " Hollywood Quarterly " (U.S.A.), Spring, 1946.
Examines recent progress of coloured artists on the screen.

HARRISON, WILLIAM : *The Negro And The Cinema.* " Sight and Sound " (London), Spring, 1939.
An examination of the inability of independent Negro producers to make satisfactory Negro films. Also deals with *Imitation of Life*, *The Emperor Jones* and the work of Paul Robeson in Hollywood and Britain.

HERRING, ROBERT : *Black Shadows.* " Close Up " (London), 97-104, August, 1929.

A plea for the production of films with Negro themes and Negro casts to contribute a needed enrichment of cinematic art. Analyses the rhythmic and dramatic qualities of the Negro race and its cultural attainments as indices of their potential contributions to the cinema. Evaluates the merits of the African travel films *Zeliv* (1928, France), *Voyage au Congo* (1926, France), and *Samba* (1929, France). Criticises the inadequacy of white players' portrayals of Negro rôles, extolling the histrionic ability of Stepin Fetchit. Includes references to *Hallelujah* (1929) and *Hearts In Dixie* (1929) as perpetuations of the " way down South " tradition of Negro life.

JABAVU, NONTANDO : *Hollywood's Celluloid Negro.* " Film Illustrated Monthly " (London), December, 1946.

A note on the colour problem in films.

JACOBS, LEWIS : In his *The Rise Of The American Film.* Harcourt, Brace. (New York), 1939.

Gives some shrewd comments on *The Birth Of A Nation* and the Negro's struggle for recognition on the screen since the making of that film.

LEDERER, JOSE : *Black Laughter.* " Picturegoer " (London), July, 1929.

Discussion about the merits of Negro comedians and black-face actors like Moran and Mack and Amos n' Andy. Very revealing in its unintelligent attitude to coloured film characters.

MACPHERSON, KENNETH : (1) *As Is.* " Close Up " (London), August, 1929.

An editorial introduction to the issue of " Close Up " devoted to the Negro in the Film. Contends that international amity and understanding is best promoted through cultural self-expression and maintains that authentic Negro films can be produced only by Negroes. Includes an appreciation of Stepin Fetchit.

(2) *A Negro Film Union—Why Not ?* In " Negro," an anthology edited by Nancy Cunard, Wishart & Co. (London), 1934.

A plea by the editor of " Close Up," for the establishment of an autonomous Negro film production group. Urges the advisability of a preliminary Interstate Academy of the Cinema for Negro students to be modelled on the principles of the State Institute of Cinematography (GIK) Moscow. Includes an examination of the author's *Borderline* (1930, Great Britain), King Vidor's *Hallelujah* (1929), and Paul Sloane's *Hearts In Dixie* (1929).

(3) *Borderline,* the script of a film starring Paul Robeson. " Close Up " (London), 1930.

MANNERS, DOROTHY : *Negro Pictures.* " Motion Picture Classic " (U.S.A.), February, 1929.

Deals with then current vogue for films with Negro themes and casts, pointing to *Hallelujah* (1929) and the *Florian Slappey* series made from the stories of Octavius Roy Cohen.

" NEW THEATRE " : (New York), July, 1935.

An issue exclusively dealing with the Negro on the stage and screen.

NOBLE, PETER : (1) *The Negro In Hollywood.* " Sight and Sound " (London), Spring, 1939.

A plea for a just depiction of Negroes on the screen, examining the manner in which some Negro actors such as Paul Robeson and Rex Ingram have succeeded in overcoming the stereotype.

(2) *The Negro In The American Film.* " Jazz Music " (London), October, 1943.

A discussion of some general principles relating to the way in which coloured peoples are portrayed in the American cinema, with notes on the treatment of Negro players in European films. Attacks Hollywood for its colour bias, and offers a solution of steps to be taken by Negroes themselves to combat the stereotyping of coloured film characters.

(3) *Colour Bar On The Screen.* " World Review " (London), June, 1944.

Examines Hollywood's anti-Negro bias in such films as *Imitation o, Life, So Red The Rose, Gone With The Wind, Tales Of Manhattan,* and others, and gives examples of how prejudice has prevented talented coloured actors from reaching deserved prominence. Advocates the formation of a Negro Screen Actors Guild to protect coloured screen players and to minimise the colour prejudice in Hollywood films.

(4) *Personality : Robert Adams.* " What's On In London," July 16th, 1943.

Deals with the rise of a West Indian actor and singer to the position of the leading coloured film actor in British films, examining his progress from *Sanders Of The River* to *An African In London ;* records his ambitions to make films of " Toussaint l'Ouverture," " Native Son " and others.

(5) *Why Not A Negro Theatre ?* In his " British Theatre " (British Yearbooks), London, 1946.

Discusses the plans of Robert Adams to form a Negro Repertory Theatre in England, and eventually to make independent Negro stage and film productions. Reviews Adams' work in the English theatre.

(6) *A Note On An Idol.* "Sight and Sound" (London), Winter, 1946. Attacks D. W. Griffith for being "the pioneer of race prejudice," citing his films *The Birth Of A Nation*, the first production to depict the Negro as a villain, and *One Exciting Night*, the first film to show the Negro as a frightened buffoon.

(7) *Katherine Dunham, Negro Dancer.* "Stage and Screen Quarterly" (London), Winter, 1946-47.

The story of the dancer and anthropologist, whose dance group has been seen in such films as *Stormy Weather* and *Carnival In Rhythm.* Also deals with Miss Dunham's dancing in such films as *Star Spangled Rhythm* and on the Broadway stage, discussing her position in the modern American dance. Gives her statements on the position of the coloured artist in American life.

(8) *Robert Adams, Negro Actor.* " Film Quarterly " (London), Spring, 1947.

Biographical study of the leading coloured actor in Europe, with appreciation of his work on the stage and in British films. Quotes Adams' own views on the screen colour bar, and his hopes for the future of the truly international cinema.

(9) *Orlando Martins.* " Film Quarterly " (London), Spring, 1947.

A note on a prominent British coloured actor whose film career began in the silent days and culminated with his magnificent study as Magole in *Men Of Two Worlds* (1946).

(10) *Colour Bar In Hollywood.* " Chelsea " (London), Spring, 1948.

(11) *Index To Negro Films 1902-1947.* British Film Institute and Dennis Dobson (London), 1948.

(12) *Lena Horne : A Tribute.* "Night Life" (London), November, 1947.

A study of the work and significance of the leading coloured film actress in Hollywood.

POTAMKIN, HARRY ALAN : (1) *The Aframerican Cinema.* " Close Up " (London), August, 1929.

A formulation of æsthetic principles for cinematic treatment of the Negro, stressing the plastic values of the material. Advocates the assimilation of primitive African sculpture and the dance, denying the artistic validity of sociological and ethnographic Negro films. Also surveys the presentation of the Negro in art, literature, and the theatre, with brief notes on Hollywood's attempts at Negro films, submitting that, for example, *The Emperor Jones* is authentic cinematic material.

(2) *The Negro.* In his " The Eyes of the Movie." International Pamphlets (New York), 1934.

Contends that the American film has consistently portrayed the Negro as an inferior individual. Cites *The Birth Of A Nation* (1915). *One Exciting Night* (1922), *Hallelujah* (1929), and the *Our Gang* comedies,

(3) *The White Man's Negro.* " Liberator " (New York), March 28th, 1931.

Surveys the rôle of the Negro in the American cinema from the pre-war production of Negro films to the release of King Vidor's *Hallelujah* (1929).

REDDICK, LAWRENCE D. : *Educational Programme For The Improvement Of Race Relations (in Films, Radio, Press and Libraries)*, "Journal of Negro Education," Summer, 1944.

STEBBINS, ROBERT : *Hollywood's Imitation of Life.* " New Theatre " (New York), July, 1935.

Protests against Hollywood's interpretation of Negro personality and psychology, emphasising as an example the misleading nature of *Imitation Of Life* (1934). Cites the Stepin Fetchit characterisations in *Hearts In Dixie* (1929), *The Ghost Talks* (1929), and *David Harum* (1934) as travesties on Negro character. Includes reference to *Hallelujah* (1929) and to *The Emperor Jones* (1933).

STERN, SEYMOUR : *The Birth Of A Nation.*

(1) A monograph published by the Museum of Modern Art in New York, and by the British Film Institute in London, 1946. Deals exhaustively with D. W. Griffith's film, and the controversy it aroused. Defends Griffith from the many critics of the film.

(2) *Index To The Creative Work of D. W. Griffith.* British Film Institute (London), 1945-46.

" THEATRE ARTS " (New York), August, 1942.

An issue devoted to the Negro on the stage and screen, written by Edith J. R. Isaacs, Rosamond Gilder, etc.

WATTS, RICHARD, JR. : *D. W. Griffith.* " New Theatre " (New York), November, 1936.

An examination of Griffith's work, in particular his biased *The Birth Of A Nation*, and its effect on public opinion all over the world.

WHITE, WALTER : *Letter from Walter White, A.* " Close Up " (London), August, 1929.

A letter from the Secretary of the National Association for the Advancement of Coloured People, anticipating the future emergence of honest interpretations of authentic Negro material.

And issues of the following journals :—

U.S.A. : " Negro Digest," " Opportunity," " Ebony," " Film Art," " New Theatre," " Hollywood Quarterly," " The Screenwriter," " Motion Picture Herald," " Our World," " Common Wealth," " The Nation."

Great Britain : " Close Up," " World Film News," " Picturegoer," " Film Weekly," " Film Pictorial," " Screen Pictorial," " Picture Show," " Film Illustrated Monthly," " Documentary News-Letter," " Kinematograph Weekly," " Daily Film Renter," " The Cinema," " Sight and Sound," " Penguin Film Review," " Film Quarterly," and " Stage and Screen."

Note : For assistance in compiling the Bibliography the author wishes to acknowledge a debt of gratitude to the Editors of " The Film Index " (published by the Museum of Modern Art Film Library, New York, 1943).

APPENDIX C

LIST OF FILMS 1902-1948 FEATURING NEGROES OR CONTAINING IMPORTANT RACIAL THEMES

AMERICAN

(*Note*: In most Hollywood musicals, from the time of " Fox Movietone Follies of 9 " onwards, coloured performers and musicians have been featured in segregated uences. The titles of these films—since there are so many—will not be listed ept where there is a *special* reason for so doing.]

IE WOOING AND WEDDING OF A COON. (1905—all-Negro).

SHTS OF A NATION. (1905).

IE MASHER. (1907).
Note : This is not to be confused with the film of the same name, made in 1910, tarring Mary Pickford and directed by *Mack Sennett*, with *D. W. Griffith* super-ising.]

IE SLAVE. Directed by *D. W. Griffith*. (Biograph, 1909).

IE RASTUS SERIES. Produced by *Sigmund Lubin*, this series of short omedies included such titles as " How Rastus Got His Turkey " and " Rastus n Zululand," made about 1910, all-Negro.

IE SAMBO SERIES. Produced by *Sigmund Lubin*, these were similar to the " Rastus " series, and were made between 1909 and 1911, all-Negro.

IE HONOUR OF HIS FAMILY. Directed by *D. W. Griffith*. (Biograph, 910).

IE THREAD OF DESTINY. Directed by *D. W. Griffith*. (Biograph, 1910).

IE HOUSE WITH CLOSED SHUTTERS. Directed by *D. W. Griffith*. With *Dorothy West*. (Biograph, 1910).

CHILD'S STRATAGEM. Directed by *D. W. Griffith*. (Biograph, 1910).

IE BATTLE. Directed by *D. W. Griffith*, from a scenario by *George Terwilliger*. hotography by *Billy Bitzer*. With *Blanche Sweet, Charles West* and other Biograph stock players. (Biograph, 1911).
Note : Seymour Stern, in his " Index To The Creative Work of D. W. Griffith," emarks : " ' The Battle ' was not the first film on the American Civil War, but probably was the first of the combination *battle-and-genre* films on this subject, which prepared the way for ' The Birth Of A Nation,' and through which Griffith generated the romantic legend of the Old South. With its appearance, the American Civil War, and, in particular, the glory of the Old South, became more prominently featured than ever before in Griffith's creative expression and output."]

R MASSA'S SAKE. With *Crane Wilbur*. (Pathe, 1911).

THE DARK ROMANCE OF A TOBACCO CAN. (Essanay, 1911).

THE JUDGE'S STORY. (Thanhauser, 1911).

THE DEBT. (Rex, 1912).

BILLY'S STRATAGEM. Directed by *D. W. Griffith.* (Biograph, 1912).

IN SLAVERY DAYS. Directed by *Otis Turner.* With *Robert Z. Leonar Margarita Fischer* and *Edna Maison.* (Rex, 1913).

THE OCTOROON. From the play by *Dion Boucicault.* With *Guy Coomb* and *Marguerite Courtot.* (Kalem, 1913).

THE BATTLE OF ELDERBUSH GULCH. Directed by *D. W. Griffit* from a scenario by *D. W. Griffith.* Photography by *Billy Bitzer.* With *M Marsh, Robert Harron, Lillian Gish, Henry B. Walthall, Dell Henderson.* (Biograp 1913).
[*Note :* This was, to quote *Seymour Stern,* " a lengthier and more ambitious o of the Civil War *battle-and-genre* films, anticipating ' The Birth Of A Nation '."]

COON TOWN SUFFRAGETTES. Produced by *Sigmund Lubin.* (1914-all-Negro).

DARK TOWN JUBILEE. The first ill-fated attempt to star a Negro in a film, this case, *Bert Williams,* the well-known New York comedian. (1914—all-Negro

THE WAGES OF SIN, THE BROKEN VIOLIN, Etc. Two titles from a seri of all-Negro films, produced by *Oscar Micheaux,* independent Negro produce about 1914.

THE BIRTH OF A NATION. Directed by *D. W. Griffith,* from the nov " The Clansman " by *Thomas Dixon.* Scenario by *D. W. Griffith* and *Fran Woods.* Photography by *Billy Bitzer.* With *Mae Marsh, Lillian Gish, Henry Walthall, Robert Harron, Wallace Reid, George Seigmann, Walter Long, Geor Reed, Ralph Lewis, Elmo Lincoln, Elmer Clifton, Donald Crisp, Raoul Wals Joseph Henaberry, Eugene Pallette, Bessie Love, Jennie Lee, Howard Gaye, To Wilson, Erich von Stroheim,* etc. (Epoch, 1915).

THE COWARD. Written and directed by *Thomas H. Ince.* With *Charles Ra Frank Keenan* and *Gertrude Claire.* (Triangle, 1915).

THE NIGGER. From the novel by *Edward Sheldon.* With *William Farmu* (Fox, 1915).

AMERICAN ARISTOCRACY. Produced by *D. W. Griffith.* Directed b *Lloyd Ingraham,* from a story by *Anita Loos.* With *Douglas Fairbanks, Jew Carmen, Al Parker.* (Triangle, 1916).
[*Note:* The hero, here, is a young Southerner who outwits some Norther munition-smugglers.]

UNCLE TOM'S CABIN. Directed by *Edwin S. Porter,* from the novel b *Harriet Beecher Stowe.* (Thomas Edison, 1903).

UNCLE TOM'S CABIN. (Thanhauser, 1909).

UNCLE TOM'S CABIN. (Imperial, 1913).

UNCLE TOM'S CABIN. Directed by *William Robert Daly.* With *Sam Luca Irving Cummings, Marie Eline* and a cast of Negro players. (World, 1914).
[*Note :* *Sam Lucas,* a Negro actor, was featured in this third version of the Beech Stowe novel, creating a precedent, since most coloured characters had, up to th time, been played by white actors in blackface.]

NCLE TOM'S CABIN. Directed by *J. Searle Dawley*. With *Marguerite Clark*. (Paramount, 1918).

NCLE TOM'S CABIN. Directed by *Harry Pollard*. With *James B. Lowe, Margarita Fischer, George Seigmann* and *Arthur Edmund Carew*. (Universal, 1927).

IE " OUR GANG " COMEDIES. Produced by *Hal Roach*. Both silent and sound, with various Negro children including *Farina, Stymie Beard, Buckwheat*, etc.

IE GREATEST THING IN LIFE. Directed by *D. W. Griffith*. (1918). [*Note* : In this film occurred the episode of the white soldier in the First World War kissing his Negro comrade-in-arms as he died. *Richard Watts, Jnr.* asserts that this was Griffith's way of atoning for the great harm he inflicted on the Negro race in " Birth Of A Nation," but this is hotly refuted by *Seymour Stern*, who replies that, (*a*) Griffith does not admit to inflicting any harm whatever in what is a faithful re-construction of actual American history, and (*b*) the scene referred to was in the script before Griffith had even read it.]

N NIGHTS IN A BAR-ROOM. With *Charles Gilpin*. (Coloured Players, about 1920—all-Negro).

NE EXCITING NIGHT. Directed by *D. W. Griffith*. With *Porter Strong* (a white actor in blackface). (1922). [*Note* : This was the first, certainly the most striking example, of a film representing the Negro as a fool and a superstitious coward.]

OBINSON CRUSOE. With *Noble Johnson*.

REE AND EQUAL. (1924).

ROKEN CHAINS. (1924).

IE GENERAL. Directed by *Buster Keaton*, from a scenario by *Charles Smith*. With *Buster Keaton* and *Helen Mack*. (Allied Artists, 1927). [*Note* : Even this Keaton comedy was violently partisan. Keaton acts a Southern train driver, who outwits dozens of villainous and stupid Northern officers and thus manages to help the South destroy the Northern armies in a battle.]

IE FLORIAN SLAPPEY SERIES. Written and produced by *Octavius Roy Cohen* (about 1925-26—all-Negro).

ELANCHOLY DAME. Written and directed by *Octavius Roy Cohen*. With *Evelyn Preer, Eddie Thompson* and *Spencer Williams*. (Cohen, 1929—all-Negro).

EARTS IN DIXIE. Directed by *Paul Sloane*. With *Clarence Muse, Stepin Fetchit, Mildred Washington*. (Fox, 1929—all-Negro).

ACK WATERS. Directed by *Herbert Wilcox*. With *John Loder, Lloyd Hamilton, James Kirkwood, Noble Johnson*. (British and Dominions—World Wide, 1929).

ALLELUJAH. Directed by *King Vidor*, from the novel by *Wanda Tuchock*. With *Daniel Haynes, Nina Mae McKinney, Victoria Spivey, William Fountain, Harry Gray, Fannie Belle de Knight* and *Everett McGarritty*. (M.G.M., 1929—all-Negro).

RAHAM LINCOLN. Directed by *D. W. Griffith*. With *Walter Huston* and *Una Merkel*. (United Artists, 1930).

RESTIGE. Directed by *Charles R. Rogers*. With *Adolphe Menjou, Melvyn Douglas, Ann Harding* and *Clarence Muse*. (R.K.O. Radio, 1932.)

ARROWSMITH. Directed by *John Ford*, from the novel by *Sinclair Lee* With *Ronald Colman, Helen Hayes, Charlotte Henry, Myrna Loy, John Qua* and *Clarence Brooks.* (Goldwyn, 1932).

THE LOST LADY. Directed by *William A. Wellman.* With *Dorothy Mack, Donald Cook, Victor Varconi, John Wray, Nina Mae McKinney, Noble Johns, Clarence Muse.* (First National, 1932).

SECRET SERVICE. Directed by *J. Walter Ruben.* With *Richard Dix, Shir Grey, Gavin Gordon, William Post, Jnr.* (R.K.O. Radio, 1932).

EAST OF BORNEO. Directed by *George Melford.* With *Charles Bickfo Rose Hobart, Lupita Tovar* and *Noble Johnson.* (Universal, 1932).
[*Note :* This is typical of the scores of jungle films of the " Trader Horn " ger made in Hollywood in the past thirty years or more, in which coloured play were featured, mostly as cannibals, head-hunters and the more repulsive types savages.]

HUCKLEBERRY FINN. Directed by *Norman Taurog*, from the novel by *M. Twain.* With *Jackie Cooper, Mitzi Green, Junior Durkin, Jackie Searle, Eug Pallette* and *Clarence Muse.* (Paramount, 1932).

THE BLACK KING. Directed by *Bud Pollard*, from the story by *Don Heywood.* With *Vivian Baber, Harry Gray, Knolly Mitchell, Mary Jane Watk* (Southland, 1932).
[*Note :* This was one of the first big independent all-Negro film productions.

FLYING DOWN TO RIO. Directed by *Thornton Freeland.* With *Dol del Rio, Fred Astaire, Gene Raymond, Ginger Rogers* and *Etta Moten.* (R.K. Radio, 1933).

THE EMPEROR JONES. Produced by *Gifford Cochran* and *John Krims* Directed by *Dudley Murphy* (under the supervision of *William C. De Mille*), fr the play by *Eugene O'Neill.* Scenario by *Du Bose Heyward.* Photography *Ernest Haller.* With *Paul Robeson, Dudley Digges, Frank Wilson, Rex Ingr George Stamper, Fredi Washington, Ruby Elzy, Brandon Evans* and *Taylor Gord* (Krimsky-Cochran, 1933).

I AM A FUGITIVE FROM A CHAIN GANG. Directed by *Mervyn Le R* from the story by *Robert E. Burns.* With *Paul Muni, Glenda Farrell, He Vinson, Preston Foster, Allen Jenkins, Edward Ellis, Edward Arnold, Sally Bl* and *Everett Brown.* (Warners, 1933).

HYPNOTISED. Directed by *Mack Sennett.* With *George Moran, Cha Mack, Ernest Torrence, Wallace Ford* and *Maria Alba.* (World Wide, 1933).
[*Note :* This was the type of film comedy featuring well-known black-f comedians, white men acting as Negroes—Moran and Mack, Amos and An Alexander and Mose, the Kentucky Minstrels, etc.—so often produced in Hol wood and New York, and occasionally in London.]

LAUGHTER IN HELL. Directed by *Edward L. Cahn.* With *Pat O'Br Merna Kennedy, Gloria Stuart, Tom Brown, Noel Madison* and *Clarence M* (Universal, 1933).

THE CABIN IN THE COTTON. Directed by *Michael Curtiz*, from the no by *Henry Kroll.* With *Richard Barthelmess, Bette Davis, Dorothy Jordan, He B. Walthall, Clarence Muse* and " *Snowflake.*" (Warners, 1933).

HELL'S HIGHWAY. Written and directed by *Rowland Brown.* With *Rich Dix, Tom Brown, Rochelle Hudson, C. Henry Gordon, Stanley Fields* and *Clare Muse.* (R.K.O. Radio, 1933).

IE HOUSE OF CONNELLY. Directed by *Henry King,* from the play by
Paul Green. With *Janet Gaynor, Robert Young, Richard Cromwell, Lionel Barry-more, Henrietta Crossman, Mona Barrie, Stepin Fetchit.* (Fox, 1934).
Note : This film concerned a Carolina family who had fallen on evil days, con-
ducting a feud with some " hated Northerners " who had come South to grow
obacco.]

Y 13. Directed by *Richard Boleslawsky.* With *Gary Cooper, Marion Davies,
Jean Parker, Katherine Alexander, Russell Hardie, Douglas Dumbrille and the
Four Mills Brothers.* (M.G.M., 1934).

IDGE PRIEST. Directed by *John Ford.* With *Will Rogers, Tom Brown,
Anita Louise, Henry B. Walthall, Rochelle Hudson, Hattie McDaniel and Stepin
Fetchit.* (Fox, 1935).
Note : The reviewer of the magazine " Film Weekly," remarked of this, " in
his new Will Rogers film, laid in the Southern States of America, the spirit and
memories of the bitter struggle between North and South take too prominent a
place."]

JANGA. Directed by *George Terwilliger.* With *Fredi Washington, Sheldon
Leonard, Philip Brandon, Marie Paxton and Winifred Harris.* (Paramount, 1935).
Note : This film was made in the West Indies with an American cast, and was
directed by *George Terwilliger,* who had written " The Battle," one of D. W.
Griffith's early films glorifying the Old South. Needless to say, the villainess in
" Ouanga," which was released in the U.S.A. as " Drums Of The Jungle," was
a half-caste !]

IITATION OF LIFE. Directed by *John M. Stahl,* from the novel by *Fannie
Hurst.* With *Claudette Colbert, Warren William, Ned Sparks, Louise Beavers,
Fredi Washington, Rochelle Hudson, Sebie Hendricks, Dorothy Black, Alan Hale
and Hazel Washington.* (Universal, 1935).
Note : This film dealt seriously with the question of the colour bar, more speci-
ically the problem of a light-skinned Negro girl who, because she resents being
treated as an inferior, makes a desperate bid to pass herself off as a white girl.]

ELLDORADO. Directed by *James Cruze.* With *Richard Arlen, Madge Evans
Ralph Bellamy, James Gleason, Henry B. Walthall and Stepin Fetchit.* (Fox, 1935).
Note : This was typical of those dozens of Hollywood films in which the Negro
character spends most of his time providing the audience with amusement by
being frightened by a " ghost."]

UBLIC HERO NUMBER ONE. Directed by *J. Walter Ruben.* With *Chester
Morris, Lionel Barrymore, Jean Arthur, Joseph Calleia, Lewis Stone, Paul Kelly,
Sam Baker and George E. Stone.* (M.G.M., 1935).
Note : Most " prison dramas " have a Negro prisoner in the cast, e.g., " Laughter
In Hell," " I Am A Fugitive," " Hell's Highway " and " The Last Mile." The
above was no exception.]

SHAUGHNESSY'S BOY. Directed by *Richard Boleslawsky.* With *Wallace
Beery, Jackie Cooper, Sara Haden, Leona Maricle, Henry Stephenson and Clarence
Muse.* (M.G.M., 1935).

D RED THE ROSE. Directed by *King Vidor,* from the novel by *Stark Young.*
With *Margaret Sullavan, Randolph Scott, Walter Connolly, Janet Beecher, Robert
Cummings, Johnny Downs, Daniel Haynes, Clarence Muse and George Reed.*
Paramount, 1936).

CAPTAIN BLOOD. Directed by *Michael Curtiz,* from the novel by *Raph. Sabatini.* With *Errol Flynn, Olivia de Havilland, Lionel Attwill, Basil Rathbo. Ross Alexander, Guy Kibbee, Robert Barrat, J. Carrol Naish* and *Gardner Jam.* (Warners, 1936).

[*Note :* This Sabatini film dealt romantically with Captain Blood, a notoric slave trader in the Carribean Sea. Needless to say, the character as played Errol Flynn was whitewashed beyond recognition.]

SHOW BOAT. Directed by *James Whale,* from the operetta by *Edna Ferber a. Jerome Kern.* With *Irene Dunne, Paul Robeson, Allan Jones, Charles Winning. Helen Morgan, Queenie Smith, Helen Westley, Donald Cook, Hattie McDaniel a. Clarence Muse.* (Universal, 1936).

FURY. Directed by *Fritz Lang.* With *Spencer Tracy, Sylvia Sydney, Walter A. Bruce Cabot, Edward Ellis, Walter Brennen, Frank Albertson* and *Morgan Wallc.* (M.G.M., 1936).

[*Note :* Lang's film, although no Negro character appeared in it, was one of most important indictments of mob rule and lynch law ever made in Ameri. studios.]

THE LITTLEST REBEL. Directed by *David Butler.* With *Shirley Tem. John Boles, Jack Holt, Bill Robinson, Karen Morley, Guinn Williams, Willie B. Frank McGlynn Snr.* and *Hannah Washington.* (Twentieth Century-Fox, 193.

[*Note :* This is a typical Hollywood Civil War picture, in which the cen. characters, Southerners, inevitably have the entire sympathy of the film. As critic in " Motion Picture Almanac " writes : " Ruthless Yankee invaders sack a. destroy the plantation home of little Shirley and her father, John Boles."]

ESCAPE FROM DEVIL'S ISLAND. Directed by *Albert Rogell.* With *Vi. Jory, Florence Rice, Norman Foster, Daniel Haynes* and *Noble Johnson.* (Colum. 1936).

THE SINGING KID. Directed by *William Keighley.* With *Al Jolson, S. Jason, Allen Jenkins, Lyle Talbot, Wini Shaw, Edward Everett Horton* and *C. Calloway.* (Warners, 1936).

THE PRISONER OF SHARK ISLAND. Directed by *John Ford.* W. *Warner Baxter, Gloria Stuart, Arthur Byron, O. P. Heggie, Harry Carey, J. Carradine, Francis Macdonald, Frank McGlynn, Snr., Ernest Whitman* and *H. McDaniel.* (Twentieth Century-Fox, 1936).

[*Note :* This was an historical film based on the imprisonment of Dr. Mu. the Southern physician, who unwittingly attended the wounds of John Wi. Booth, the assassin of Abraham Lincoln. Mudd's descendants claim (see " F. Weekly," August 29th, 1936) that he was not treated so badly by his North. captors as this film implies.]

THE PETRIFIED FOREST. Directed by *Archie Mayo,* from the play *Robert E. Sherwood.* With *Leslie Howard, Bette Davis, Genivieve Tobin, Humpi. Bogart, Dick Foran, Joseph Sawyer, Charley Grapewin, Porter Hall, Slim Joh. and John Alexander.* (Warners, 1936).

[*Note :* There is an interesting scene between *Slim Johnson* as the Negro gang and *John Alexander* as the obsequious coloured chauffeur in this excellent intelligently directed picture of the Sherwood play.]

:GION OF TERROR. Directed by *C. C. Coleman.* With *Bruce Cabot, Marguerite Churchill, Ward Bond, Arthur Loft, John Tyrell* and *Charles Wilson.* (Columbia, 1937).
[*Note :* This film was concerned with the revival of the hooded secret society on Ku Klux Klan lines, which menaced the U.S.A. in the middle nineteen 'thirties.]

HITE HUNTER. Directed by *Irving Cummings.* With *Warner Baxter, June Lang, Wilfrid Lawson, Gail Patrick, Alison Skipworth, Ernest Whitman* and *Ralph Cooper.* (Fox, 1937).

'IRIT OF YOUTH. With *Joe Louis* and *Clarence Muse.* (Independent— all-Negro, 1937).

,AVE SHIP. Directed by *Tay Garnett.* With *Warner Baxter, Wallace Beery, Elizabeth Allen, Mickey Rooney, George Sanders, Joseph Schildkraut* and *Miles Mander.* (Twentieth Century-Fox, 1937).

:NROD AND SAM. Directed by *William McGann.* With *Frank Craven, Billy Mauch, Craig Reynolds, Spring Byington* and *Philip Hurlic.* (Warners, 1937).
[*Note :* This film was one of a series, an extension of the " Our Gang " type of movie, in which Penrod's gang was composed of several white boys and one Negro child, played engagingly by Philip Hurlic.]

REN OF THE TROPICS. Produced and directed by *Jack* and *Dave Goldberg.* With *Josephine Baker.* (Goldberg, 1937—independent all-Negro).

HE BLACK LEGION. Directed by *Archie Mayo.* With *Humphrey Bogart, Dick Foran, Erin O'Brien Moore, Ann Sheridan, Robert Barrat, Joseph Sawyer, Paul Harvey, Henry Brandon* and *John Litel.* (Warners, 1937).
[*Note :* Another film based on the story of the " Black Legion," a degenerate successor to the Ku Klux Klan, which flourished in the Middle West in the 1930's.]

HE GREEN PASTURES. Directed by *William Keighley* and *Marc Connelly.* With *Rex Ingram, Oscar Polk, Eddie Anderson, Frank Wilson, Ernest Whitman, William Cumby, Edna Mae Harris, Al Stokes, David Bethea, George Reed* and *Clinton Rosemond.* (Warners, 1937—all-Negro).

HEY WON'T FORGET. Directed by *Mervyn Le Roy,* from the novel " Death In The Deep South " by *Ward Greene.* With *Claude Rains, Allyn Joslyn, Edward Norris, Gloria Dickson, Otto Kruger, Lana Turner, Elisha Cook, Jnr., Clinton Rosemond, Trevor Bardette, Elliot Sullivan* and *Frank Faylen.* (Warners, 1937).

HITE BONDAGE. Directed by *Nicholas Grinde.* With *Jean Muir, Gordon Oliver, Joseph King, Harry Davenport, Virginia Brissac, Addison Richards, Eddie Anderson* and *Trevor Bardette.* (Warners, 1937).

:NNIES FROM HEAVEN. Directed by *Norman McLeod,* from a screenplay by *Jo Swerling.* With *Bing Crosby, Madge Evans, Edith Fellowes, Donald Meek, John Gallaudet, Louis Armstrong* and *Charles Wilson.* (Columbia, 1937).

NE MILE FROM HEAVEN. Directed by *Allan Dwan.* With *Claire Trevor, Sally Blane, Douglas Fowley, Fredi Washington, Ralf Harolde, Bill Robinson, Ray Walker, Chick Chandler* and *Eddie Anderson.* (Twentieth Century-Fox, 1938).
[*Note : Fredi Washington* gave an outstanding portrayal (see " Film Weekly," January 8th, 1938) as the coloured foster-mother of a white child.]

F HUMAN HEARTS. Directed by *Clarence Brown,* from a screenplay by *Bradbury Foote.* With *Walter Huston, James Stewart, Beulah Bondi, John Carradine, Guy Kibbee, Leatrice Joy Gilbert* and *Charley Grapewin.* (M.G.M., 1938).

The Negro in Films

JEZEBEL. Directed by *William Wyler*, from the play by *Owen Davis*. Wit Bette Davis, Henry Fonda, George Brent, Margaret Lindsay, Donald Crisp, Fa Bainter, Richard Cromwell, Lew Payton, Eddie Anderson and Stymie Bear (Warners, 1938).

A NATION AFLAME. Directed by *Victor Halperin*, from the story by *Thoma Dixon*. With *Noel Madison, Lila Lee, Douglas Walton, Harry Holman, Sn Pollard* and *Norma Trelvar*. (Halperin, 1938).
[*Note :* This story, from a book by *Thomas Dixon*, whose novel " The Clansman was made as " The Birth Of A Nation," concerned a " fake " secret socie organised on the lines of the Ku Klux Klan, and the efforts of a reporter to expo the crooked politicians who had " perverted " the secret society and used i " legitimate " framework for their own ends !]

MYSTERY IN SWING. Produced and directed by *Arthur Dreifuss*. Wit Monte Hawley, Marguerite Whitten, Bob Webb, Sybil Lewis, Josephine Edward F. E. Miller, Halley Harding and Jess Lee Brooks. (Goldberg, 1938—independer all-Negro).

NOTHING SACRED. Directed by *William Wellman*, from a screenplay by *Be Hecht*. With *Fredric March, Carole Lombard, Charles Winninger, Walter Connoll Frank Fay, Monty Woolley, Troy Brown* and *Hattie McDaniel*. (Selznick, 1938

DOUBLE DEAL. Directed by *Arthur Dreifuss*, from a screenplay by *Arth Hoerl*. With *Jeni LeGon, Monte Hawley, Florence O'Brien, Edward Thompso Maceo Sheffield, F. E. Miller, Edgar Washington, Freddie Jackson, Charles Hawki* and *Shelton Brooks*. (Goldberg, 1938—independent all-Negro).

YOU CAN'T TAKE IT WITH YOU. Directed by *Frank Capra*, from the pla by *George S. Kaufmann* and *Moss Hart*. With *Jean Arthur, Lionel Barrymor James Stewart, Edward Arnold, Mischa Auer, Ann Miller, Spring Byington, Dona Meek, Lilian Yarbo* and *Eddie Anderson*. (Columbia, 1939).

STAND UP AND FIGHT. Directed by *W. S. Van Dyke II*. With *Robe Taylor, Wallace Beery, Florence Rice, Helen Broderick, Barton MacLane, Charl Grapewin, John Qualen* and *Clinton Rosemond*. (M.G.M., 1939).

PARADISE IN HARLEM. Directed by *Joseph Seiden*, from a story by *Fra Wilson*. With *Frank Wilson, Mamie Smith, Edna Mae Harris, Sidney Easto Norman Astwood, Alex Lovejoy, George Williams* and *Merritt Smith*. (Goldber 1939—independent all-Negro).

ST. LOUIS BLUES. Directed by *Raoul Walsh*. With *Dorothy Lamour, Llo Nolan, Jessie Ralph, Jerome Cowan, Mary Parker, Tito Guizar, William Frawl* and *Maxine Sullivan*. (Paramount, 1939).

THE ADVENTURES OF HUCKLEBERRY FINN. Directed by *Richa Thorpe*, from the novel by *Mark Twain*. With *Mickey Rooney, Walter Connoll William Frawley, Rex Ingram, Lynne Carver, Elizabeth Risdon, Victor Kilia Minor Watson* and *Clara Blandick*. (M.G.M., 1939).

HARLEM ON THE PRAIRIE. Produced and directed by *Jed Buell*, and claime as " the first independent all-Negro Western film." (Buell, 1939).

WAY DOWN SOUTH. Directed by *Bernard Vorhaus*, from a story and scree play by *Clarence Muse* and *Langston Hughes*. With *Bobby Breen, Clarence Mus Allan Mowbray, Ralph Morgan, Steffi Duna, Sally Blane, Lilian Yarbo, Stym Beard, Jack Carr, Marguerite Whitten* and *Hall Johnson Choir*. (Sol Lesser, 1939

MAN ABOUT TOWN. Directed by *Mark Sandrich*. With *Jack Benny, Dorothy Lamour, Eddie " Rochester " Anderson, Binnie Barnes, Edward Arnold, Monty Woolley, Isabel Jeans, Phil Harris* and *Theresa Harris*. (Paramount, 1939).
[*Note :* This was the type of Benny-" Rochester " comedy made successfully in the period 1939-44.]

YOUNG MR. LINCOLN. Directed by *John Ford*. With *Henry Fonda, Alice Brady, Marjorie Weaver, Arleen Whelan, Richard Cromwell, Eddie Quillan* and *Ward Bond*. (Twentieth Century-Fox, 1939).

TELL NO TALES. Directed by *Leslie Fenton*. With *Melvyn Douglas, Louise Platt, Gene Lockhart, Douglass Dumbrille, Halliwell Hobbes, Harlan Briggs, Hobart Cavanagh, Theresa Harris* and *Clinton Rosemond*. (M.G.M., 1939).

GONE WITH THE WIND. Directed by *Victor Fleming*, from the novel by *Margaret Mitchell*. With *Vivien Leigh, Clark Gable, Leslie Howard, Olivia de Havilland, Thomas Mitchell, Evelyn Keyes, Barbara O'Neill, Hattie McDaniel, Oscar Polk, Adrian Morris, Ben Carter* and *Eddie " Rochester " Anderson*. (Selznick, 1939).

MR. WASHINGTON GOES TO TOWN. Produced and directed by *Jed Buell*. With *Mantan Moreland*. (Buell, 1940—independent all-Negro).

BROKEN STRINGS. Produced and directed by *Bernard B. Ray*. With *Clarence Muse*. (Harold Flavin, 1940—independent all-Negro).

SWANEE RIVER. Directed by *Sydney Lanfield*. With *Don Ameche, Andrea Leeds, Al Jolson, Felix Bressart, Hall Johnson Choir* and *George Reed*. (Twentieth Century-Fox, 1940).
[*Note :* Al Jolson appeared as E. P. Christy, the man who founded one of the first " nigger minstrel " troupes.]

GOLDEN BOY. Directed by *Rouben Mamoulien*, from a play by *Clifford Odets*. With *Barbara Stanwyck, William Holden, Adolphe Menjou, Lee J. Cobb, Joseph Calleia, Sam Levene, Don Beddoe* and *Clinton Rosemond*. (Columbia, 1940).

CHASING TROUBLE. Directed by *Howard Bretherton*, from a screenplay by *Mary McCarthy*. With *Frankie Darro, Mantan Moreland, Majorie Reynolds, Milburn Stone* and *Cheryl Walker*. (Monogram, 1940).
[*Note :* Darro and Negro actor Moreland were co-starred in this film, and also in others in the series, which included : " In The Night," directed by *Jean Yarborough*, from a story by *Edmond Kelso*, 1941 ; " Amateur Detective," directed by *Howard Bretherton*, 1940 ; " Farewell To Fame," directed by Yarborough, from a story by Kelso, 1941 ; " You're Out Of Luck," directed by *Howard Bretherton*, 1941 ; " Up In The Air," directed by *Howard Bretherton*, 1941, etc.]

ONE TENTH OF OUR NATION. Directed by *Henwar Rodakiewiecz*. Documentary showing inadequate conditions of education among Negroes in the South. (American Film Centre, 1940).

SPIRIT OF THE PEOPLE. Directed by *Max Gordon*, based on the play " Abe Lincoln In Illunois," by *Robert E. Sherwood*. With *Raymond Massey, Ruth Gordon, Gene Lockhart, Alan Baxter, Howard da Silva, Dorothy Tree, Harvey Stephens, Herbert Rudley*. (Gordon-R.K.O. Radio, 1940).

OF MICE AND MEN. Directed by *Lewis Milestone*, from the play by *John Steinbeck*. With *Burgess Meredith, Lon Chaney, Betty Field, Charles Bickford, Roman Bohnen, Bob Steele, Noah Beery, Jnr.* and *Leigh Whipper*. (Hal Roach, 1940).

AROUSE AND BEWARE. Directed by *Leslie Fenton*, from the book by *MacKinlay Kantor*. With *Wallace Beery, John Howard, Dolores del Rio, Dona Meek, Robert Barrat, Addison Richards, William Haade* and *John Wray*. (M.G.M 1940).

THE GHOST BREAKERS. Directed by *George Marshall*. With *Bob Hope Paulette Goddard, Richard Carlson, Paul Lukas, Willie Best, Pedro de Cordob Anthony Quinn, Lloyd Corrigan, Virginia Brissac* and *Noble Johnson*. (Paramoun 1940).
[*Note :* Typical Hollywood comedy with *Willie Best* as coloured comic relief.]

THE DARK COMMAND. Directed by *Raoul Walsh*. With *Claire Treve John Wayne, Walter Pidgeon, Roy Rogers, George Hayes* and *Porter Ha* (Republic, 1940).
[*Note :* Story of American Civil War intrigue ; both hero and heroine we (inevitably) Southerners.]

VIRGINIA CITY. Directed by *Michael Curtiz*. With *Errol Flynn, Miria Hopkins, Humphrey Bogart, Alan Hale, Frank McHugh* and *Guinn Willian* (Warners, 1940).
[*Note :* *Errol Flynn* plays the conventional hero, a handsome Southern office in this romance of the American Civil War.]

SAFARI. Directed by *Edward H. Griffith*, from a story by *Paul Hervey Fo* With *Douglas Fairbanks, Jnr., Madeleine Carroll, Tullio Carminati, Lynne Overma Muriel Angelus, Clinton Rosemond* and *Ben Carter*. (Paramount, 1940).

KEEP PUNCHING. With *Henry Armstrong*. (1941—independent all-Negro).

NO TIME FOR COMEDY. Directed by *William Keighley*, from the play b *S. N. Behrman*. With *James Stewart, Rosalind Russell, Genevieve Tobin, Charl Ruggles, Allyn Joslyn* and *Louise Beavers*. (Warners, 1941).

ARIZONA. Directed by *Wesley Ruggles*, from the story by *Clarence Buddingto Kelland*. With *Jean Arthur, William Holden, Warren William, Porter Ha Paul Harvey, Regis Toomey, Edgar Buchanan* and *Addison Richards*. (Columbi 1941).
[*Note :* This was one of the rare American films in which the hero is a Northerne and a soldier in the Union Army.]

MARYLAND. Directed by *Henry King*, from the screenplay by *Ethel Hill an Jack Andrews*. With *Walter Brennan, Fay Bainter, Brenda Joyce, John Payn Charlie Ruggles, Hattie McDaniel, Marjorie Weaver, Sydney Blackmer, Claren Muse, George Reed, Ben Carter, Ernest Whitman, Zack Williams Thaddeus Jone Clinton Rosemond* and *Jesse Graves*. (Twentieth Century-Fox, 1940).
[*Note :* In this romance of the South several Negro players were, as usual, feature prominently as comedy relief. *Lionel Collier*, film critic of " Picturegoer," o reviewing the film, shrewdly noted : " Support comes from *Hattie McDaniel,* the inevitable black mammy and from *Ben Carter*, as a shiftless Negro who always in trouble."]

KING OF THE ZOMBIES. Directed by *Jean Yarborough*, from a screenpla by *Edmond Kelso*. With *Dick Purcell, Mantan Moreland, John Archer, Henr Victor, Joan Woodbury, Marguerite Whitten,* and *Leigh Whipper*. (Monogran 1941).
[*Note :* Negro Moreland was co-starred with white actor Purcell in this " zombi comedy," and in others in the series including : " The Phantom Killers," directe by *William Beaudine*, 1943.]

URDER ON LENOX AVENUE. Directed by *Arthur Dreifuss*, from a story by *Frank Wilson*. Lyrics and music by *Donald Heywood*. With *Mamie Smith, Alex Lovejoy, Dene Larry, Norman Astwood, Gus Smith, Edna Mae Harris, Alberta Perkins* and *George Williams*. (Goldberg, 1941—independent all-Negro, produced in Florida).

PLACE TO LIVE. Directed by *Irving Lerner*. Documentary on housing conditions among Negroes and whites in Philadelphia. (Philadelphia Housing Association, 1941).

UNDAY SINNERS. Directed by *Arthur Dreifuss*, from a story by *Frank Wilson*. Lyrics and music by *Donald Heywood*. With *Mamie Smith, Norman Astwood, Edna Mae Harris, Alex Lovejoy, Cristola Williams, Sidney Easton, Earl Sydnor, Gus Smith* and *Alberta Perkins*. (Goldberg, 1941—independent all-Negro, produced in Florida).
[*Note :* *Donald Heywood*, writer and composer, has been prominently associated with independent Negro films since 1932, when he wrote the screenplays of several *Bud Pollard* pictures, including " The Black King."]

UCKY GHOST. Produced and directed by *Jed Buell*. With *Mantan Moreland*. (Buell, 1941—independent all-Negro).

IRTH OF THE BLUES. Directed by *Victor Schertzinger*, from the story by *Harry Tugend*. With *Bing Crosby, Mary Martin, Brian Donlevy, Eddie " Rochester " Anderson, J. Carrol Naish, Warren Hymer, Horace MacMahon* and *Ruby Elzy*. (Paramount, 1941).

FFECTIONATELY YOURS. Directed by *Lloyd Bacon*, from the screenplay by *Fanya Foss* and *Aleen Leslie*. With *Merle Oberon, Dennis Morgan, Rita Hayworth, Ralph Bellamy, George Tobias, James Gleason, Hattie McDaniel* and *Butterfly McQueen*. (Warner, 1941).

IRGINIA. Directed by *Edward H. Griffith*, from a story by *Griffith* and *Virginia Van Upp*. With *Madeleine Carroll, Fred MacMurray, Sterling Hayden, Helen Broderick, Paul Hurst, Marie Wilson, Leigh Whipper, Louise Beavers* and *Darby Jones*. (Paramount, 1941).
[*Note :* The " traditional feud " between the North and South, even in 1941, formed the basis of yet another story in which the hero is a young Southerner.]

ENTLEMAN FROM DIXIE. Directed by *Al Herman*, from an original story by *Fred Myton*. With *Jack La Rue, Marian Marsh, Clarence Muse, John Holland, Phyllis Barry* and *Monte Blue*. (Monogram, 1942).

HE PITTSBURGH KID. Directed by *Jack Townley*, from the novel by *Octavius Roy Cohen*. With *Jean Parker, Billy Conn, Veda Ann Borg, Dick Purcell, Alan Baxter, Jonathan Hale, Ernest Whitman, Etta McDaniel* and *Henry Armstrong*. (Republic, 1942).

HEY DIED WITH THEIR BOOTS ON. Directed by *Raoul Walsh*, from the screenplay by *Wallace Kline* and *Aeneas MacKenzie*. With *Errol Flynn, Olivia de Havilland, Arthur Kennedy, Charley Grapewin, Anthony Quinn, Gene Lockhart, Stanley Ridges, John Litel, Sydney Greenstreet* and *Hattie McDaniel*. (Warners, 1942).

THE BODY DISAPPEARS. Directed by *D. Ross Lederman*, from the screen play by *Scott Darling* and *Erna Lazarns*. With *Jeffrey Lynn, Jane Wyman, Edward Everett Horton, Marguerite Chapman, Willie Best* and *David Bruce*. (Warner 1942).
[*Note :* Typical " who-dunnit " comedy with *Willie Best*, who (to quote " Film Weekly," June 27th, 1942) " adequately supplies coloured comedy."]

SYNCOPATION. Directed by *William Dieterle*, from a story by *Valentine Davies*. With *Adolphe Menjou, Jackie Cooper, Bonita Granville, George Bancroft Ted North, Todd Duncan, Frank Jenks* and *Mona Barrie*. (R.K.O. Radio, 1942).

SANTA FE TRIAL. Directed by *Michael Curtiz*, from a screenplay by *Robert Buckner*. With *Errol Flynn, Olivia de Havilland, Raymond Massey, Ronald Reagan, Alan Hale, William Lundigan, Van Heflin, Guinn Williams, Alan Baxter, John Litel, David Bruce, Ward Bond* and *Erville Alderson*. (Warners, 1942).

IN THIS OUR LIFE. Directed by *John Huston*, from the novel by *Ellen Glasgow* With *Bette Davis, Olivia de Havilland, George Brent, Dennis Morgan, Charles Coburn, Frank Craven, Billie Burke, Lee Patrick, Hattie McDaniel* and *Ernest Anderson*. (Warners, 1942).

HENRY BROWN, FARMER. Directed by *Roger Barlow*. Music by *Gene Forrall*. Narration by *Canada Lee*. A documentary on the life of a Negro farmer in Alabama. (Produced by the U.S. Department of Agriculture, at Inskerger Alabama, 1942).

THE TALK OF THE TOWN. Directed by *George Stevens*, from a story by *Sydney Harmon*. With *Jean Arthur, Ronald Colman, Cary Grant, Edgar Buchanan Glenda Farrell, Charles Dingle, Rex Ingram, Leonid Kinsky* and *Don Beddoe* (Columbia, 1942).

MEN OF DESTINY. Directed by *Ray Enright*, from the screenplay by *Harold Shumate*. With *Robert Stack, Broderick Crawford, Jackie Cooper, Anne Gwynne Ralph Bellamy, Leo Carrillo, John Litel, William Farnum* and *Addison Richards* (Universal, 1942).

CAIRO. Directed by *W. S. Van Dyke* II, from the screenplay by *John McClain* With *Robert Young, Jeanette Macdonald, Ethel Waters, Reginald Owen, Lionel Atwill, Dooley Wilson, Mona Barrie* and *Rhys Williams*. (M.G.M., 1942).

GALLANT LADY. Directed by *William Beaudine*, from a story by *Octavius Roy Cohen*. With *Rose Hobart, Sydney Blackmer, Claire Rochelle, Vince Barnet* and *Ruby Dandridge*. (Monogram, 1943).

PANAMA HATTIE. Directed by *Norman Z. McLeod*, based on the play by *Herbert Fields* and *B. G. de Sylva*. With *Ann Sothern, Red Skelton, Rags Raglano Ben Blue, Marsha Hunt, Virginia O'Brien, Carl Esmond, The Berry Brothers, Nyas James* and *Warren*, and *Lena Horne*. (M.G.M., 1943).

STORMY WEATHER. Directed by *Andrew Stone*, from a story by *Jerry Horwin* and *Seymour Robinson*. With *Lena Horne, Bill Robinson, Cab Calloway Katherine Dunham, Harold* and *Fayard Nicholas, Ada Brown, Dooley Wilson Babe Wallace, Ernest Whitman, Zuttie Singleton, F. E. Miller* and *Nicodemus Stewart*. (Twentieth Century-Fox, 1943—all-Negro).

DIXIE. Directed by *Edward Sutherland*, from a story by *Karl Tunberg* and *Darrell Ware*. With *Bing Crosby, Dorothy Lamour, Billy de Wolfe, Marjorie Reynolds Lynne Overman, Raymond Walburn* and *Eddie Foy, Jnr*. (Paramount, 1943).
[*Note :* This was a biography of Daniel Emmett, the first blackface minstrel and the composer of " Dixie," later to become the marching song of the Confederate Army.]

HE VANISHING VIRGINIAN. Directed by *Frank Borzage*, from a book by *Rebecca Yancey Williams*. With *Frank Morgan, Kathryn Grayson, Spring Byington, Douglas Newland, Elizabeth Patterson, Leigh Whipper* and *Louise Beavers*. (M.G.M., 1943).
[*Note :* This film, according to " Film Weekly," February 20th, 1943, " depicts the kindly feelings between the Virginian aristocrats and the Negroes and the impact of the First World War on their community."]

ASABLANCA. Directed by *Michael Curtiz*. With *Humphrey Bogart, Ingrid Bergman, Paul Henreid, Claude Rains, Conrad Veidt, Sydney Greenstreet, Peter Lorre, Dooley Wilson, John Qualen, Helmut Dantine* and *Marcel Dalio*. (Warnersl 1943).

ALES OF MANHATTAN. Directed by *Julian Duvivier*. With *Charles Boyer, Rita Hayworth, Ginger Rogers, Henry Fonda, Charles Laughton, Edward G. Robinson, Paul Robeson, Ethel Waters, Eddie " Rochester " Anderson, Thomas Mitchell, Caesar Romero, Gail Patrick, Roland Young, George Sanders, Clarence Muse, George Reed, Cordell Hickman* and *The Hall Johnson Choir*. (Twentieth Century-Fox, 1943).
[*Note :* In " Picturegoer and Film Weekly," May 1st, 1943, film critic *Lione, Collier* writes : " I can imagine that Negroes will not be too well pleased by the manner in which their countrymen are presented as half-wits in ' Tales Of Manhattan ! ' "]

OMETHING TO SHOUT ABOUT. Directed by *Gregory Ratoff*. With *Don Ameche, Janet Blair, Jack Oakie, William Gaxton, Cobina Wright, Jnr., Veda Ann Borg* and *Hazel Scott*. (Columbia, 1943).

TRANGE INCIDENT. Directed by *William Wellman*, from the novel " The Ox Bow Incident " by *Walter Van Tilberg Clark*. With *Henry Fonda, Dana Andrews, Anthony Quinn, William Eythe, Mary Beth Hughes, Henry Morgan, Jane Darwell, Frank Conroy, Francis Ford, Marc Lawrence, Paul Hurst* and *Leigh Whipper*. (Twentieth Century-Fox, 1943).

RASH DIVE. Directed by *Archie Mayo*, from the original story by *W. R. Burnett*. With *Tyrone Power, Anne Baxter, Dana Andrews, James Gleason, Dame May Whitty, Henry Morgan, Ben Carter, Frank Conroy* and *John Archer*. (Twentieth Century-Fox, 1943).
[*Note :* This film is particularly notable for Mayo's sympathetic treatment of *Ben Carter*, who plays a Negro hero.]

WALKED WITH A ZOMBIE. Directed by *Jacques Tourneur*, based on a story by *Inez Wallace*. With *James Ellison, Frances Dee, Tom Conway, Edith Barrett, James Bell, Theresa Harris, Darby Jones, Sir Lancelot* and *Jeni LeGon*. (R.K.O. Radio, 1943).

ATAAN. Directed by *Tay Garnett*, from an original screenplay by *Robert D. Andrews*. With *Robert Taylor, George Murphy, Thomas Mitchell, Lloyd Nolan, Lee Bowman, Robert Walker, Desi Arnaz, Philip Terry, Kenneth Spencer* and *Tom Dugan*. (M.G.M., 1943).

RIME SMASHER. Directed by *James Tinling*. With *Frank Graham, Mantan Moreland* and *Richard Cromwell*. (Monogram, 1943).
[*Note :* Moreland was co-starred in this, as in others in the series.]

CABIN IN THE SKY. Directed by *Vincente Minnelli.* With *Lena Horn Eddie " Rochester " Anderson, Ethel Waters, Rex Ingram, Kenneth Spencer, Ern Whitman, Mantan Moreland, Louis Armstrong, Oscar Polk, " Buck and Bubbles Duke Ellington, John Sublett* and *Willie Best.* (M.G.M., 1943—all-Negro).

CARNIVAL IN RHYTHM. A short film devoted to *Katherine Dunham* and h Negro Ballet. (Warners, 1944).

LIFEBOAT. Directed by *Alfred Hitchcock.* With *Tallulah Bankhead, Jo Hodiak, Henry Hull, Walter Slezak, Canada Lee, Hume Cronyn, Mary Anders* and *Heather Angel.* (Twentieth Century-Fox, 1944).

THE NEGRO SOLDIER. Produced, written and narrated by *Carleton Mo* Directed by *Frank Capra.* Documentary, produced by the U.S. War Depar ment, 1944.

BOOGIE WOOGIE DREAM. Produced by *Jack* and *Dave Goldberg.* Wi *Lena Horne, Albert Ammons, Pete Johnson* and *Teddy Wilson.* (Goldberg, 1944 independent all-Negro).

SAHARA. Directed by *Zoltan Korda.* With *Humphrey Bogart, Bruce Benne Rex Ingram, Lloyd Bridges, Dan Duryea, J. Carroll Naish, Richard Nugent, C Harbord* and *Kurt Kreuger.* (Columbia, 1944).

THE CURSE OF THE CAT PEOPLE. Directed by *Gunther Fritsch* a *Robert Wise,* from the screenplay by *De Witt Boden.* With *Simone Simon, Ke Smith, Jane Randolph, Ann Carter* and *Sir Lancelot.* (R.K.O. Radio, 1944).
[*Note :* This film was distinguished by the remarkably sympathetic treatment the relationship between a Negro—*Sir Lancelot*—and a little girl, *Ann Carter.*]

THE NEGRO SAILOR. Directed by *Henry Lieven.* With *Leigh Whipper* a *Joel Fluellyn.* Documentary, produced by the U.S. War Department, 1945.

THE HOUSE I LIVE IN. With *Frank Sinatra.*
[*Note :* This film, directed at racial intolerance, won an Academy Award in 194 Sinatra is well-known for his work in combatting race prejudice.]

DARK WATERS. Directed by *Andre de Toth,* from the story by *Frank a Marian Cockrell.* With *Merle Oberon, Franchot Tone, Thomas Mitchell, F Bainter, Elisha Cook, Jnr., Rex Ingram, Nina Mae McKinney, John Qualen* a *Alan Napier.* (Benedict Bogeaus, 1945).

DIXIE JAMBOREE. Directed by *Christy Cabanne,* from the screenplay *Sam Neumann.* With *Frances Langford, Eddie Quillan, Guy Kibbee, Char Butterworth, Lyle Talbot, Fifi D'Orsay, Frank Jenks, Louise Beavers, Ben Car* and *Gloria Jetter.* (P.R.C., 1945).

BOWERY TO BROADWAY. Directed by *Charles Lamont,* from a screenpl by *Edmund Joseph* and *Bart Lytton.* With *Jack Oakie, Maria Montez, Susann Foster, Turhan Bey, Ann Blyth, Donald Cook, Louise Allbritton, Ben Car Mantan Moreland, Andy Devine, Evelyn Ankers, Thomas Gomez, Frank McHu* and *Rosemary de Camp.* (Universal, 1945).

NEGRO COLLEGES IN WARTIME. Produced by the Office of War I formation, 1945.

DR. GEORGE WASHINGTON CARVER. With *Clinton Rosemond.* Doc mentary based on the life and work of the Negro scientist. (M.G.M., 1945).

AMMIN' THE BLUES. Directed and photographed by *Gjon Mili*. A semi-documentary of a " jam-session " in a Negro club. (Warners, 1945).

ENTLE ANNIE. Directed by *Andrew Marton*, from the novel by *MacKinlay Kantor*. With *James Craig, Donna Reed, Marjorie Main, Henry Morgan, Barton MacLane, Noah Beery, Snr.* and *Paul Langton*. (M.G.M., 1945).
[*Note :* Yet another pro-South film (see " Picturegoer," September 15th, 1945).]

E'VE COME A LONG LONG WAY. Produced and directed by *Jack Goldberg*. A documentary cavalcade of the Negro race, with narration by *Elder Michaux*. (" Negro Marches On," 1945).

NCLE TOM'S CABANA. Produced by *Fred Quimby*. A typical comedy short film emphasising the stereotype, which have been made in scores by Hollywood. (M.G.M., 1947).

REWSTER'S MILLIONS. Directed by *Allan Dwan*, from the novel by *George Barr McCutcheon*. With *Dennis O'Keefe, Helen Walker, Eddie " Rochester " Anderson, June Havoc, Gail Patrick, Mischa Auer, Joseph Sawyer, John Litel, Herbert Rudley* and *Neil Hamilton*. (Edward Small, 1946).

EMORY FOR TWO. Directed by *Del Lord*, from the story by *John Gray*. With *Phil Harris, Eddie " Rochester " Anderson, Leslie Brooke, Walter Catlett, Frank Sully, James Burke* and *Pierre Watkin*. (Columbia, 1946).

ARATOGA TRUNK. Directed by *Sam Wood*, from the novel by *Edna Ferber*. With *Ingrid Bergman, Gary Cooper, Flora Robson, Jerry Austin, John Warburton, Florence Bates, Curt Bois, John Abbott* and *Cecile Cunningham*. (Warners, 1946).
[*Note :* An important coloured role, Angelique Pluton, was played by white actress *Flora Robson* in blackface, a psychological throwback to the time of *D. W. Griffith.*]

EGFELD FOLLIES. Directed by *Vincente Minnelli*. With *William Powell, Virginia O'Brien, Lucille Ball, Esther Williams, James Melton, Marion Bell, Victor Moore, Fred Astaire, Lucille Bremer, Keenan Wynn, Lena Horne, Red Skelton, Judy Garland, Gene Kelly, Kathryn Grayson, Edward Arnold, Cyd Charisse, Robert Lewis* and *Avon Long*. (M.G.M., 1946).
[*Note :* Lena Horne and Avon Long were featured in a sequence—inevitably Jim Crow—of this giant musical.]

OLD THAT BLONDE. Directed by *George Marshall*, from a play by *Paul Armstrong*. With *Eddie Bracken, Veronica Lake, Willie Best, Frank Fenton, Albert Dekker, George Zucco, Donald MacBride* and *Norma Varden*. (Paramount, 1946).
[*Note :* This is a typical innocuous Hollywood comedy, in which a Negro, in this case *Willie Best*, plays the amiable manservant to the hero, as in " The Ghost Breakers," " The Bride Wore Boots," etc.]

IE SCARLET CLUE. Directed by *Phil Rosen*, based on stories by *Earl Derr Biggers*. With *Sydney Toler, Mantan Moreland, Ben Carter, Benson Fong,* and *Virginia Brissac*. (Monogram, 1945).
[*Note :* This is a typical Toler-Moreland " Charlie Chan " feature ; other titles include " Dark Alibi," " The Jade Mask," " Charlie Chan In Black Magic," etc., in all of which Moreland plays " Birmingham," Chan's coloured chauffeur-stooge.]

MILDRED PIERCE. Directed by *Michael Curtiz*, based on the novel by *Jam M. Cain*. With *Joan Crawford, Jack Carson, Zachary Scott, Eve Arden, Bru Bennett, Ann Blyth, Lee Patrick, Butterfly McQueen, Moroni Olsen, Charles Trou bridge* and *Chester Clute*. (Warners, 1946).

[*Note :* *Butterfly McQueen* played a coloured servant-girl, invariably stupid, this, and in others like " Gone With The Wind " and " Duel In The Sun." Sh has recently announced that she will henceforth refuse all " stupid maid " parts.]

SMOOTH AS SILK. Directed by *Charles Barton*. With *Kent Taylor, Virgin Grey, Jane Adams, Milburn Stone, John Litel, Charles Trowbridge* and *There Harris*. (Universal, 1946).

[*Note :* *Theresa Harris* tried valiantly to infuse life into her role of a Negro ma in this, as in many other films.]

THE MAN ON AMERICA'S CONSCIENCE. (released in the U.S. " Tennessee Johnson "). Directed by *William Dieterle*, from a story by *Milt Ginsberg* and *Alvin Meyers*. With *Van Heflin, Lionel Barrymore, Ruth Husse Marjorie Main, Regis Toomey, J. Edward Bromberg, Grant Withers, Dane Clar Charles Dingle, Carl Benton Reid, Noah Beery, Snr., Robert Warwick, Llo Corrigan, William Farnum, Charles Trowbridge, Lynne Carver* and *Morris Ankrur* (M.G.M., 1944—released in England in 1946).

THE SAILOR TAKES A WIFE. Directed by *Richard Whorf*, from a play *Chester Erskine*. With *Robert Walker, June Allyson, Eddie " Rochester " Anderso Audrey Totter, Hume Cronyn, Reginald Owen* and *Gerald Oliver Smith*. (M.G.M 1946).

BEWARE. Produced and directed by *Bud Pollard*. With *Louis Jordan, Fra Wilson, Valerie Black, Ernest Calloway, Milton Woods* and *Emory Richardso* (Astor, 1946—independent all-Negro).

[*Note :* *Bud Pollard* began making all-Negro films in 1932, and has continued the present time. The above film, one of a series featuring trumpet-vocali *Louis Jordan*, is typical of his more recent output.]

THE BROTHERHOOD OF MAN. A colour cartoon based on " The Races (Mankind " by *Ruth Benedict* and *Gene Weltfish*. (Brandon, 1946).

[*Note :* This is " a noble attempt to combat race prejudice through the imaginativ use of cartoon technique." See " Theatre Arts," February, 1947.]

NIGHT AND DAY. Directed by *Michael Curtiz*, based on the life story of *C Porter*. With *Cary Grant, Alexis Smith, Monty Wooley, Ginny Simms, Ja Wyman, Eve Arden, Donald Woods, Paul Cavanagh, Selena Royle, Henry Stephenso Victor Francen, Clarence Muse, Dorothy Malone, Alan Hale, Tom d'Andrea an Hazel Scott*. (Warners, 1946).

[*Note :* This is another film in which Hazel Scott appears as " Hazel Scott," t only screen role she has so far consented to play.]

TILL THE END OF TIME. Directed by *Edward Dmytryk*, from a screenpl by *Allen Rivkin*. With *Dorothy McGuire, Robert Mitchum, Guy Madison, B Williams, Tom Tully, Jean Porter, William Gargan, Loren Tindall, Ruth Nelso* and *Selena Royle*. (R.K.O. Radio, 1946).

ANGEL ON MY SHOULDER. Directed by *Archie Mayo*, from a story *Harry Segall*. With *Paul Muni, Anne Baxter, Claude Rains, Onslow Steve George Cleveland, Hardie Albright, James Flavin* and *Erskine Sanford*. (Unit Artists, 1946).

ONG OF THE SOUTH. Produced by *Walt Disney*, based on the "Uncle Remus" stories. With *Ruth Warrick, James Baskett, Lucille Watson, Hattie McDaniel, Luana Patten* and *Bobby Driscoll*. (R.K.O. Radio-Disney, 1947).

EW ORLEANS. Directed by *Arthur Lubin*. With *Arturo de Cordova, Dorothy Patrick, Marjorie Lord, Irene Rich, Richard Hageman, Louis Armstrong* and *Billie Holliday*. (Majestic-United Artists, 1947).

EET, PETITE AND GONE. With *Louis Jordan*. (Astor, 1947—all-Negro).

BONY PARADE. With *Cab Calloway, Count Basie, The Mills Brothers, Mantan Moreland, Mable Lee, Dorothy Dandridge, Ruby Hill* and *Vanita Smythe*. (Astor, 1947—all-Negro).

EPIA CINDERELLA. Directed by *Arthur Leonard*, from a screenplay by *Vincent Valentini*. With *Billy Daniels, Sheila Guyse, Ruble Blakey, Walter Fuller, John Kirby* and *Fred Gordon*. (Herald-Jack Goldberg, 1947—all-Negro).

HE BURNING CROSS. Directed by *Walter Colmes*. With *Hank Daniels, Virginia Patton, Joel Fluellyn, Dick Rich, Raymond Bond* and *Matt Willis*. Described by the producers as a "daring exposure of the infamous Ku Klux Klan." (Somerset-Screen Guild, 1947).

ROSSFIRE. Directed by *Edward Dmytryk*. Screenplay by *John Paxton*. With *Robert Young, Robert Ryan, Robert Mitchum* and *Sam Levene*. This is notable as the first Hollywood film ever to be made dealing with anti-Semitism, and therefore deserves a place in this list of films touching on problems of racial intercourse. (R.K.O. Radio, 1947).

BRITISH

ORDERLINE. Directed by *Kenneth Macpherson*. With *Paul Robeson* and *Eslanda Goode Robeson*. (Pool, 1930).

IGER BAY. Directed by *J. Elder Wills*. With *Anna May Wong, Ralph Richardson, Orlando Martins, etc*. (British Lion-Wyndham, 1933).

ENTUCKY MINSTRELS. Directed by *John Baxter*. With *Scott* and *Whaley, C. Denier Warren, Wilson Coleman* and *Norman Green*. (Universal, 1935).
[*Note :* This was an example of the repellent blackface film of the British " nigger minstrel " variety.]

MIDSHIPMAN EASY. Directed by *Carol Reed*, from the story by *Captain Marryat*. With *Margaret Lockwood, Hugh Green* and *Robert Adams*. (British Lion, 1935).

ANDERS OF THE RIVER. Produced by *Alexander Korda*. Directed by *Zoltan Korda*, from the novel by *Edgar Wallace*. With *Paul Robeson, Leslie Banks, Nina Mae McKinney, Robert Cochran, Martin Walker, Toto Ware, Richard Gray, Allan Jeayes, Eric Maturin* and *Charles Carson*. (London, 1935).

SONG OF FREEDOM. Directed by *J. Elder Wills*, from the story by *Doroth Holloway* and *Claude Wallace*. With *Paul Robeson, Elizabeth Welch, Geor Mozart, Esme Percy, Joan Fred Emney, Robert Adams, Ronald Simpson, Conn Smith, Alf Goddard, Orlando Martins, James Solomon* and *Toto Ware*. (Britis Lion-Hammer, 1937).

KING SOLOMON'S MINES. Directed by *Robert Stevenson*. With *Pa Robeson, Cedric Hardwicke, Roland Young, Anna Lee, John Loder, Arthur Sinclai Robert Adams* and *Arthur Goullett*. (Gaumont British, 1937).

CALLALOO. Directed by *Irene Nicholson* and *Brian Montagu*. Songs by *Edr Connor*. With *Ursula Johnson*. (A documentary made for the " Trinida Guardian," 1937).

JERICHO. Directed by *Thornton Freeland*. With *Paul Robeson, Henry Wilcoxo Wallace Ford, John Laurie, Princess Kouka, James Carew, Lawrence Brown, I Hatch, Rufus Fennell, Frank Cochrane, George Barraud, Orlando Martins an Eslanda Goode Robeson*. (Buckingham, 1937).

JAVA HEAD. Directed by *J. Walter Ruben*. With *Anna May Wong, Elizabet Allan, Edmund Gwenn, John Loder, Ralph Richardson, Herbert Lomas, an Orlando Martins*. (A.T.P.).

BIG FELLA. Directed by *J. Elder Wills*, from the story by *Dorothy Holloway* an *Claude Wallace*. With *Paul Robeson, Elizabeth Welch, Roy Emerton, James Hayte Lawrence Brown, Eldon Grant, Marcelle Rogez, Eric Cowley* and *Joyce Kenned* (British Lion-Hammer, 1938).

ON VELVET. Directed by *Widgey Newman*. With *Nina Mae McKinney, Wal Patch, Leslie Bradley, Vi Kaley, Garland Wilson, etc.* (Columbia, 1938).

OLD BONES OF THE RIVER. Directed by *Marcel Varnel*. With *Will Ha Robert Adams, Moore Marriott, Graham Moffatt, Wyndham Goldie* and *Jac Livesey*. (Gainsborough, 1939).

MURDER IN SOHO. Directed by *Norman Lee*, from a screenplay by *McGre Willis*. With *Jack La Rue, Sandra Storme, Bernard Lee, Martin Walker, Jam Hayter, Googie Withers, Drue Tartière, Francis Lister, Renée Gadd* and *Orlana Martins*. (Associated British, 1939).

MEN OF AFRICA. Produced by *Basil Wright*. Directed by *Alexander Shau Photography by *Jo Jago* and *Harry Rignold*. Narration by *Leslie Mitchell*. documentary illustrating the principles of British administration in the healt education and agricultural services of East Africa. (Colonial Marketing Boar 1939).

THE PROUD VALLEY. Directed by *Pen Tennyson*, from a story by *Herber Marshall* and *Fredda Brilliant* ; screenplay by *Louis Golding* and *Roland Pertwe With *Paul Robeson, Edward Chapman, Simon Lack, Rachel Thomas, Edward Rigb Janet Johnson, Clifford Evans, Charles Williams, Jack Jones, Allan Jeayes* an *Edward Lexy*. (Ealing, 1940).

THE THIEF OF BAGDAD. Produced by *Alexander Korda*. Directed b *Michael Powell, Ludwig Berger* and *Tim Whelan*, from a screenplay by *Lajos Bir With *Conrad Veidt, Sabu, June Duprez, John Justin, Rex Ingram, Mary Morris Miles Malleson, Hay Petrie, Adelaide Hall* and *Allan Jeayes*. (London, 1941).

AN AFRICAN IN LONDON. Directed by *George Pearson*. With *Rober Adams*. (Colonial Film Unit, 1943).

EAD OF NIGHT. Directed by *Cavalcanti, Charles Crichton, Basil Dearden, Robert Hamer.* With *Michael Redgrave, Mervyn Johns, Googie Withers, Roland Culver, Frederick Valk, Sally Anne Howes, Judy Kelly, Michael Allan, Ralph Michael, Basil Radford, Naunton Wayne, Elizabeth Welch, Hartley Power, Garry Marsh* and *Miles Malleson.* (Ealing, 1945).

HE MAN FROM MOROCCO. Directed by *Max Greene*, from a story by *Rudolph Cartier.* With *Anton Walbrook, Margaretta Scott, Mary Morris, Hartley Power, Reginald Tate, Peter Sinclair, David Horne, Charles Victor, Paul Demel, John McLaren, David Baxter, Orest Orloff, Orlando Martins, Harold Lang* and *Peter Noble.* (Associated British, 1945).

T HAPPENED ONE SUNDAY. Directed by *Karel Lamac.* With *Robert Beatty, Barbara White, Judy Kelly, Marjorie Rhodes, Ernest Butcher* and *Robert Adams.* (Associated British, 1945).

OLD COAST JOURNEY. Produced by *Maxwell Munden.* (Horizon-Cadbury's, 1946.)
[Documentary, produced by Horizon Film Unit for Cadbury's—one of a series.]

HE LISBON STORY. Directed by *Paul L. Stein*, from the musical play by *Harold Purcell* and *Harry Parr-Davies.* With *Walter Rilla, David Farrar, Patricia Burke, Lawrence O'Madden, Austin Trevor, Paul Bonifas, Ralph Truman, Harry Welchman, Esme Percy, Allan Jeayes, Uriel Porter, Frederick Wendhausen* and *Fela Sowande.* (British National, 1946).

ALKING ON AIR. Directed by *Aveling Ginever*, from a story by *Johnny Worthy* and *Val Guest.* Music and lyrics by *Peter Noble.* With *Johnny Worthy, Bertie Jarrett, Billy Thatcher, Maudie Edwards, Freddie Crump, Ray Ellington, Sonny Thomas, Carol Fenton, Susan Shaw, Gordon Edwards, Jill Allen, Miki Hood, Jasmine Dee, Lauderic Caton* and *Coleridge Goode.* (Michael Goodman, 1946).

EN OF TWO WORLDS. Directed by *Thorold Dickinson*, from a screenplay by *Joyce Cary, Herbert Victor* and *Thorold Dickinson* (from an idea by *C. Arnot Robertson*). With *Eric Portman, Robert Adams, Phyllis Calvert, Arnold Marlé, Cathleen Nesbitt, David Horne, Cyril Raymond, Orlando Martins, Sam Blake, Napoleon Florent, Viola Thompson, Eseza Makumbi, Tunji Williams, Rudolph Evans, Uriel Porter, James Rich* and *Berto Pasuka.* (Two Cities, 1946).
[*Note :* This film made history as the first important feature-length production to give a coloured actor a co-starring part with a white star ; it was a lesson to Hollywood, and pointed the way to future developments in filmic relations between black and white peoples.]

HE END OF THE RIVER. Directed by *Derek Twist.* With *Sabu, Bibi Ferreira, Robert Douglas, Raymond Lovell* and *Orlando Martins.* (Archers, 1947).

CONTINENTAL

E GRAND JEU. Directed by *Jacques Feyder.* (French, 1935).

ONI. Directed by *Jean Renoir.* (French, 1935).

A MORT DU CYGNE. Directed by *Jean Benoit-Levy* and *Marie Epstein.* (French, 1937).

'ALIBI. Directed by *Pierre Chenal*, from a story by *Marcel Achard.* With *Erich von Stroheim.* (French, 1938).

AR IS HELL. Directed by *Victor Trivas.* (German, 1933).

HE CIRCUS. Directed by *Alexandrov.* (Russian, 1937).

OUNG PUSHKIN. (Russian, 1935).

APPENDIX D

GRIFFITH'S DEFENCE OF " THE BIRTH OF A NATION."

" From the very beginning, *The Birth Of A Nation* became the subject of an extremely bitter controversy. Both Dixon and Griffith, as authors of the novel and the scenario, respectively, were accused of libelling 10,000,000 Americans, and thus of inciting to racial hatred. The film made front-page headlines, when political organisations, seeking the Negro vote, attacked it from many sides—from the pulpit ; in the press ; on the lecture platform ; through advertisements ; in drives for mass-boycott ; and inevitably, later, through the agency of " socially-conscious " hoodlums, hired to wreck the screens, create turmoil in the theatres, provoke street-fights, incite riots ; or, in a word, to foment inter-racial strife, which then could be blamed on the picture.

Griffith's defence of the film was based on seven main lines of evidence and rebuttal, as follows :—

(1) First and foremost, it was based on the story. Of whatever excesses or outrages the blacks may be guilty, these they commit as the blind and misguided, if violent, pawns of their satanic new masters from the North. But of an attack on " race " or on the Negro race as such, Griffith contended, there is no hint, no scene or sign, no taint whatever, anywhere in *The Birth Of A Nation* ; and he offered in proof the scenario of the finished film.

(2) He further pointed out, that the personal " heavy " is not Silas Lynch, the mulatto leader, but the white senator, the Hon. Austin Stoneman, denoted in a sub-title as the " uncrowned king of Capitol Hill."

(3) Stoneman is the fictional counterpart of Thaddeus Stevens, a Nineteenth Century rabble-rouser and demagogue, whose political extremism and maniacal ambition very nearly wrecked Lincoln's post-war programme of unionization. Stoneman's devilry and mania in the film parallel Stevens's machinations and fanaticism in history.

(4) On the Reconstruction Period in general, and the Ku Klux Klan in particular, as depicted, Griffith cited documentation from Woodrow Wilson's "*History of the American People*."

(5) In defence of his showing the Negroes gaining control of the South Carolina legislature, and then running amuck, Griffith cited the records of the State House of Representatives, Columbia, S.C., and also of the State Supreme Court of South Carolina, 1868-1871.

(6) In support of certain other scenes of alleged Negro misbehaviour, he cited records of the same period from the higher courts throughout the South. This testimony included documentary evidence.

(7) Finally, Griffith defended his own right as a free American citizen to dramatise history in the light of his own understanding."

(*An excerpt from " The Birth Of A Nation," a monograph by*

Seymour Stern, July, 1945.)

A LETTER FROM D. W. GRIFFITH

To the Editor, " Sight and Sound."

DEAR SIR,

My attention has been directed to Mr. Peter Noble's attack against myself and certain of my films (" The Birth Of A Nation," etc.) in the Autumn, 1946 issue of *Sight and Sound*. This attack charges me with having projected in these films bias against, and hatred of, the Negro race. I have also read an advance copy of a reply which Mr. Seymour Stern, author of the Griffith Index and my biographer, has written to Mr. Noble refuting his charges. Mr. Stern informs me that this reply is scheduled for publication this Spring in *Sight and Sound*.

Mr. Stern has, I believe, presented the facts adequately and effectively. I have nothing to add to them, but for myself, I will take this occasion of Lincoln's birthday to request that you permit me to say just this : I am not now and never have been " anti-Negro " or " anti " any other race. My attitude towards the Negroes has always been one of affection and brotherly feeling. I was partly raised by a lovable old Negress down in old Kentucky and I have always gotten along extremely well with the Negro people.

In filming " The Birth Of A Nation," I gave to my best knowledge the proven facts, and presented the known truth, about the Reconstruction Period in the American South. These facts are based on an overwhelming compilation of authentic evidence and testimony. My picturization of the history as it happened requires, therefore, no apology, no defence, no " explanations." I regret that Mr. Noble, whose remarks do not appear to be based either on historic fact or personal experience, has made even this statement of the self-evident truth of my film necessary.

Very truly yours,

David Wark Griffith.

February 12th, 1947,

Beverley Hills,
California, U.S.A.

* * * * * *

SEYMOUR STERN REPLIES

Note.—Below is a condensation of the salient points of a reply by Seymour Stern (published in *Sight and Sound*, Spring, 1947), headed " Griffith Is Not Anti-Negro," to a detailed criticism, by Peter Noble, of " The Birth Of A Nation " (published in *Sight and Sound*, Autumn, 1946.)

Is D. W. Griffith guilty of anti-Negro bias in " The Birth Of A Nation " ? Is he guilty of having consciously maligned the Negro race ? The answer is emphatically " no."

The truth is, that with Woodrow Wilson's *History of the American People* as his principal academic authority, Griffith depicts the history of the tragic and turbulent Reconstruction Period in the South with a degree of authenticity, documentation, objectivity and scholarship seldom if ever equalled on the screen. What is more important, he carefully explains, and in the action itself makes it unmistakably clear, that the real villains of Southern history from 1865-72 (the Reconstruction Period) were not the uneducated and newly-freed Negroes but the *doctrines* of certain fanatical and vengeful Northern whites, who duped the Negroes with glittering promises of wealth and power.

The reign of terror which swept the South in the wake of Lincoln's assassination and which forms the basis of the second half of " The Birth Of A Nation," was launched by Northern whites—by Thaddeus Stevens (" Stoneman " in the film) and the " carpet baggers," white exploiters, who swarmed into the South, and, by every known method of brutality, chicanery, deception, duplicity, falsehood, fraud and political hoax or trickery, organised the Negro vote in support of an economic political and social revolution. The Negroes devoid of previous political experience and, therefore, easy prey for the Northern politicos, became unwitting but efficient pawns. These are the known facts of this stormy and trying period of American history—facts which appear to have escaped Mr. Noble. Similarly, the rise of the old Ku Klux Klan as filmed by Griffith is based on solid documentation. Much of the documentary material used by Griffith in filming the wild and stirring scenes of the clansmen has since been more fully embodied in the standard work on this subject, Stanley F. Horn's *The Invisible Empire* (Houghton, Mifflin, 1940).

In a word, all the major scenes and episodes of " The Birth Of A Nation," especially those of the second half of the film, are solidly documented.

For the information of Mr. Noble and other anti-Griffith mud-slingers let these facts stand on the record : Mr. Griffith was at no time driven to remorse by the storm which followed the showing of his film, as Mr. Noble, and others like Mr. Lewis Jacobs and Mr. Richard Watts, Jnr., naively suggest. Mr. Griffith has never " relented," never has tried to " make up " for anything, for the simple reason that he did not, and to this day does not, consider that he was, or is, guilty of the charges so maliciously imputed to him.

* * * * * *

WITHOUT COMMENT

" It is by our own decision that D. W. Griffith's " The Birth Of A Nation " will not appear in this cycle. Fully aware of the greatness of the film, of its artistic and historic importance, we have also had sufficient and repeated evidence of the potency of the anti-Negro bias and believe that exhibiting it at this time of heightened social tensions cannot be justified."

Page 3, Introductory Note, to a pamphlet issued by the Museum of Modern Art, in 1946, containing the programme of a season entitled " The History of The Motion Picture, 1895-1946."

INDEX

DAVID GLENN HUNT
MEMORIAL LIBRARY
GALVESTON COLLEGE

UNIVERSITY

WITHDRAWN

DAVID GLENN HUNT
MEMORIAL LIBRARY
GALVESTON COLLEGE